More Than a Century of Investment Banking

More Than a Century of Investment Banking

The Kidder, Peabody & Co. Story

VINCENT P. CAROSSO
Kenan Professor of History
New York University

McGRAW-HILL BOOK COMPANY
New York St. Louis San Francisco Auckland Bogotá
Düsseldorf Johannesburg London Madrid Mexico
Montreal New Delhi Panama Paris São Paulo
Singapore Sydney Tokyo Toronto

In memory of

RALPH W. HIDY
Friend and Colleague

Library of Congress Cataloging in Publication Data

Carosso, Vincent P
More than a century of investment banking.

Includes bibliographical references and index.
1. Kidder, Peabody, and Company. I. Title.
HG4930.C35 332.1'0973 78-24019
ISBN 0-07-010136-1

1234567890 DODO 7865432109

The editors for this book were W. Hodson Mogan and Virginia Fechtmann Blair, the designer was Naomi Auerbach, and the production supervisor was Teresa F. Leaden. It was set in Electra by University Graphics, Incorporated.

Printed and bound by R. R. Donnelley & Sons Company.

ENDPAPER ILLUSTRATION: *View of Boston in 1848, from East Boston.*
(Reproduced for Goodspeed's Book Shop from the original, 1971. Copyright 1971, Goodspeed's Book Shop.)

Contents

Preface

This is a story of success, near failure, and spectacular recovery. It begins almost two generations before the Civil War, when John E. Thayer, a young minister's son from Lancaster, Massachusetts, settled in Boston, went into business for himself, starting in trade then expanding into banking and brokerage. The same mix of functions—commercial and travelers' letters of credit, foreign exchange, banking, brokerage—was continued by his brother, Nathaniel, who headed the house after the elder Thayer's death in September 1857, some three weeks after the onset of that year's brief but severe financial panic. The firm weathered the storm easily, continued to grow and prosper so that when Nathaniel Thayer decided to retire and turn the business over to three of his clerks (Henry P. Kidder and the brothers Francis H. and Oliver W. Peabody), the new partnership, Kidder, Peabody & Co., set up in April 1865, inherited the accounts of a large and loyal clientele.

During the next half-century the new firm, building upon foundations laid by the Thayers, made itself one of the country's foremost private international banking houses. By the eve of World War I its commercial and travelers' letters of credit, issued jointly with Baring Brothers & Co. of London, circulated throughout the world and, in the United States, its reputation as an underwriter and distributor of corporate and government securities placed it among the half-dozen most prominent and influential investment firms in the country. The policies that had made for growth and success in the past ceased to work in the radically different economic and financial environment of the post-war years. Kidder, Peabody's failure to adjust to the new era and the aggressive competitors that it spawned deprived the firm of substantial business and profits, losses made much worse by the severe business contraction that followed the stock market debacle of October 1929. By the end of 1930, when the first steps were taken to save Kidder, Peabody from bankruptcy, the chief asset of this once eminent banking house was its still widely respected name, one associated with years of business integrity and financial conservatism that continued to command the loyalty of its many individual and corporate clients seeking investment advice and services.

The three new partners who took over Kidder, Peabody in March 1931—Edwin S. Webster, Jr., Albert H. Gordon, and Chandler Hovey—used the old firm's name and reputation, together with the financial assistance and goodwill of its friends and associates on and off Wall Street, to salvage and rehabilitate the badly ailing house. The job of rebuilding Kidder, Peabody, begun at the depth of the worst depression in the nation's history, at a time when the public image of Wall Street financiers was at its lowest, proved long and difficult, almost as long as it had taken the three founding partners to establish Kidder, Peabody as a major national investment house. It was not until after the close of World War II that Kidder, Peabody once again regained the respected position it had held at the beginning of the twentieth century, when it was generally recognized as one of the country's leading financial houses.

The purpose of this study is to describe the growth and

development, adjustments and readjustments of one of today's top Wall Street investment banking houses. It is not a comprehensive history of the firm or its business. The surviving records do not permit the kind analytic treatment that a firm history normally would include. The evidence—correspondence among the partners and between them and the firm's clients, ledgers and other account books—is too scanty to show the way decisions were reached and executed, what alternatives were available, and why certain policies were adopted and others rejected. Nor does the written record permit much discussion of two other important aspects of the firm's business: its internal operations, such as the relationships among the partners and between them and the senior staff, and the way it approached, planned, and served enterprises in need of long-term capital. Enough internal evidence does exist, however, to show the main lines of Kidder, Peabody's development, the way it adapted to more than a century of widespread, fundamental changes in the world of business and finance, from the expansive days of the post-Civil War era, when some of Wall Street's most legendary figures first made headlines, to the recent past, what Michael C. Jensen of *The New York Times* called "the go-go years, the go-slow years and the shakeout years" of the 1960s and 1970s.

A few words on the preparation of this book are in order. Kidder, Peabody's officers not only allowed me free access to the firm's records, but also spent much time and effort collecting information from outside sources and arranging scores of interviews with present and retired members of the staff, as well as with some of Kidder, Peabody's current and former clients. Albert H. Gordon, the chairman of the board, spent hours answering questions on a wide variety of subjects, from the way Kidder, Peabody recruited some of its first corporate clients to recent changes in the firm's back-office procedures; Ralph D. DeNunzio, president, also made available much material; and several other earlier partners, current officers, and employees—most notably, Amyas Ames, John R. Chapin, Richard F. Coons,

Robert A. Krantz, William N. Loverd, Frederick L. Moore, and Donald Ward—searched their memories and personal files for needed information. But no one did more to make this book possible than Alfred E. Borneman, a former general partner and presently a vice president. A veteran of a half-century on Wall Street, all of it spent with Kidder, Peabody & Co., Borneman not only secured my access to records and answered all my questions willingly and with good humor, but also with his recollections of people and events in the financial district added immeasurably to my knowledge of the firm and the evolution of the securities business. Together with several other present and past members of the firm, he read and re-read various drafts of the manuscript for factual accuracy, but neither he nor anyone else at Kidder, Peabody suggested changes in interpretation or emphasis. The views expressed herein are mine alone.

A few other acknowledgments remain to be recorded. Marian Sears Chaffin, formerly Associate in Research at the Harvard Graduate School of Business Administration, worked long and effectively analyzing the few surviving records of the Thayers and those of Kidder, Peabody's early years; my son, Steven, spent a summer collecting statistics on the firm's corporate and municipal underwritings and direct sales; and my wife, Rose, as always, worked with me throughout the preparation of this book, from the initial research to the final typing and proofreading. I have received much valuable help. Any errors in fact or interpretation are mine.

April 1978 *Vincent P. Carosso*

Foreword

Kidder, Peabody & Co., one of the oldest investment banking houses in the United States, was organized on April 1, 1865, a week before Robert E. Lee and Ulysses S. Grant met at Appomattox Court House and agreed upon the terms that ended the Civil War. Even then the firm was new in name only. Its three founding partners—Henry P. Kidder, Francis H. Peabody, and Oliver W. Peabody—were experienced and well-known Boston bankers. Each had served more than 15 years of apprenticeship with J. E. Thayer & Brother, a private banking and brokerage house on State Street, the center of Boston's financial district. Association with this firm provided Kidder, Peabody with a tradition and experience that went back to the beginnings of American investment banking.

As intermediaries between the users and suppliers of capital, Kidder, Peabody's partners and officers have provided a host of financial services to more than six generations of business and government leaders both at home and abroad. The firm has been associated with some of the country's most important public and private enterprises. It has helped governments raise funds to pay for wars and internal improvements; it has participated actively in supplying capital to many of the country's most important transportation, industrial, utility, and financial corporations, among them the Atchison, Topeka & Santa Fe Railroad, United States Steel, American Telephone & Telegraph, and Boston's National Shawmut Bank; and through its important foreign exchange and letter of credit business, the firm also played a leading role in financing international trade. Kidder, Peabody's varied financial and investment activities helped provide the rapidly developing American economy with the ever growing amounts of capital required to finance and service the increasingly large and complex business organizations that transformed the United States from an agricultural, rural, and debtor country into an industrialized, urban, and creditor nation. For more than a century, during periods of prosperity and depression, war and peace, the firm has occupied a leading position at the key centers of American finance, helping to develop new techniques and reshaping old ones to meet the ever-changing, ever-growing demands for investment capital, not only in the United States but in Europe and elsewhere as well. Few of today's investment banking houses have been so intimately associated with so many of the nation's major business and financial developments.

PART
ONE

Private Bankers

CHAPTER ONE

Pre-Civil War Origins

Kidder, Peabody's roots in American finance go back to 1824, at the time James Monroe was concluding his second term as President of the United States and Henry Clay, the Kentucky statesman who hoped to succeed him, called for a "genuine American System," a program designed to promote the nation's economic growth and development. In that year John Eliot Thayer, a twenty-year-old native of Lancaster, Massachusetts, moved to Boston and opened his own private banking and brokerage house. The son of a Unitarian minister and descendant of John Cotton, the seventeenth-century Massachusetts religious leader, Thayer grew up in a rural, unpretentious but cultivated home. His formal education was limited. Unlike his father, young Thayer did not attend Harvard College. He chose to go into business, starting on his career in Lancaster at an unusually young age.

There is no record of Thayer's early activities. It is possible he may have been associated with relatives, for at the time there were Thayers in Lancaster who were engaged in trade with China. The fact that he established his own business on Boston's Central Wharf, where many of the city's merchants maintained countinghouses, also suggests that his experience may have been in foreign commerce.[1] Thayer kept his wharf location only two years. In 1826 he moved to 47 State Street, the center of Boston's financial district, where most other stock and exchange brokers and all but one of the city's fifteen chartered commercial banks had offices. He continued in business on State Street until his death in 1857.

Like many other private banking and brokerage houses at the time, Thayer's appears to have been a one-person organization. The firm's initial capital is unknown, but it was believed to have been small. At the time of his death, the *Boston Evening Transcript* noted that Thayer had started in business "with no inheritance except a good name."[2]

Other aspects of the firm's early years are equally obscure. Staff size is unknown as is its composition and turnover. The business probably was conducted with no more than one or two clerks, almost certainly with no more than six, the number employed at the time the firm was dissolved in 1865.

Contemporary business directories classified the firm as a brokerage house, usually listing it with "stock and exchange" brokers. Its functions, however, included many other activities beyond those commonly associated with present-day brokerage firms. Some of Thayer's services, such as raising new capital for business and governments, buying and selling securities for clients, and providing financial advice to corporations and counseling wealthy individuals on their investments, foreshadowed on a small scale some of the functions of present-day investment bankers. Others were typically those of pre-Civil War and later nineteenth-century private bankers. Thayer dealt in foreign exchange, but did not participate actively in foreign trade. He accepted some deposits, chiefly from clients seeking investments. These funds, together with some of his own, he invested in a variety of enterprises, mostly New England banks, insurance companies, cotton manufacturing firms, real estate, as well as railroads.[3]

Massachusetts law prohibited private bankers from issuing their own notes for circulation as money, and Thayer, unlike some of his contemporaries in other states, appears to have adhered strictly both to the intent and letter of the law. His apparent refusal to engage in any money-creating activities probably was the only significant difference in functions between his banking house and Boston's chartered commercial banks.[4]

But it was Thayer's services to a relatively small group of elite Boston business managers and investors that augmented his reputation and fortune and, according to the *Boston Evening Transcript,* made him "the head of a banking house second to none in the country."[5] Thayer shared many of his clients' values and outlook; his family background was similar to theirs, and so was that of his wife, Anna Francis, the daughter of Ebenezar Francis, one of Boston's richest men, a shipowner, merchant, and financier.[6]

Thayer was a conservative banker and cautious investor. His involvement with railroad enterprises illustrates these qualities. At a time when railroads were widely hailed as the solution to the country's pressing need for cheap and improved land transportation, Thayer, like many other Boston bankers and capitalists, was neither an active supporter of nor a heavy investor in these projects. His railroad interests in the 1830s included three Massachusetts carriers. In two of them, the Boston and Worcester (incorporated in 1831) and the Western (chartered in 1833), Thayer was a small initial investor, subscribing to five shares of the former and twenty of the latter. For the third road, the Eastern (incorporated in 1836), he was a late investor. His first purchase of this road's stock occurred in 1839, after its viability had been proved and further state aid was forthcoming. Thayer's involvement in early railroad finance was modest and largely passive.[7]

The same cannot be said of Thayer's other activities. These

were growing rapidly and were widespread. During the later 1830s, he had accounts with some eighteen brokerage firms in nine different cities, from Amherst, New Hampshire, to New Orleans, Louisiana. Six of his correspondents were in New York City, one of the more important of whom was Cammann & Whitehouse, a highly respected and energetic firm. In Washington, D.C., Thayer's correspondent was William Wilson Corcoran, who was then operating his own brokerage house.[8]

There is no evidence to indicate the nature of Thayer's transactions with his correspondents, but his ledger shows that several of his accounts were active and involved sizable sums. Such was the one with Cammann & Whitehouse. A sample month in 1839 recorded thirteen entries with total debits of nearly $125,000. Another of Thayer's active accounts was with A. H. Dorr & Co., a New York City brokerage firm. For January 1839, Thayer's total debits with this house amounted to nearly $370,000, with some twenty-eight transactions involved. These and other ledger entries substantiate contemporary opinion that Thayer's business was relatively large, widespread, and profitable. Earlier in the decade his wealth had been estimated at $200,000; a few years before his death a contemporary chronicler claimed Thayer was worth about $1.5 million. Bostonians considered him an influential capitalist, "the possessor of a most ample fortune," in the words of the *Boston Evening Transcript.*[9]

State Street bankers and brokers regarded Thayer as a leading figure in the financial district. He was one of thirteen brokers who helped establish the Boston Stock Exchange in 1834, then called the Boston Broker's Board. Its original quarters, on the upper story of the Washington Bank Building at 47 State Street, were at the same address Thayer occupied at the time. In 1854 he also took an active part in organizing the Boston Board of Trade.[10]

Thayer continued in business for himself until 1839. In that year he admitted to the firm his younger brother, Nathaniel, who was then a few months shy of his thirty-first birthday. Educated at the Lancaster Academy, Nathaniel, like his brother, also violated family tradition by opting for a business career instead of attending Harvard. Nathaniel Thayer was sixteen years old when he moved to Boston to accept a clerkship with a Long Wharf merchant trading with the West Indies. He stayed with this firm six years, long enough to learn the business and accumulate some capital. In 1830, at age twenty-two, he became a partner of Elisha Preston, another prominent Long Wharf trader dealing in West Indian goods. During his years with Preston, young Thayer also engaged in other profitable activities. In 1832, together with his partner and three other Boston merchants, he joined a syndicate organized to hunt whale in the Pacific, Indian, and Atlantic oceans. The group purchased four ships and operated them profitably until 1840, a year after young Thayer had left Long Wharf to join his brother on State Street.[11]

J. E. Thayer & Brother, the new partnership, was organized on June 1, 1839. Little is known about the firm's original capital or the amount each brother contributed to it. An entry in John Thayer's cash book dated December 1840 seems to indicate that he took three-fourths of the profits plus interest on his investment. On the basis of these figures, the firm's capital at the time appears to have been about $200,000.[12]

The Thayer firm never had more than two partners, and its office staff never numbered more than a half-dozen clerks. John Thayer continued as senior partner until his death on September 29, 1857, at which time Nathaniel became head of the firm. By then his share of the business and profits had increased to 50 percent.[13]

At this time the firm was located in the Union Bank Building at 40 State Street. Also occupying quarters in that three-story corner structure were five banks, four insurance companies, nine "loan and fund associations," several private banking and brokerage houses, as well as the Boston Stock and Exchange Board, the latter having moved there from its old location in March 1853.[14]

Contemporary directories, which previously had classified J. E. Thayer & Brother as brokers, increasingly listed the firm as a banking house. The change in classification appears to have been meaningless. No significant alterations occurred in its functions. The firm continued to engage in a wide variety of banking and brokerage activities, much as it had done when the elder Thayer was in charge.[15]

Like many other Atlantic seaboard banking and brokerage houses at the time, J. E. Thayer & Brother was a diversified, unspecialized house. Its most important functions included carrying investment accounts for individuals, acting as brokers for individuals, estates, and institutions (The Massachusetts Hospital Life Insurance Company was a Thayer client), and bidding for state and federal bonds. The firm also invested and traded in Massachusetts real estate and Western lands as well as in new and old securities of banks, insurance companies, and railroads. Dealing in foreign exchange was still one of its principal activities. During the early 1840s the firm was the largest seller of exchange in Boston, competing vigorously with the American representative of London's Baring Brothers & Co.[16]

Although the sum total of Thayer & Brother's activities continued essentially unchanged, after 1840 the firm and its partners personally became increasingly involved in railroad affairs. The elder Thayer's originally hesitant interest and small investments in railroad properties grew substantially after his brother Nathaniel joined the firm. In 1846 the firm, together with John Murray Forbes, a thirty-three-year-old wealthy former China trader, helped launch the private corporation that bought the state-owned Michigan Central Railroad and made itself the financial representative of the new company.[17]

Nathaniel Thayer was an even more active railroad promoter and financier. Not only did he invest his own money in these enterprises, but it was largely through his efforts that the firm became an important distributor of railroad securities and, on occasion, also accepted the task of serving as transfer agent of the roads it helped finance. Unlike the elder Thayer, who appears to have served only on the directorate of two roads—the Eastern and the Hannibal and St. Joseph—Nathaniel was on the board of at least six by the time he retired from the banking and brokerage business.

Financing railroads widened Thayer & Brother's business to include some important investment banking functions. To protect its investments and those of its clients, the firm assumed an increasing responsibility toward the companies it financed. In addition to accepting railroad directorships, the partners, as individuals, also served as the companies' financial advisers and, through the firm, provided them with various other banking facilities.[18]

Thayer & Brother's growing importance as railroad promoters and bankers occurred at a time when the firm was becoming increasingly active in other business and financial areas as well. During the 1850s and early 1860s the firm developed strong ties with several banks in Boston and with others elsewhere in New England, either through a personal investment of a partner or by securing representation on their directorates. Both partners took an active role in organizing the Boston Five Cents Savings Bank in 1854. Meanwhile the firm continued its earlier correspondent relationship with several banking and brokerage houses in New York City. It developed close ties with McCalmont & Co. of London, a competitor of the Barings in the sale of American securities in England. In the late 1850s McCalmont became the Thayer firm's chief English correspondent in exchange and securities transactions. Association with this house gave Thayer & Brother improved access to the London capital market just at the time when Nathaniel Thayer himself and his house became increasingly occupied with railroad finance.[19]

As a railroad financier, Nathaniel Thayer operated on two levels. He was a partner and then head of an important, well-connected house that dealt extensively in railroad securities and provided the companies that issued them with a wide variety of advisory and banking services. At the same time, he was also a heavy individual investor in many of these enterprises. The two roles remained largely separate, with the latter becoming increasingly more important, especially after his brother's death in 1857.[20]

Nathaniel Thayer's railroad interests expanded greatly during the Civil War. He invested in more lines, not only in New England, but in New York, Pennsylvania, and in several Middle Western states, including Michigan, Missouri, Illinois, and Ohio. The amounts he invested also grew substantially. Most of his purchases, which included both stocks and bonds, were made in 1863 or later. Some of his largest railroad holdings at the beginning of 1865 were in securities of the Chicago, Burlington & Quincy ($540,000), Pittsburgh, Fort Wayne & Chicago ($380,000), and Hannibal and St. Joseph ($200,000). Except for his investments in two middle Atlantic carriers (the Philadelphia & Reading [$365,000] and the Philadelphia, Wilmington, & Baltimore [$380,000]), Thayer's principal holdings were in western roads. His growing interest in these properties stemmed in no small part from his close association with John Murray Forbes.[21]

Besides his railroad holdings, Thayer also was interested in several land companies, mines, and textile firms. In 1864 he added to his investments by buying into the Chicago Rolling Mill Company, the first industrial securities he purchased other than textile issues. That same year he also bought into the American Telegraph Company, which subsequently was made part of the Western Union system. Thayer's growing personal investments, which amounted to some $3 million in 1865, led him to relinquish his other business responsibilities and devote himself entirely to managing his holdings and participating more actively in the affairs of the companies in which he invested, particularly railroads.[22]

Thayer's decision to become an active capitalist on his own account in the Forbes tradition necessitated a reorganization of his banking and brokerage business. On April 1, 1865, Thayer left his State Street office and moved to 62 Exchange Place, where he continued to operate the firm as a trust estate. At the time of his death, on March 7, 1883, he was worth some $16 million. "How wonderfully the property rolled up, since the trial-balance we took in 1857," Francis H. Peabody wrote his brother Oliver.[23] Both men certainly were in a position to appreciate the spectacular growth of Thayer's fortune, each having served as a clerk in J. E. Thayer & Brother for almost twenty years from the mid-1840s until 1865, when the firm was reorganized and a new one, Kidder, Peabody & Co., was established to take over the "exchange and stock business" of the old one.

At the time of the reorganization, J. E. Thayer & Brother was one of Boston's leading private banking and brokerage houses, well-known and respected in American and English financial circles. Brown, Shipley & Co., the London house of Brown Brothers & Co., at the time one of America's most prestigious and influential international banking partnerships, considered the Thayer firm as "possessed of good means."[24] The firm's resources, the knowledge, experience, reputation, and connections of its partners, attracted to Thayer & Brother a distinguished clientele of prominent and wealthy Bostonians who depended upon the firm for investment advice and services. Business executives, particularly railroad officials, also turned to Thayer & Brother for the capital they needed to improve and expand their properties. The firm's banking experience, traditions, and business practices, as well as many of its clients, passed to Kidder, Peabody & Co.

CHAPTER
TWO

A New Firm with an Old Experience

Kidder, Peabody & Co. opened for business on April 1, 1865, at 40 State Street, the offices previously occupied by J. E. Thayer & Brother. "We retain the exchange accounts of J. E. Thayer & Brother," the new firm informed the public by mail and newspaper notices, "and shall be represented at the Stock Board by one of our partners, who will give personal attention to the purchase and sale of stocks, bonds, and gold, in New York, Philadelphia, or Baltimore."[1] The three services Kidder, Peabody advertised at the time of its organization—"banking, brokerage, and exchange business"—also were provided by many of the city's other financial institutions. Boston, with a population of some 192,000 inhabitants in 1865 and property (real and personal) valued at close to $382 million, counted upwards of 200 financial institutions, among them 18 private banks (including Kidder, Peabody), 77 stock and exchange brokers, and 43 nationally chartered commercial banks.[2] What distinguished Kidder, Peabody and firms like it, such as Lee, Higginson & Co., from other State Street intermediaries was the ability of these houses to recruit the great amounts of capital needed to finance a rapidly developing economy composed of increasingly large and complex business organizations.

Kidder, Peabody's success in securing funds for railroads and industry stemmed from the confidence wealthy Bostonians had in the integrity and experience of its founding partners—Henry P. Kidder, Francis H. Peabody, and Oliver W. Peabody. All three were natives of Massachusetts, well-known among the state's business and financial leaders through their long association with J. E. Thayer & Brother, a firm that had enjoyed close ties with Boston's affluent elite for nearly two generations.

The three partners themselves came from families of modest circumstances. None of them had attended college, each having gone into business when quite young. Kidder, the son of a Boston fish and meat inspector, was one of twelve children. He attended The Roxbury Latin School and worked for several years as a clerk in Coolidge & Haskell, auctioneers of promissory notes, real estate, drygoods, and miscellaneous other articles, mostly imports. From there he went to the Boston & Worcester Railroad where he served as a clerk in the forwarding department. In 1845, at the age of twenty-three, he joined J. E. Thayer & Brother as Nathaniel Thayer's confidential clerk, was made head clerk in 1857, and a partner the next year.[3]

Francis and Oliver Peabody were the sons of a Unitarian minister. Their father was the pastor of a church in Springfield, Massachusetts, where they were born. Francis, the oldest, went to public schools and worked for two years in the Chicopee Bank in which the Thayers had an interest. In 1847, at the age of sixteen, he moved to Boston to become a clerk in the Thayer firm.[4]

Three years younger than his brother, Oliver Peabody was the only one of the firm's founding partners to have started in business with the Thayers. He joined their house as a clerk in 1849, immediately upon leaving Phillips Exeter Academy. Fifteen years old at the time, he stayed with the Thayers until 1862, leaving to enlist in the Forty-fifth Regiment, Massachusetts Volunteers. When the regiment was disbanded, he joined another, the Second Massachusetts Volunteer Militia, and served in it through the war, rising to the rank of lieutenant colonel. After Lee surrendered to Grant, Peabody returned to Boston and joined his brother and Kidder in the newly organized firm.[5]

Kidder, forty-two years old at the time the firm was organized, was the senior partner. He headed the house until his death in 1886. The terms of agreement made no mention of the firm's capital or the amounts contributed by each partner. A statement on the division of profits suggests what may have been the relative size of their contributions. Kidder was to receive 50 percent, Francis Peabody 30 percent, and his brother 20 percent. Toward the end of the century it became firm policy to admit new partners without requiring them to put up any new capital, but this probably was not true at the start.[6]

Profits were calculated on the same accounting principle employed by the Thayers. Earnings were charged with 6 percent interest on the capital before profits were derived.

The firm's staff, composed of four clerks in 1865, was headed by Frank G. Webster who had been hired to close the books of J. E. Thayer & Brother. Born on June 11, 1842, Webster was the son of a carriage maker in Canton, Massachusetts, a Boston suburb. He went to public schools; then worked as a bookbinder and in a wallpaper store in Providence, Rhode Island. After a few years he returned to Canton and accepted a clerkship in a local bank. In 1862 he enlisted in the Fifty-fourth Massachusetts Volunteers, serving until 1864. On his return to Boston he worked for a short time in the National Shoe and Leather Bank, and in March 1865 joined J. E. Thayer & Brother. The next month, when Kidder, Peabody was organized, Webster became its senior clerk. In 1886, at the age of forty-five, he was made a partner.[7]

Webster opened Kidder, Peabody's books and he continued

to be solely responsible for keeping the accounts and supervising the entire office staff until December 1868. By then the number of clerks had doubled and Webster was assigned an assistant, a Mr. Sibley. Webster continued to be in charge of the firm's correspondence and bond accounts; Sibley assumed oversight of the gold and currency books; and the two of them, the only two employees "authorised to deal with customers at the counter," also supervised the work and conduct of the other "young gentlemen" on the staff, making certain that they arrived promptly "at half-past eight, A.M., do their duty faithfully . . . and do not leave without . . . approval." Webster and Sibley also were charged with enforcing the partners' rules on "general deportment in the office" which, according to the firm's "regulations," meant no "profanity, rough play, coarse language and disrespect to the members of the firm, to themselves, or to each other."[8]

From the time it was organized, Kidder, Peabody was and remained a diversified banking house. It was only natural that this should be the case. The founding partners had been trained in this tradition and it was common practice for private banks in major metropolitan centers to offer a wide variety of financial services. This was as true of firms founded before the Civil War, such as Winslow, Lanier & Co., with which Kidder, Peabody had close ties, as it was of those that achieved prominence in the later decades of the nineteenth century, like Drexel, Morgan & Co. and Kuhn, Loeb & Co.

Like many private banking houses in Boston, New York, and other major Atlantic seaboard cities, Kidder, Peabody's business fell into two broadly defined categories: banking and investments. The firm conducted both types of operations not only in Boston but also in out-of-state cities through correspondents. Within each of these classifications, Kidder, Peabody provided a variety of services. As bankers it accepted deposits of corporations and individuals subject to check. Nearly all these accounts were those of clients for whom the firm also conducted other business. It dealt in gold and specie, made secured call and time loans, bought and sold foreign exchange on a commission basis, and issued commercial and travelers' letters of credit.[9]

The firm was particularly active in the foreign exchange and letter of credit business. Daniel Curtis, the manager of Brown Brothers & Co.'s Boston branch, reported to his firm's New York office that Kidder, Peabody was incessantly "drumming our customers." The newly organized house, Curtis wrote in March 1871, was "ingenious in invention of small inducements to such of our Credit and Exchange customers as are open to them."[10] Kidder, Peabody was equally forceful in developing its letter of credit business. New England merchants turned to the firm to finance substantial shares of their imports with Kidder, Peabody letters of credit. In November 1878 the firm opened an account with Baring Brothers & Co., London, then one of the world's most prestigious and influential private banking houses. The account proved so mutually advantageous that in January 1886 the English bankers made Kidder, Peabody their exclusive American agents. The negotiations leading to these arrangements also resulted in Thomas Baring becoming a partner in Kidder, Peabody. From then on the Boston firm's circular letters of credit were issued jointly with Barings. Kidder, Peabody's foreign banking business was sufficiently important that letters of credit and foreign exchange received major attention in the firm's advertisements until the early 1890s. Foreign banking continued to be important into the 1920s, but it ceased to receive special attention.[11]

During the years of Kidder, Peabody's emergence as a foreign banking house serving the needs of business people buying and selling throughout the world, the firm also expanded its investment operations. These involved several functions: dealing in federal, state, and municipal securities; buying and selling corporate bonds and stocks on commission in Boston and other markets; trading and investing in securities on its own account; originating and distributing new issues, mostly railroad offerings; acting as fiscal agents for the companies the firm had helped finance; and when it appeared necessary, participating in the management of the corporations whose securities it had helped distribute or in which the firm had invested. Little was added to those operations after 1865, particularly in the half century before World War I.

All of these functions had been performed by J. E. Thayer & Brother; Kidder, Peabody increased their volume and modified them to meet the changing needs of its clients. Since its founding the firm had a partner on the Boston Stock and Exchange Board and since 1886 a representative on the New York Stock Exchange. During the Civil War J. E. Thayer & Brother dealt and invested in the federal government's bond offerings, particularly the "five-twenties" and "seven-thirties." After Appomattox Kidder, Peabody, along with other private bankers, participated in the Treasury's funding of its short-term obligations. In the 1870s the firm also helped the government refund its Civil War loans, selling federal bonds in Boston and elsewhere in Massachusetts.[12]

Most of the firm's ventures on its own account were conducted jointly with the Barings and wealthy Bostonians. Typical of these transactions was one Francis Peabody proposed early in December 1883, when it appeared there might be a brief credit panic. Writing to Kidder, who was then in London conferring with the Barings on a new offering for the Atchison, Topeka & Santa Fe Railroad, Peabody suggested that if security prices dropped substantially, as was anticipated, the firm should buy a large block of Ottawa Railroad stock, using its own funds and those of an undisclosed local capitalist. The road had been showing a steady profit; the price of its stock would recover from any momentary loss it might suffer. The venture Peabody proposed was large, involving some $2 million, so he wanted Kidder's approval. If he consented, Kidder was to instruct the Barings to include the word "ADELITA" in their next communication to Boston; if, however, he deemed it "wiser to forego embarking on so large an enterprise," then the Barings should "telegraph the word 'NIRVANA,' upon receipt of which we shall drop the idea."[13] Kidder's reply is missing from the record, and there is no other evidence to indicate that the firm purchased the stock.

As was true of so many of its operations, Kidder, Peabody's activities in originating and distributing new corporate issues also grew out of the partners' earlier experience with the Thayers. Some of the firm's earliest bond offerings, such as those for the Chicago, Burlington & Quincy, were for carriers with which Nathaniel Thayer had been associated. Kidder, Peabody built upon these ties and developed others.

The firm emerged as a major American banking house during the railroad boom of the late 1870s when the economy started to recover from the long depression that followed the panic of 1873. Between 1870 and the onset of the next severe crisis in 1893, total railroad mileage in the United States nearly tripled, while the combined total outstanding issues of railroad bonds and stocks more than doubled, increasing from $4.8 billion to $9.9 billion. During these years of rapid railroad building and improvements, Kidder, Peabody helped finance more than sixty carriers, among them some of the major transcontinental systems and principal eastern trunk lines, as well as the Mexican Central Railroad. The services it performed for these companies ranged from nothing more than selling their securities to choosing their officers and advising them on how to operate the properties.[14]

Bankers like Kidder, Peabody played an important role in reorganizing railroads in financial trouble. The fees and commissions earned in these transactions often were "very large," as Frank Webster, then a partner, wrote to the elder Peabody who was on his way to Europe. Webster believed the firm should cultivate this business, and he urged Peabody to impress upon the Barings the profits and safety in these operations. It was imperative, he said, that Barings understand "that for the making of large profits," Kidder, Peabody should be permitted to use the funds the two firms held in joint account "without any feeling of restraint or misunderstanding." Peabody illustrated the point by referring to Drexel, Morgan & Co.'s reorganization of the Philadelphia & Reading Railroad, in which Kidder, Peabody had been given an opportunity to participate by Franklin B. Gowen, the president of the carrier. "I was satisfied that the property could be safely reorganized," Webster wrote, and on a basis "upon which the new securities would be perfectly good." Webster refused the business, he said, because of Thomas Baring's "apprehension and uneasiness" concerning reorganizations. Such fears were baseless, he reported. Had Baring shown more "confidence in our conservatism and judgment in the matter," Webster concluded, he would have accepted a share of the business and Kidder, Peabody, the Barings, and Drexel, Morgan would have divided "a commission of over $1,000,000 . . . without a particle of risk to anyone."[15] There were far fewer dangers and much greater profit in reorganizing railroad properties than in the letter of credit business. Peabody should stress to the Barings that "there is no basis of a security so sound or so capable of intelligent understanding, as the basis of the reorganization of a large property; as you have all the history, the condition of the property, and what it can safely be depended upon to do under the worst circumstances before you upon which to form your judgment." He concluded that the two firms should concentrate more of their attention on serving the financial needs of large corporations.

The close relationship that developed between Kidder, Peabody and the Atchison, Topeka & Santa Fe Railroad during the late 1800s illustrates both the kind of business Webster wanted the firm to emphasize and the range of services private bankers came to provide their issuer clients. Kidder, Peabody's association with the Santa Fe began in September 1870, when the road was in financial difficulties and in desperate need of capital to build from Atchison, Kansas, to the Colorado border in order to satisfy the terms of its congressional land grant. The president of the railroad and several of the directors as well as most of its investors were Bostonians. It was only natural that the Santa Fe should turn to a Boston house for the funds it required. From 1870 until 1888 Kidder, Peabody, usually in collaboration with the Barings and occasionally with one or two American houses, financed much of the construction and acquisition of new properties that turned the Santa Fe from a sectional railroad, with most of its mileage in Kansas, into a major transcontinental system.[16]

Financing the Santa Fe's expansion was only one of Kidder, Peabody's services to this company. The firm also acted as the carrier's transfer agent, bank of deposit, and financial consultants. It was in this latter capacity that Kidder, Peabody exercised its greatest influence over policy. In 1871 Francis Peabody joined the Santa Fe's directorate, rising to become chairman of the finance committee and vice president. But even after he relinquished these posts and the firm no longer was represented in an official capacity, Kidder, Peabody continued to be actively concerned with company affairs.[17] In part this stemmed from the fact that for a time Kidder, Peabody and the Barings were among the Santa Fe's largest stockholders, having secured most of their shares in payment for originating and marketing the carrier's securities. In addition to these holdings the two banking houses sometimes also found themselves with a large volume of the road's unsold securities. In October 1887, for instance, the amount of unsold Santa Fe securities held in joint account by Kidder, Peabody and Baring Brothers stood at nearly $5.9 million.[18]

Protection of its own investment was not the only reason Kidder, Peabody sought to maintain its ties with the Santa Fe. Nor was it due chiefly to Kidder, Peabody's sense of responsibility toward the investors who had bought the railroad's securities, important as this consideration was to everyone concerned. Kidder, Peabody's continuing interest in the property derived in no small part from the pride and satisfaction of having played a vital role in launching a major transcontinental railroad. "The property is increasing rapidly and largely in value and influence," Webster wrote Francis Peabody, "and has, on the whole, I think, the most honest and able management that I know of, of any railroad property here. We ought to keep it to ourselves."[19]

Kidder, Peabody's hopes for the continued success and integrity of the Santa Fe were to be seriously shaken. Rapid construction westward and expansion of its facilities brought a sharp increase in the road's bonded debt, from $52 million in 1883 to $154 million in 1888. Interest payments strained the company's resources, while an appreciable drop in earnings added to its financial troubles.

Pressed by problems, the railroad called on Kidder, Peabody for advice and assistance. The bankers responded at once, recommending measures to cut costs and improve the company's credit. When these proved inadequate, Kidder, Peabody prepared to institute more drastic reforms. The first step was to seek and win Baring Brothers' approval. Once this had been accomplished, Kidder, Peabody then arranged to have a partner placed on the road's finance committee and to have its authority over disbursements greatly extended. These measures, together with a $7 million loan floated by Kidder, Peabody, proved immediately useful but did not solve the Santa Fe's long-term problems.[20]

A comprehensive program designed to restore the Santa Fe's credit and assure the road's successful operation in the future was initiated in the spring of 1889. Kidder, Peabody, with the support of the Barings, instituted a series of changes in the carrier's management and financial structure that gave the bankers a commanding voice in making policy. They achieved this position at the Santa Fe's annual meeting on May 9, 1889. On that day Thomas Baring, the American representative of the London banking house and a Kidder, Peabody partner since January 1, 1886, voted his huge block of shares (some 71 percent of those represented) in favor of the "Kidder, Peabody ticket," giving the Boston bankers an easy victory. The newly elected board was composed of six directors, two of whom (Thomas Baring and Oliver Peabody) were Kidder, Peabody partners. A few months later a third partner, Francis Peabody, who previously had served a term as a Santa Fe director, returned to his old place on the board. A fourth Kidder, Peabody partner, George C. Magoun, the firm's expert on corporate reorganizations, was named chairman of the board.[21] By the end of August 1889, four of the Santa Fe's six directors were Kidder, Peabody partners and the bankers also held majorities on the road's executive and finance committees.[22]

Once Kidder, Peabody and the Barings were in control of the Santa Fe's top management, the bankers then proceeded to reorganize the carrier's finances. The plan, involving some $250 million of new securities, was designed to achieve several objectives: reduce fixed charges, simplify the capital structure, retire some $1.7 million of floating debt, and provide the company with about $5 million of new capital. To achieve these objectives, Kidder, Peabody proposed converting a great variety of outstanding bond issues into two types: general first mortgage bonds and income bonds, the former paying 4 percent and the latter 5 percent. The plan, which Kidder, Peabody persuaded the bondholders to accept, caused them no loss of income. The major concession they were asked to accept was "to have part of their interest payments depend upon current earnings, if available, rather than on a legal obligation."[23] For the Santa Fe the exchange of securities involved a saving of $3.8 million. Contemporary observers hailed Kidder, Peabody's reorganization. *The Commercial & Financial Chronicle,* crediting Magoun for his skill and ingenuity in planning and executing the project, called the reorganization "a brilliant conception."[24]

The bankers sought to perpetuate their reforms by having the Santa Fe's stock put into a voting trust "for the protection of the property." The original plan, set forth by Francis Peabody, called for a three- or five-year arrangement. But shortly thereafter, when it appeared Jay Gould might try to win control of the road, Peabody suggested a ten-year trust. "If he should do so," Peabody wrote Magoun, "it would not only be a great disaster to the property, but a terrible mortification for K.P. & Co., who would practically have cooked the goose for him to eat."[25] No such device was effected and Kidder, Peabody's influence over the Santa Fe lasted until 1893, when the panic of that year and the long depression that followed it forced the road into bankruptcy, along with one-fourth of the country's carriers.

Kidder, Peabody's principal American associates or syndicate partners were private bankers with strong connections to the European capital markets. The firm joined Drexel, Morgan & Co. in financing many of the United States' principal railroads and in the reorganization of the Baltimore & Ohio; it cosponsored with Winslow, Lanier & Co. and J. & W. Seligman & Co. large bond offerings for the Atlantic & Pacific Railroad; and it participated with its Boston rivals, Lee, Higginson & Co., in financing the Chicago, Burlington & Quincy. What distinguished these houses and others like them, such as Kuhn, Loeb & Co. and Brown Brothers & Co., firms with which Kidder, Peabody also cooperated and competed, was their access to large amounts of capital, both foreign and domestic.[26] Kidder, Peabody's alliance with the Barings and its ties to Boston wealth gave the firm strong advantages in competing for corporate accounts.

Equally important in attracting clients were the firm's own growing capital resources. In December 1886 Oliver Peabody reported to the Barings that the firm had distributed $25,000 to the clerks, "the usual percentage . . . we can safely divide from [$] 450,000 to [$] 500,000 for the year, or rather since the 1st of Feby." The next year, in submitting its regular statement to its London associates, Kidder, Peabody reported that the joint account stood at $13.8 million and suggested using some $5 million or $6 million "for a speculation" in Santa Fe stock, "buying upon a declining market to the amount, possibly, of 25,000 shares . . . to be carried . . . until we realize the profit, which we feel is quite sure to come." Meanwhile, the firm reported it was continuing to add to its capital. By the end of the century the amounts often were substantial. "You will be grateful to know," Francis Peabody informed the Barings early in

January 1893, "that after making up our accounts to Jan. 1st on a very conservative basis, we have added $500,000 to our capital during the past year."[27]

Since relatively few American banking houses were able to satisfy the huge demand for capital that railroads needed to expand, improve, and reorganize their systems, firms like Kidder, Peabody occupied a strategic position in the economy. During the last quarter of the nineteenth century most of the principal railroads and many other large corporate borrowers, notably the new industrial combinations that were launched in the 1890s, developed and maintained close ties with one or more banking houses, depending upon them for financial assistance in times of prosperity as well as depression.

The growing needs of these corporations led the bankers that financed them to concentrate increasingly upon providing investment services to the users and suppliers of capital. Although few firms, if any, specialized exclusively in what came to be known as the investment banking business, most of them, while continuing to offer a diversity of financial services, came to be associated chiefly with corporate finance and the securities business, specifically with the job of originating, underwriting or purchasing, and distributing new issues. In performing these functions investment firms, like Kidder, Peabody, extended and revised practices developed earlier, many of them in the 1850s when railroad securities first appeared in substantial volume. Growth in the number and size of these offerings in the post-Civil War years led to the institutionalization of practices previously employed informally. In the 1850s J. E. Thayer & Brother and similar firms like Winslow, Lanier & Co. had provided financial advice to railroad managements on an ad hoc basis; in the 1880s the more common practice was to have the banker sponsoring a company's securities represented on its board of directors.

Nor was the custom of bankers joining together in groups, or syndicates, to pool their resources and spread the risk a post-Civil War innovation. Associations of this type had been employed before, especially in the sale of government bonds. The change came in the frequency with which these groups were employed and the variety of uses to which they were put. Kidder, Peabody, for instance, organized and participated in many types of syndicates, some to purchase securities, others to underwrite new offerings, and still others designed to distribute blocks of bonds and stocks to brokers, investors, or both.[28]

The ability of firms like Kidder, Peabody to raise capital through the sale of securities rested, of course, on the confidence of investors. To protect the interest of those who entrusted their funds to them as well as their own reputation, investment bankers employed various devices. They accepted representation on the boards and finance committees of the companies whose securities they sponsored, hoping that their presence there would prevent the adoption of policies that might endanger the solvency of the corporation. Because investors believed banking representation of this type meant that their interests would be served better, company officials encouraged the practice since it helped the sale of their securities. Some corporations, railroads as well as industrial companies, valued these arrangements sufficiently to advertise the name of the bankers on their board, hoping the prestige of the banking house would spill over to them.

There were other reasons beyond the need for self-protection that led partners in investment houses to maintain their association with the companies they sponsored. The banker that originated a corporation's securities often became its transfer agent or bank of deposit. Familiarity with the corporation's affairs and the ties the banker established with its officials also made it likely that his firm would be called upon the next time the company needed new capital. Kidder, Peabody's intervention in the Santa Fe, like the reorganizations negotiated by other bankers, was designed not only to restore the company's credit and inspire confidence in its securities but also to permit the firm to earn a fee for its various services.

The stands Kidder, Peabody's partners took on public issues reflected their concern with maintaining credit, aiding business, and attracting capital investments. Francis Peabody, writing to John Murray Forbes in August 1882, said he had "no interest in Republican politics" because he disapproved of the party's tariff and tax policies. "I do not expect to feel any interest in politics until some party arises whose principal object is a reform of the Civil Service and a considerable diminution in Government revenue, and in the number of officials now employed to collect it."[29] The partners' views on these and other major issues of the day, notably attempts to get Congress to regulate the railroads and inflate the currency, both of which they strongly opposed, placed them solidly in the ranks of the more conservative elements of the business and financial community.

During the 1880s Kidder, Peabody was considered one of the country's more cautious and responsible banking houses. In May 1882 the *Boston Evening Transcript*, criticizing several Wall Street firms for having "smirched their names" in various transactions, proudly proclaimed that "there is no house in New York of equal standing with that of Messrs. Kidder, Peabody & Co. of Boston." Four years later, at the time of Kidder's death, *The New York Times* described the firm as the "leading banking house in New England," occupying a position in American finance "analgous to that of Drexel, Morgan & Co."[30]

J. Pierpont Morgan, then the head of Drexel, Morgan, also considered Kidder, Peabody a major banking house. In January 1889 he invited it to participate in a conference to be attended by officials of the country's major railroads. The only other banking firm invited to the meeting, officially known as the Interstate Commerce Railway Association, was Brown Brothers & Co. The purpose of the conference was twofold: to establish a committee to enforce the Interstate Commerce Act, which Congress had passed in 1887, and reach an agreement on rates that would ensure profits and put an end to the destructive competition that threatened the solvency of various roads. Morgan failed to achieve his objectives, but many of the suggestions made by the bankers were effected after the panic of 1893.[31]

Kidder, Peabody's partners attributed the crisis that broke with the stock market crash of June 1893 to private greed and mismanagement, as exemplified by some of the nation's railroad and business leaders, together with lack of confidence in the government's monetary policies, specifically Congress' failure to repeal the Sherman Silver Purchase Act of 1890. Six months before the stock market break Francis Peabody wrote President Benjamin Harrison that the government and the country were headed for serious trouble. He cautioned the President, who had just been defeated in his bid for reelection, that the Treasury's continued silver purchases under the terms of the Sherman Act were checking the flow of foreign capital to the United States, "which impresses me as an unnecessary evil to us all." Buying silver, he told the President, also would drive gold to a premium, precipitating a severe panic "from which it would take the country years to recover."[32] Repeal of the Sherman Act was accomplished by Harrison's successor, President Grover Cleveland, who summoned Congress into special session on June 30, three days after the stock market collapse. By then it was too late to stem the tide and by the end of the year more than 400 banks and some 15,000 businesses had failed.

Kidder, Peabody weathered the crisis easily. "Business is of course quiet," Francis Peabody wrote his brother at the height of the panic, "and we are neither making nor losing much money." One of the firm's important services during the worst month of the crisis was to import $1.5 million in gold to help relieve the critical need for currency.[33]

Meanwhile, the firm tried to influence its representative in Congress to adopt measures it considered necessary to restore confidence and prosperity. It sought, among other things, to persuade its member of Congress to press for a revision of the Interstate Commerce Act, one which would allow certain types of railroad pools. "A large part of the loss and disaster which we have all suffered," Oliver Peabody wrote Congressman William Everett, "has come from the prohibition of pooling. It keeps Western railroads in perpetual warfare and makes peace impossible. Furthermore, it keeps them all busy with offering secret rebates to important customers, as for instance the wealthy cattle dealers of Chicago. This practice not only impoverishes the railroads, and demoralizes their employees, but it gives the wealthy shippers a great advantage over the smaller ones. The larger the business is, the bigger the rebates [that] can be got. The consequence is that the small dealers are obliged to pay higher rates for transportation than the larger ones. In other words, the pooling prohibition creates the very trouble that it was intended to cure."[34]

Asked for its views on various proposals to alter the currency, Kidder, Peabody replied that the "present banking system, based upon U.S. Bonds, is certainly the best currency ever possessed by any nation upon the face of the earth, so long as our government maintains its determination and possesses the ability to keep up gold payments. . . . This may seem a strong statement, but it is true; whether in Norway, Turkey, Africa, India, Japan, or any other country, a U.S. national bank note is par or about par. For safety and convenience combined, I repeat that it is unequalled by any currency existing on the face of the earth." The operation of the system needed to be improved so that "the currency would contract on a plethoric money market and expand on a tight money market," but Kidder, Peabody doubted the times allowed for the careful thought and study required to achieve sound changes in the banking laws.[35]

Like most other conservative banking houses, Kidder, Peabody was disturbed and frightened by various demands to inflate the currency. William Jennings Bryan's silver crusade and his capture of the Democratic nomination for President in July 1896 brought business to a near halt. "The feeling of uneasiness is very general, and it wouldn't surprise me if the thing culminated in a panic," Francis Peabody wrote his brother. The firm had taken the necessary precautions: "Are keeping Barings fully remitted, have all our Bank loans now on long time, and ample cash balances in hand so that I suppose we can stand it as well as the rest if it comes," Peabody reported.[36] No crisis occurred, and Bryan's defeat in the November election dissipated Peabody's remaining fears.

By the time William McKinley entered the White House in March 1897, the economy had started on its recovery and public confidence in the securities markets was beginning to be restored. Industrial corporations as well as railroads turned to investment houses for financial advice and assistance.

The techniques bankers had developed to finance railroads now were employed to launch the industrial giants and mergers of the 1890s and early years of the twentieth century. Kidder, Peabody participated in many of the transactions that transformed privately held enterprises into publicly owned companies. Before 1900 the Boston Stock Exchange was the principal market for industrial securities and Kidder, Peabody was among the first of the major houses to offer these issues. It participated in converting Procter & Gamble from a family partnership into a publicly owned corporation, and the firm took an active part in sponsoring, planning, and helping distribute the securities of several major consolidations, among them the American Sugar Refining Company, P. Lorillard & Co., New England Cotton Yarn, a company with which the firm remained closely associated, National Shawmut Bank, an early bank merger, and American Telephone & Telegraph (AT&T), one of the first major utility holding companies.[37]

At a time when telephone securities were not widely held outside New England and the company and its subsidiaries needed huge amounts of capital for expansion and improvements—an estimated $200 million in five years—Kidder, Peabody was one of the first major houses to develop a national and international market for AT&T bonds. The firm negotiated its first offerings for the company in 1899, an issue of collateral trust bonds for $7 million and another for $3 million, followed by still another for $5 million the next year.

But Kidder, Peabody did more than finance the company's early expansion. It also helped AT&T strengthen its position in a rapidly growing and, at the time, highly competitive business. In 1901, together with AT&T president Frederick P. Fish, Kidder, Peabody helped plan the reorganization of the Erie Telegraph & Telephone Co., a financially troubled corporation with subsidiaries in six Middle Western states and Texas. The reorganization not only extended AT&T's facilities but, more important still, virtually eliminated its most powerful rival, the Telephone, Telegraph, and Cable Co., an independent corporation that had sought to use the Erie Company to challenge the Bell System's dominance of the telephone business.[38] Except for a $20 million issue of notes sold competitively to Speyer & Co. and Lee Higginson & Co. in 1904, Kidder, Peabody continued to serve AT&T as its principal Boston bankers. In 1905 the firm, together with Baring Brothers, submitted the winning bid for $25 million of AT&T bonds, $5 million of which Kidder, Peabody sold privately. The Barings took $6.5 million, with the remainder being offered for public subscription in Boston, New York, and through correspondents, in Chicago, St. Louis, and Amsterdam.[39] AT&T's continuing and mounting need for capital, amounts far greater than could be obtained from its traditional sources, led Kidder, Peabody to secure the assistance of J. P. Morgan & Co. and Kuhn, Loeb & Co. The three firms, together with Baring Brothers, became AT&T's chief bankers, heading most of the syndicates that sold the company's securities, the first of which was organized in March 1906 to distribute $150 million of convertible bonds. The issue was offered to the public in installments over a two-year period, with Kidder, Peabody responsible for sales in New England.[40] Meanwhile, the firm also helped sell the securities of AT&T's subsidiaries. Between November 1909 and September 1912, Kidder, Peabody distributed nearly $68.5 million of bonds for the New York Telephone Co.[41] The firm's expanding role in the financial affairs of AT&T and its operating subsidiaries, particularly its activities in enlisting the aid of Chicago brokerage houses to use their "best efforts" to develop new markets for telephone securities, made Kidder, Peabody one of the largest distributors of these issues in the United States.[42]

During the early years of the twentieth century when Kidder, Peabody was making a specialty of telephone securities, the firm also participated in launching the United States Steel Corporation, the nation's first billion-dollar corporation. Kidder, Peabody was one of the two private banking houses (Morgan's firm was the other) that was included in the underwriting syndicate to distribute United States Steel's common stock. The firm also sponsored and distributed the securities of other smaller companies, not only in New England but throughout the United States. The corporations served by Kidder, Peabody included interurban trolley lines, gas and electric utilities, light and heavy industrials, regional railroads, textiles, mines, as well as banks and trust companies.[43]

When foreign governments first started borrowing in the United States, Kidder, Peabody also participated in these operations. In 1900 and 1901 the firm, together with J. P. Morgan & Co. and its Philadelphia partnership (Drexel & Co.), distributed millions of British consols. During the next few years Kidder, Peabody helped sell four other foreign government loans, all sponsored by groups headed by either Morgan & Co. or Kuhn, Loeb. These included issues for Japan (1905), Argentina (1909), Austria (1912), and in the latter year a small offering by the city of Tokyo. Kidder, Peabody's foreign exchange, letter of credit, and acceptance business also contributed to the firm's reputation as a foreign banking house. In 1907 the Italian government made Kidder, Peabody its bank of deposit, an account which the firm was to hold until 1931.[44]

Unlike some private banks, notably the House of Morgan and Kuhn, Loeb, which were primarily originators and wholesalers of new securities, Kidder, Peabody was one of the few national firms that provided a full range of investment banking services. It originated, purchased, and underwrote securities, sold some of them in large blocks to wealthy individuals, to institutions such as life insurance and trust companies, and to brokerage houses across the country, which resold them to investors. And it also kept sizable amounts of the issues it sponsored for its own clients, many of whom were individuals of modest means. Not a few of these small sales involved only one or two bonds or a few shares of stock.[45]

Boston continued to remain Kidder, Peabody's principal office, even though New York City had been the nation's investment banking center for almost a half century. But as the firm's securities business expanded so did its New York operations, and the representative office at 45 Wall Street that was opened by Magoun in 1868 was made a branch three years later and operated under the Kidder, Peabody name.[46]

Like most other private banking houses of the late nineteenth and early twentieth centuries, Kidder, Peabody's policies were determined entirely by the partners, whose numbers always remained small. At no time did the firm have more than a dozen partners, and it only reached that number in 1928. The first new partner, Magoun, was admitted in 1872, a year after he had been put in charge of Kidder, Peabody's New York City branch. No one else was invited to join the partnership until January 1886, when Thomas Baring joined Magoun in New York as a general partner "on the same basis" as the others. Later that year five additional partners entered the firm, three in Boston and two in New York City.[47]

The new arrangement—five partners in Boston and four in New York—continued until April 30, 1891, when the firm was dissolved and re-formed the next day as two separate partnerships: the one in Boston kept the Kidder, Peabody name; the New York firm styled itself Baring, Magoun & Co. Each continued to be the agent of the other.[48]

At the time of the dissolution Kidder, Peabody's capital "was understood to be" about $5 million, of which approximately $3 million was allocated to the Boston firm and the balance assigned to the New York branch. Thomas Baring, who withdrew from the Boston firm to become a partner in New York, contributed an additional $2 million, giving Baring, Magoun an initial capital of $4 million. The New York firm also added a new partner, Cecil Baring.[49]

The organization of Baring, Magoun left Kidder, Peabody with four partners: Webster and three Peabodys (the two surviving founders and Francis' son Frank).[50] Five others were added in the next twenty years, three in Boston and two in New York. Robert Winsor, the son of a prominent Winchester, Massachusetts, physician and Harvard classmate of Theodore Roosevelt, was made a partner in January 1894. Winsor had started as a clerk with Kidder, Peabody in July 1880 immediately after graduating from Harvard.[51] After Francis Peabody, the last of the founders, died in September 1905, the sixty-three-year-old Webster became official head of the house, but "most of the detail and management of the concern's many important transactions fell on Winsor's shoulders," reported *The Bankers Magazine*.[52]

New partners were not expected to contribute to the firm's capital nor to pay anything for the goodwill of the business, and none of Kidder, Peabody's did so. Webster, who had opened the firm's accounts in 1865 and "witnessed the first and only written articles of co-partnership . . . ever drawn," explained the accepted policy. It was understood, Webster said, "that we [new partners] should pay no consideration to the other partners for the purpose of entering the firm, nor should we receive any consideration when we retire, either voluntarily or by death, for any other items than our deposit of moneys with the firm, the interest to which we might be entitled as the result of such deposit from the date of the last payment of interest up to the date of our retirement or death, and a sum of money for our share of the earned profits of the concern from the date of the last division up to the date of our retirement or death."[53]

All arrangements among the partners were and remained verbal, including each one's percentage of the profits. When a partner retired or died his interest in the firm was settled by payment in cash and securities. "I think it a wonderful record," Webster recalled after more than a half century with the firm, that "at no time has any question arisen in respect to the partnership in which we were not all in accord."[54]

The small staff of clerks, which grew from four in 1865 to seventy-five at the turn of the century, assisted the partners in operating the business. Almost all of them had started with the firm as young men, with many recruited from among the partners' relatives, friends, and business associates. Starting salaries were low, even for 1900: $4 a week for errand boys, the usual starting position. When they reached the status of clerks with two or three years' experience, the weekly stipend was $12. Clerks were instructed not to speculate. The firm's regulations on this subject, originally set forth in December 1868, were specific. "Nothing is more injurious to young men than to indulge in ideas of speculative prosperity. It perverts the judgment and destroys habits of industry, and leads to almost certain ruin, and no clerk can be allowed to take part in speculative operations of any kind." The opportunity of being given an interest in the firm compensated, to some extent, for the low stipends and the "years of patient preparation, industry, and self-denial" the partners expected of the clerical staff. Of the seventy-five clerks in 1905, eight subsequently became partners while several others rose to prominent positions in affiliated firms. The rest of the office staff was composed of women stenographers, of whom there were ten in 1905.[55]

Since April 1882, when Kidder, Peabody left its first location in the Union Bank Building at 40 State Street, the firm had occupied offices at 113 Devonshire Street. The *Boston Evening Transcript,* commenting on Kidder, Peabody's new "banking rooms," called them "the finest and best-appointed . . . in the world."[56] But as the business expanded and the staff almost doubled in size, from 50 in 1882 to nearly 100 in 1905, the partners acquired some adjoining property and erected a building for their own exclusive use. Completed in 1905, the imposing structure, rising 2½ stories, was considered one of the most modern and comfortable banking houses in the nation. A notable feature, *The Bankers Magazine* reported, was "a tastefully furnished ladies' room," facilities rarely found in private banks at the time.[57]

By the time Kidder, Peabody moved into its new offices, the firm was one of a half-dozen top private banking partnerships in the United States, with a capital of some $6.8 million and assets of nearly twice as much.[58] Experienced in financing the needs of large borrowers, both public and private, the firm's services were eagerly solicited by big business and governments dependent upon raising capital from the public. Despite its acknowledged expertise as an investment banking house, Kidder, Peabody continued to provide a variety of domestic and foreign banking services, much as it had done in the beginning. It served as a bank of deposit for corporations, governments, and a few wealthy individuals. After 1907 one of its largest depositors was the Italian government; this account alone amounted to some $10 million or more.[59] The firm also continued to deal extensively in foreign exchange, and its letter of credit business placed Kidder, Peabody among the nation's most prominent foreign bankers. None of these activities, important as they were, brought to Kidder, Peabody the wide public attention generated by its securities operations and close connections with some of the country's largest financial institutions—the great life insurance and trust companies—that the contemporary press liked to call the reservoirs of the people's money.

The assistance of these financial giants was vital in effecting a successful flotation of new security issues, and Kidder, Peabody, like the other major investment banking houses, sought and maintained close ties with moneyed institutions in Boston, New York, and elsewhere. Nearly all of the firm's partners were directors, trustees, or officers of several large institutional investors. Magoun was on the board of the Equitable Life Assurance Society and the Union Trust Company; Endicott's affiliations included five Massachusetts trust companies, as well as the Employers' Group Association and the Employers Liability &

Assurance Corporation; and Webster was a director of the Boston Safe Deposit & Trust Company. Other partners held similar positions with comparable institutions. Furthermore, the firm itself invested in the stock of banks and trust companies.

Since investment bankers often needed short-term loans to carry securities during a flotation, they also tried to maintain close ties with commercial banks. Webster and Winsor were directors of the National Shawmut Bank and Winsor also was a board member of the First National Bank of Boston, while Endicott was a vice president and director of Boston's National Bank of Commerce. The firm also held stock in all three institutions, among the largest and most important banks in Boston.[60]

Affiliations and interlocks among the partners of the major investment houses and the nation's key moneyed institutions spread the influence of these firms far beyond the narrow confines of the financial districts in which they were located. This, together with the alleged power they exercised over the great railroad, industrial, and utility corporations, gave rise to public suspicion and charges that the country was being controlled by a small, all-powerful group of financiers.

Criticism of the moneyed interests, especially of eastern bankers, has been a constant in American history, going back to the earliest days of the republic. From the time of Alexander Hamilton's fight to get Congress to charter the first Bank of the United States on down through the recent past, many Americans—farmers, workers, small business people, and a myriad of reformers—blamed the moneyed power for most of the country's problems, both real and fancied. Early in the twentieth century some people, frightened by the rise of giant enterprise and the methods bankers used to launch and finance them, looked to the government to moderate the trauma of industrialization and correct the sordid and depressing conditions of urban life that accompanied the vast economic changes of the post-Civil War decades. No small part of the evidence muckrakers and progressive reformers used to castigate the forces of wealth and privilege came from the findings of the Industrial Commission, which Congress had authorized to investigate the great trusts, mergers, and consolidations that disturbed so many Americans at the turn-of-the-century. Even before the Commission published its *Final Report* in 1902, critics of big business and high finance had warned against the powerful Wall Street moneyed interests they believed were gaining control of the economy. Others soon joined the attack, and a great reform impulse designed to save the people from the "interests" swept the country.

Public demand for reform and protective legislation was fed by a series of brief but severe stock market crises. The first of these, in May 1901, was precipitated by a major battle for control of the Northern Pacific Railroad. Two years later the so-called trust panic was attributed to speculative orgy and the loss of confidence that accompanied the offering of a large volume of new, slow-selling securities. Neither of these crises created the degree of public fear and indignation that followed the more severe and widespread panic set off by the suspension of the Knickerbocker Trust Company in October 1907. J. P. Morgan's intervention, which proved so effective in preventing the panic from turning into a major financial disaster, also helped confirm the fears of all those who believed that a few powerful Atlantic Coast financiers, led by "Old Jupiter," controlled the nation's economic life and destiny.

This view was strengthened still further by the disclosures of several government investigations. The New York legislature's probe into the affairs of the life insurance companies doing business in the state, which included some of the largest and most important companies in the nation, disclosed a close and mutually advantageous community of interests between these concerns and the country's leading investment houses. Although the investigating committee's chief counsel, Charles Evans Hughes, then a forty-three-year-old corporation lawyer, found no fraud or other irregularities, the mere existence of such relationships disturbed him and many other people concerned with the ethics of partners in investment houses selling securities they sponsored to companies of which they were officials.

How could such individuals, many people asked, serve the best interests of both parties? The bankers who testified before the committee insisted no such conflict existed. Hughes, the legislature, and much of the public thought otherwise. In April 1906 the New York legislature enacted a series of comprehensive reform statutes that destroyed the many close ties that had developed between the life insurance companies and the investment banking community.

Neither this investigation nor a subsequent one conducted by New York State into speculation in the securities and commodities markets attracted the widespread attention that accompanied the probe presided over by the Louisiana Democrat, Arsène Pujo. Unlike the other investigations, which were not primarily concerned with investment banking practices, the Pujo inquiry was directed specifically at the way in which the nation's principal bankers conducted their affairs and the consequences their policies and actions had upon the country's largest businesses. The purpose of the probe which the Banking and Currency Committee of the House of Representatives authorized on April 25, 1912, was to investigate "the concentration of money and credit in the United States." The hearings climaxed more than a decade of protest against high finance, and when they came to a close at the end of February 1913, most of the country's leading bankers had been called to testify. The Committee's findings, made popular by Louis D. Brandeis in *Other People's Money and How the Bankers Use It* (1914), became an accepted part of American folklore, influencing all subsequent Wall Street probes.[61]

As members of one of America's most prominent private banking houses, Kidder, Peabody's partners were called to testify at most of these investigations as well as at others, such as the Interstate Commerce Commission's probe into the reorganization of the New York, New Haven & Hartford Railroad.

In none of these inquiries was the firm's name featured so prominently as it was at the Pujo hearings. Kidder, Peabody, asserted Samuel Untermyer, the subcommittee's chief counsel, was one of the half-dozen "most active agents in forwarding and bringing about the concentration of control of money and credit." The others singled out for this dubious distinction were three private and two commercial banks, all but one headquartered in New York City.[62]

Untermyer and the subcommittee documented their charges with evidence provided by the bankers themselves. Kidder, Peabody responded to the subcommittee's request for information reluctantly, "in order not to unnecessarily delay the Committee," but the partners wanted "it clearly understood that we do not admit the right of the Committee to require the production from us of any of the information desired, and we reserve the right if we are so advised to refuse to produce before the Committee any or all of the information asked for until the Courts have decided that the Committee have the right to require its production."[63] The subcommittee's right to secure the information never was challenged, and Kidder, Peabody supplied Untermyer with forty pages of detailed data dealing with the firm's securities transactions for interstate corporations during the years 1907 through 1912, together with its investments and corporate affiliations and those of individual partners.

The evidence collected was impressive. Between 1907 and 1912 Kidder, Peabody purchased, underwrote, and distributed, sometimes alone but more often with other bankers, the securities of some 100 interstate corporations valued at more than $1.1 billion. Kidder, Peabody's five Boston partners held nine directorships in six Massachusetts banks and trust companies, and the firm itself owned stock in five of these institutions, with the largest holdings in two of the three most important Boston banks, the National Shawmut Bank ($679,200 par value) and the Old Colony Trust Co. ($358,700 par value). On the basis of these findings, the subcommittee concluded that Kidder, Peabody wielded a dominant influence over New England's principal financial institutions.[64]

Similarly close ties were disclosed between Kidder, Peabody and some of the largest railroad, industrial, mining, and utility corporations. The firm served as "bankers, fiscal agents, or as depositary of the funds" of eight interstate corporations, and its partners held a dozen directorships in eight nonfinancial corporations including American Telephone & Telegraph Co., United States Steel, and Western Union Telegraph Co.[65]

There was nothing illegal in these relationships. Nor did the subcommittee uncover any evidence to show that Kidder, Peabody or any of the other major banking houses investigated had misused or abused their affiliations with the corporations they served. On the contrary, the subcommittee's *Report* acknowledged the vital service these bankers had provided American business. "Without the aid of their invaluable enterprise and initiative and their credit and financial power the many requirements of our vast ventures could not have been financed in the past, and much less so in the future."[66] But the fact that financial concentration existed and that a relatively few investment houses sponsored most of the security offerings of the largest corporations aroused widespread fear of a dangerous money power directed by a few powerful financiers or, as the *Report* labeled them, a "handful of self-constituted trustees of the national prosperity."[67]

Alarmed by the extent of the public criticism leveled against them, disturbed by threats of federal regulation, and concerned with improving their own image, representatives of almost 200 banking houses met at the old Waldorf Astoria Hotel in New York City early in August 1912 and organized the Investment Bankers Association. Plans for such an organization had been in the making since 1910, a year before the Kansas legislature enacted the first comprehensive law regulating the sale of securities within its borders. Other states soon followed Kansas' lead, and the era of expanded state regulation of the securities business, the so-called Blue Sky movement, had become a reality. Kidder, Peabody was one of the new trade association's 347 charter members, as were all the other firms that Pujo's subcommittee had singled out as belonging to the "inner group" of financiers accused of dominating the country's economic life.[68]

Pujo's disclosures, whatever their merits, underscored the significant position Kidder, Peabody had come to occupy in the nation's financial and business system since its founding a half century earlier. During that fifty-year period the firm, which started as a regional house serving mostly the investment needs of Boston's wealthy citizens and corporations that looked to State Street for new capital, transformed itself into a national and international banking partnership. The firm continued to remain a potent force in New England finance, but as American business turned more and more to Wall Street rather than State Street for its financial requirements, Kidder, Peabody originated fewer new issues of interstate corporations domiciled outside of its region and participated more frequently than previously in underwriting and distributing syndicates led by New York City bankers. The firm's transition into a national underwriter and distributor rather than an originator of the securities of the great interstate corporations reflected, of course, the vast post-Civil War changes in the nation's economic life and the financial institutions that served it. Kidder, Peabody's adjustment to these changes was delayed and complicated by the outbreak of World War I.

CHAPTER THREE

War, Boom, and Bust

August 1914, the month Europe went to War, was a difficult time for American business. The stock market reflected the general depression in trade—a marked increase in the number of business failures, dividend suspensions, and an equally pronounced decline in bank clearings and merchandise exports. Sales on the New York Stock Exchange, which had totaled 131.1 million shares in 1912, fell to slightly less than 83.5 million in 1913 and continued to fall through the first seven months of 1914. Contemporary business opinion blamed President Woodrow Wilson's "misguided attempts . . . to carry through a scheme of radical legislation intended to revolutionize business methods" for the fact that "business was lame and halt and enterprise and energy crippled and paralyzed, with confidence at a low ebb."[1] Kidder, Peabody & Co., like so many other businesses, suffered from the downturn. "As you will see, the year has been a poor one," the firm wrote Baring Brothers early in 1914.[2] It was not only the decline in profits that concerned the partners; what disturbed them just as much was the uncertainty created by the continuing decade-long mood of reform and the newly enacted state and federal laws and regulations affecting their own operations and business generally. The outbreak of World War I added new uncertainties and undermined confidence still further.

The first shock came on July 28, 1914, with the Austro-Hungarian declaration of war against Serbia, followed by another blow the next day when Tsar Nicholas II ordered general mobilization. Europe's stock exchanges, badly demoralized since the onset of the crisis, responded to these events by closing their doors. The New York Stock Exchange was one of the last major markets to continue operations. It had suffered a week of heavy liquidations at disastrously declining prices, with still more selling orders pouring in from all parts of the world. To avoid panic and protect the reserves of New York City's banks, badly depleted by earlier gold exports, stock market officials conferred with several prominent Wall Street bankers and early on the morning of July 31 decided not to open the exchange. It remained closed for more than three months, and even then it opened only on a limited basis. Full operations were not resumed until April 1915. Exchanges in other cities, following New York's lead, also closed their doors.

With no market for securities, investment banking came to a near halt. New issues, which had totaled some $1.9 billion during the first six months of 1914, fell to slightly less than $861.4 million during the last half of the year; trading in existing securities came to a near standstill.[3] Unlisted securities continued to be traded, but even these transactions were limited and regulated by special committee. It was not until mid-autumn that orderly trading began to be restored, and a few new issues started to appear, mostly short-term notes.

Security markets were not the only ones to be disrupted by war. Foreign exchange operations were hit just as hard, causing immediate and widespread distress not only to business people but to American tourists stranded in Europe, unable to draw on their letters of credit or cash traveler's checks. Congress immediately appropriated an initial $250,000 (subsequently adding another $2.5 million) to relieve their distress, and several Atlantic Coast bankers, including Kidder, Peabody as well as American Express, contributed an additional $3 million. Early in August 1914, to ease the pressure on exchange rates, Kidder, Peabody helped arrange a shipment of gold to London aboard the battleship *Tennessee*.[4]

As one of the country's leading international banking houses, with particularly strong ties in England, Kidder, Peabody was heavily involved in all kinds of foreign exchange transactions. It cooperated with the Treasury and other bankers in trying to restore the value of the dollar in foreign exchange and promote the recovery of American trade, which had been totally demoralized by the outbreak of war. William L. Benedict, the Kidder, Peabody partner who managed the firm's New York office, was among the bankers, business executives, shippers, and government officials called together by Treasury Secretary William G. McAdoo to devise a plan to help the country's hard-hit cotton growers, nearly all of whom faced disaster unless they could resume exports. It was this group, led by McAdoo, that in November 1914 established a $135 million loan fund to help cotton growers survive the crisis.[5]

No sooner had these emergency activities been completed than investment bankers were called upon to satisfy the belligerents' pressing needs for credit and assistance in making war purchases in the United States. Kidder, Peabody played an important role in these operations. Almost six months before the Wilson administration officially approved private loans to belligerents, the Barings had queried Kidder, Peabody on the possibility of Britain borrowing in the United States. No loans to belligerents were possible, Kidder, Peabody replied, without the consent of the United States government.[6]

Once the Wilson administration relaxed its original prohibitions against private credits and loans to the belligerents, American bankers proceeded immediately to finance the combatants.

Between October 30, 1914, when New York's National City Bank extended to France a $10 million credit to pay for its war purchases and April 6, 1917, when the United States declared war on Germany, the warring countries borrowed almost $2.7 billion through American bankers. Except for some $35 million that went to the Central Powers, the balance was loaned to the Allied governments, with the largest amounts going to Britain ($1.25 billion) and France ($640 million), followed by Russia ($107 million), Japan ($102 million), and Italy ($25 million).[7] Kidder, Peabody helped underwrite and distribute many of these loans, particularly the great $500 million Anglo-French loan of October 1915. The firm comanaged a syndicate organized by J. P. Morgan & Co. in June 1916 to sell a $50 million loan for Russia, and it also participated in many other foreign offerings, among them the French cities and Paris loans of 1916 and a Canadian bond issue in 1917.[8]

Kidder, Peabody's services to the Allies were not limited to selling their bonds. Equally important were its activities in assisting companies producing arms, munitions, and other war goods. The Winchester Repeating Arms Company of Connecticut was one of the companies that turned to Kidder, Peabody for capital to expand its production of guns and cartridges to meet greatly increased orders, particularly from Britain and France. The company had borrowed $8 million from the House of Morgan and an equal amount had been advanced to it by the British government. These sums proved inadequate, and in March of 1916 Kidder, Peabody managed a syndicate offering $16 million of Winchester's two-year notes. Slightly more than half of the money from this issue went to pay earlier loans made by Morgan & Co. Charles S. Sargent, a Kidder, Peabody partner, became a Winchester director, serving the company as its financial consultant.[9]

Allied war purchases also increased the deposit liabilities of bankers arranging payments for these orders. Kidder, Peabody was no exception. Its deposit accounts grew appreciably during 1915 and 1916. The firm was fully aware of the risks and advantages resulting from these increases. Writing to the Barings at the end of January 1916, Kidder, Peabody attributed some of the firm's profits to the "temporary increase" in foreign deposits, and assured its London correspondent that the partners were using these funds cautiously, "keeping a large amount of cash in banks and [investing the balance in] the quickest kind of short time notes and quick securities."[10]

With the exception of about a half-dozen corporate underwritings—the largest an $80 million bond issue for the American Telephone & Telegraph Company offered in December 1916—most of Kidder, Peabody's major transactions during the period of American neutrality involved assisting the Allied governments, selling their securities, and financing their suppliers in the United States. These and other war-related activities, such as distributing foreign-held American securities traded on the New York Stock Exchange before and after its closing, contributed significantly to transforming the United States from a debtor to a creditor nation and moving the financial capital of the world from London to New York.

Once the United States entered the war, the federal government called on investment firms to provide it with many of the same services they previously had performed for the Allies. One of the most important of these was to assist the Treasury in selling an unprecedented volume of war bonds. In less than two years—between June 1917 when the first Liberty Loan was launched and April 1919 when the Victory Loan was offered—the Treasury issued a total of $20.5 billion of bonds. Not since the Civil War had Americans been asked to respond to such enormous calls on their savings in so short a time. That the loans were successful was due in no small part to the assistance and cooperation of the nation's bankers.

Kidder, Peabody participated actively in all five of these loans, soliciting its clients by letter and circular. Several weeks before the first Liberty Loan was floated, the firm informed its clients that it had purchased $10 million of short-term Treasury notes. Kidder, Peabody recommended these to its clients, suggesting that later they exchange them for bonds. The notes, yielding 3 percent, were being sold at cost, the firm informed prospective buyers. A year later at the time of the third Liberty Loan, Kidder, Peabody advised women with "any means at all" to buy the government's new bonds, and in January 1918 announced it had made a specialty of buying and selling the Treasury's securities.[11]

Investment houses also cooperated with the government's efforts to conserve capital and direct it into essential war industries. Early in January 1918, at the request of Treasury Secretary McAdoo and with the enthusiastic support of the Investment Bankers Association, the Federal Reserve Board established a Capital Issues Committee (CIC) on an informal basis. Four months later it was given statutory authority under Title II of the War Finance Corporation Act. The CIC's chief task, to review all new security offerings in excess of $100,000 and determine whether they contributed to the war effort, was accomplished through special subgroups organized in each Federal Reserve District. Only issues approved by the CIC as "compatible with the national interest" were allowed to be floated and then only at times when they did not compete with the Treasury's bond drives. Many of the circulars announcing the half-dozen offerings underwritten by Kidder, Peabody in 1918, such as the one for a $50 million note offering of the Bethlehem Steel Corporation, included the statement: "Passed by the Capital Issues Committee as not incompatible with the national interest, but without approval of legality, validity, worth, or security."[12] The CIC's efforts to conserve capital proved effective. Between May and December 1914, the months its restrictions were in force, the CIC disallowed some $450 million of new issues, slightly less than 20 percent of those proposed. Total corporate offerings fell from nearly $2.2 billion in 1916 to $1.3 billion in 1918. During the same period state and municipal bond issues declined by nearly 53 percent, from nearly $498 million to slightly less than $263 million.[13]

Like all businesses, investment houses had to adjust to the

loss of employees to the armed forces and other war-related activities. Kidder, Peabody endured a large turnover of clerks, some sixty-five leaving the firm and nearly twice as many being hired between 1914 and 1919. None of the partners took on full-time government assignments, but many of them served on Liberty Loan committees and assisted the Treasury in other ways as well.

Unlike a few private banking houses, notably Morgan & Co., which added new partners to help meet expanded wartime operations, Kidder, Peabody admitted no new partners during the war either in Boston or New York. In January 1919 Albert S. West, who had started with the firm as a clerk in 1877, was admitted to the partnership following the death three months earlier of Frank E. Peabody, the last partner to bear the name of a founder.[14]

World War I brought about important changes in the way investment bankers conducted their affairs and accelerated others already in the making before the onset of hostilities. The size and frequency of Allied war loans during the period of American neutrality led to the formation of larger underwriting syndicates, bringing new firms into an aspect of the securities business previously restricted to a relatively few Atlantic Coast firms. Underwriting and selling groups became nationwide. After the United States entered the war, the Treasury's huge bond drives sparked the organization of new firms, just as had occurred during the Civil War. Sales of Liberty bonds also revealed a new group of potential investors, one which many investment bankers came to consider essential to the successful flotation of large issues. Kidder, Peabody was one of the first major houses to appeal to middle-income investors. In April 1918 for the first time the firm called on women specifically to invest in Liberty bonds; less than a year later in January 1919 it advised anyone with $100 or any larger sum" to buy American Telephone & Telegraph Company seven-year convertible 6 percent bonds.[15] These developments, together with the emergence of the United States as the world's leading creditor nation, altered the financial environment in which investment houses operated and provided new challenges and opportunities.

Transition from war to peace was accompanied first by a steep price and credit inflation (1919), then by a brief but severe eighteen-month depression, with recovery well on its way by early 1922. From then until the October 1929 stock market crash, except for slight interruptions in 1924 and 1927, most businesses prospered and a larger proportion of Americans shared in the affluence of those years than had been the case in earlier periods of "good times." Both gross national product and personal income, measured in current prices, rose steadily; the former climbed from a 1921–1922 low of $74 billion to a high of $104.4 billion in 1929, while the latter rose from $62 billion in 1922 to $85.8 billion in 1929, with an estimated one-third of the annual total going to the top 5 percent of all recipients.[16] Rising individual incomes, together with relative price stability after 1923, added to the amount of money available for investment not only in the securities of domestic corporations but in those of foreign governments and companies as well. Confidence in an expanding economy and optimism about its continued growth contributed significantly to the decade's flourishing market for new and old securities. Trading on the New York Stock Exchange soared from 173 million shares in 1921 to 577 million shares in 1927 and more than 1.2 billion in 1929; total new corporate offerings increased more than fourfold, from $2.27 billion in 1923 to nearly $9.4 billion in 1929; the volume of new state and municipal issues more than doubled between 1920 ($683 million) and 1927 ($1.51 billion); and the amount of foreign issues sold in the United States rose steadily from $421 million in 1923 to $1.3 billion in 1927, falling off to $1.25 billion in 1928 and then dropping precipitously to $671 million in 1929.[17] The huge increase in new security offerings of American and foreign corporations and governments provided investment houses with an unprecedented volume of business.

Increased underwriting, sales, and brokerage were not the decade's only new developments. The character of the securities markets itself changed significantly, with stocks becoming increasingly popular, particularly toward the end of the decade when more and more corporations adopted the practice of paying regular dividends. Another important development was the change in size and makeup of the investment banking community as more and more metropolitan commercial banks organized wholly-owned security affiliates to provide users and suppliers of capital, both individuals and corporations, with all the financial services commonly performed by long-established firms like Kidder, Peabody. In addition to the security affiliates whose resources and facilities exceeded by far those of the largest old-line private banks, prewar investment firms also had to face the additional competition of new houses, some of which got their start financing regional and other enterprises overlooked or avoided by the industry's leaders. These changes, together with others designed to attract new investors with little capital, forced most firms to adopt policies suited to the changing demands of a new era.

Adjustment to the new conditions varied widely. Some firms adapted to the changing times more easily than others. Kidder, Peabody was not one of them. In some respects it remained highly conservative; in others, it followed the expansive and optimistic trends of the boom years.

Kidder, Peabody's ambivalent adjustment to the new era was reflected in many of its policies and practices. To a large extent this was due to Robert Winsor, officially the senior partner since 1919. He was sixty-one years old then, and one of the last major pre-World War I financiers still actively engaged in business. Most of the other great names of Winsor's era were either dead or in retirement. Leadership had passed to a new generation. To many of Wall Street's new chieftains, unfamiliar with his record or reputation in New England (some State Street bankers referred to him as "the J. P. Morgan of Boston"), Winsor represented an older era with a different ethic. His decision to keep Kidder, Peabody's headquarters in Boston instead of centering the firm's activities in New York City reflected Winsor's adherence to tradition and strong commitment to New England enterprises. New York was the world's financial center in the 1920s, but Winsor spent only one day a week—Mondays—at the firm's 17 Wall Street office on the third floor of the New York Stock Exchange building at the corner of Broad and Wall, directly across the street from J. P. Morgan & Co., probably the greatest bastion of conservative banking in the 1920s. Winsor, a friend of J. P. (Jack) Morgan, who had succeeded his father as head of the house in March 1913, shared similar views on what was proper banking practice.[18]

Winsor's conservatism also showed itself in the types of securities Kidder, Peabody sponsored. At a time when equities were growing in public favor, the firm continued to underwrite chiefly bonds and notes, principally for railroads and public utilities. Among the latter, those of the American Telephone & Telegraph Company represented a substantial share of the firm's total corporate debt offerings. Kidder, Peabody also sold foreign bonds. Included among these were issues of several South American and Far Eastern governments. But the firm did not emphasize these securities, and Winsor himself was skeptical of the merits of many of the foreign loans sold. "I think we have invested too much capital abroad and must pay the penalty," he told Clarence Barron in August 1928.[19]

The same caution was apparent in Kidder, Peabody's attitude toward most common stock. At no time during the 1920s did these issues account for more than 25 percent of the firm's total yearly corporate offerings, with that volume not being reached until 1929. Prior to then Kidder, Peabody's yearly common stock offerings amounted to considerably less. The figure for 1927 was 9 percent, rising to 13 percent in 1928, the year of the great bull market. Nor were the firm's common stock offerings obviously risky or speculative. Most of them were the issues of financial institutions, mainly banks and insurance companies, with Kidder, Peabody's own investment trust shares becoming more important toward the end of the decade. The firm's offerings of industrial common lagged behind its sponsorship of shares in financial institutions until 1927; that year the two became equal and in 1928 the volume of industrials exceeded the other, only to drop again to second place in 1929.[20]

Caution and conservatism also was displayed in Kidder, Peabody's advice to its clients. This was especially true of its recommendations concerning equities. Winsor's lukewarm endorsement of common stocks, however, did not extend to the shares of the American Telephone & Telegraph Company (AT&T), which Kidder, Peabody advertised in May 1921 as "one of the soundest stocks in the world."[21]

Until then Kidder, Peabody's association with AT&T had been chiefly as a comanaging underwriter of the company's debt offerings. During the 1920s the firm also became a major retailer of its capital stock. Early in 1921, as part of its long-term financial planning and also to dispel some recent unfavorable newspaper comments about the quality of its common stock, the company called on Kidder, Peabody to help it raise new equity capital by widening the market for its stock, which AT&T's directors made more attractive by voting a yearly $9-a-share dividend. Winsor and Sargent, the two Kidder, Peabody partners in charge of the firm's campaign to publicize AT&T common, started by adding forty young women to the staff of the Boston office with no responsibilities other than writing to every telephone subscriber in the greater Boston area advising them to buy the company's shares and use the dividends to pay their telephone bills.[22] Kidder, Peabody also circularized its correspondents and other brokerage houses throughout New England, New York, northern New Jersey, and Illinois—the territory agreed upon by Winsor and the company—urging them to recommend AT&T common as an investment security.

The 1921 campaign proved highly effective. "I think Winsor has performed a service of the greatest possible value to the Company, with extraordinary skill," Charles Francis Adams, the Boston lawyer who later became Herbert Hoover's Secretary of the Navy, informed Harry B. Thayer, AT&T's chief. Thayer agreed, and in a letter to Winsor asking him to continue the publicity and sales campaign another year, praised the banker's work saying his "efforts to produce wider distribution of the shares have accomplished noteworthy results."[23] After September 1921, when AT&T organized the Bell Telephone Securities Company to promote the sale of the entire system's securities, Kidder, Peabody coordinated its efforts with those of the newly organized corporation. In November 1922, a month before Kidder, Peabody's campaign came to a close, Thayer wrote Winsor a personal letter thanking him for putting his reputation behind AT&T at a time when some "investment houses and investment advisers" had suggested that it might have to cut its dividend. You told "the world that the Company was all right," Thayer wrote, "and the world believes."[24]

No other common stock enjoyed Winsor's similar confidence. Nor was he impressed by booming stock prices. The more they rose, the more fearful he became. In June 1928 Kidder, Peabody circularized its clients warning them that while the firm was "not predicting a big crash," they should take note that the market was "in a relatively high area." "No one is competent to say that common stocks, good or bad, will not go higher," the circular stressed. All it was intended to do was "to give the facts of the situation," which it did by citing the Dow-Jones averages. The decision to hold or sell was up to the investor. Should the decision be to sell, Kidder, Peabody suggested alternative ways to employ funds. The investor might keep them on deposit with the firm, which then was paying 3.5 percent "on time deposits of reasonable size," or reinvest them. The only securities Kidder, Peabody recommended at that time were bonds and notes, mostly railroads, public utilities, and various AT&T debt issues.[25]

Winsor's adherence to tradition also accounts for the fact that throughout the 1920s, when many investment firms concentrated almost exclusively on investment banking services, Kidder, Peabody, like the house of Morgan, remained a diversified private banking house much as it had been at the time of its organization. It continued to accept deposits, mainly those of its corporate and government clients. The Italian government's account continued to be one of its largest. During the war when Kidder, Peabody was appointed paying agent for some of Italy's war purchases in the United States, the account exceeded $100 million; in the 1920s it fell to less than $10 million, with the funds being used chiefly in foreign exchange operations, maintaining a market for the Italian lira, and paying Italy's war debt installments to the American government.[26] Some of the firm's other foreign deposit accounts, all of them substantially smaller than the Italian government's, were those of the Anglo-Czechoslovak Bank for which Kidder, Peabody served as one of its paying agents, the Banco di Napoli, the National Bank of Egypt, and the Banque Belge, all of which were used mostly for foreign exchange and in the remittance business.[27] Among the firm's domestic corporate accounts, AT&T's was one of the largest. Opened in July 1921, the $11 million deposit was used to finance Winsor's campaign to widen ownership of AT&T stock, and subsequently for the company's securities transactions.[28] Kidder, Peabody paid interest on these deposits and invested the funds in the call money market.

The firm also continued trading in foreign exchange and issuing commercial letters of credit. Kidder, Peabody's letters of credit, issued jointly with Baring Brothers, were used by many American businesses importing raw products from abroad. Some of the firm's most important clients included Goodyear Tire, Remington Rand, Allied Kid, Roger Pyatt Shellac, and the Amoskeag Manufacturing Company. The firm's foreign business occupied almost all the time and attention of four partners, two in Boston and two in New York, and accounted for some $10 million of Kidder, Peabody's annual business, rivaling underwriting as the chief source of earnings. Before World War I the firm also had dealt in bankers' acceptances, but in the 1920s the business of providing commercial credits in dollars to finance imports and exports was assigned to the Kidder, Peabody Acceptance Corporation, the first of the banking house's several affiliates to be organized during that decade.[29]

Next to its banking services, which contributed so significantly to sustaining Kidder, Peabody's profits and reputation in the 1920s, the firm's other principal activity was underwriting. This combination of banking and underwriting, the two pillars upon which the firm had been built and which had served so well in the pre-World War I era, fitted perfectly with Winsor's image of the firm as a "prudent and conservative" private banking partnership similar to J. P. Morgan & Co., Kuhn, Loeb & Co., and a few others like them. But whereas in the previous half century Kidder, Peabody had been among the half-dozen or so leading originators and underwriters of new issues, the firm ceased to belong to that select group of houses in the 1920s. Not only did it originate fewer prime issues, but it also participated less frequently in underwriting syndicates. Between 1925 and 1930, when the value of new corporate offerings more than doubled, Kidder, Peabody served as sole or chief manager of only seventeen offerings, most of which were for companies domiciled in New England, such as the region's three major railroads—the Boston & Maine, Maine Central, and the New York, New Haven & Hartford. Some of the other important financings originated and managed by Kidder, Peabody in those years were for Winchester Repeating Arms Co., United Drug, Inc., United Merchants & Manufacturers, Inc., and Commercial Credit, the last being a jointly managed account.[30]

None of these financings, however, was as profitable or as prestigious as Kidder, Peabody's participation in the syndicates organized to distribute the debt offerings of AT&T and its associated companies. Between 1920 and 1930 the Bell System sold $797 million of bonds and notes, for which the bankers syndicating these issues received $26.9 million in gross commissions. Kidder, Peabody headed the New England group that sold these securities and, in addition, the firm itself had a 15 percent underwriting participation of its own, an amount second only to the managing banker, J. P. Morgan & Co., with 20 percent.[31]

Kidder, Peabody did not occupy as prominent a position in

any of the other choice offerings of the 1920s. Not only did its total underwriting participation fall off badly, but the firm's name appeared in only 14 percent of the 102 offerings managed by Morgan & Co. and less than 2 percent of those headed by Kuhn, Loeb & Co.[32]

Kidder, Peabody's total underwriting performance in the 1920s was spotty. While the Boston office showed a yearly underwriting profit from 1925 through 1930 with the peak—nearly $736,500—reached in 1928, the New York City branch during these years registered its largest gain in 1926, some $210,000. Twice, in 1927 and 1929, the underwriting losses at the Wall Street office were so large that they wiped out whatever profits Boston had made in this area of the firm's business. Such was the case in 1927, when New York's losses (almost $543,500) forced Kidder, Peabody's underwriting account into the red by nearly $19,500.[33] The firm's underwriting losses helped weaken its capital position and contributed to its search for other ways to generate new funds.

It was the need to add to its capital that led Kidder, Peabody to shed some of its conservatism and adopt some of the more expansive practices of the times. Brokerage, that is, the buying and selling of securities for clients, was one of the first activities to be expanded. The firm always had conducted a brokerage business and retailed some of its underwritings to individuals of relatively small means. In the early 1920s, particularly after its successful campaign to distribute AT&T common, the firm started to stress its retail capabilities. "We try to serve the small individual investor as well as the large bank and insurance company, and to serve them all with equal care and interest," Kidder, Peabody advised the public in 1923. The ten-page booklet advertising the firm's services also notified the potential "customer who does not find it convenient to come to our office" that Kidder, Peabody representatives were prepared to make "personal calls" and provide at the client's office or home the "same careful conscientious assistance and advice as may be obtained at our office."[34] To improve its sales effort, the firm added new countermen to its staff—by the end of the decade they constituted the single largest group of employees—and opened several new offices. In 1922 Kidder, Peabody started a branch at Providence, Rhode Island, and later added another at Newark, New Jersey, as well as in midtown Manhattan. Still others were opened in and around Boston, including one at Harvard Square. Besides its own branches the firm organized three Kidder corporations to operate brokerage offices in Springfield, Lowell, and New Bedford, Massachusetts, with the partnership holding an interest in each of them. And the firm also expanded the number of its correspondents at home and abroad while continuing its joint account with the Barings in London.[35]

Expansion of Kidder, Peabody's retail sales organization was initiated by the Boston partners, and by the end of the decade all of the branches had added new personnel to their brokerage operations. In 1927 the Wall Street office started its own in-house sales school, which soon "graduated" about a dozen salespeople who bought and sold mostly AT&T shares and those of Kidder, Peabody's own investment trusts. The firm did not seek or carry margin accounts. In terms of its total profits, brokerage trailed considerably behind the firm's banking and underwriting business.[36]

Increased attention to sales was not Kidder, Peabody's most important concession to the "New Era's" financial optimism. The firm's most obvious departure from its old ways came with the decision to organize affiliated corporations of its own. There was nothing new in the practice of banks setting up separate entities to perform functions that the parent firm did not want to provide or could not legally do. Commercial banks had employed securities affiliates to extend their securities operations in the years immediately before World War I, and they greatly expanded these activities in the 1920s. Kidder, Peabody employed the same technique, though for different reasons, when it established the Kidder, Peabody Acceptance Corporation in April 1922.

Originally intended to provide commercial credits in dollars to manufacturers and merchants for the purchase of raw materials in both domestic and foreign markets, as well as to assist the financing of imports and exports generally, the Acceptance Corporation became the vehicle through which Kidder, Peabody subsequently launched its own investment trusts. This occasioned no surprise, for the Acceptance Corporation itself was not an entirely new entity. Its origins went back to the turn-of-the-century.

The Acceptance Corporation evolved out of the New England Cotton Yarn Company (NECY), a merger of nine Massachusetts textile companies organized by Kidder, Peabody in July 1899. The consolidation never proved profitable, although it aroused widespread comment at the time and was labeled a trust and monopoly by critics of big business. In 1903 NECY, a New Jersey corporation, was recapitalized and reorganized under a Massachusetts charter. When the new corporation proved no more profitable than the original consolidation, it was liquidated. By the end of 1917 NECY had sold all its physical properties. The funds received were invested mostly in securities of the spun-off companies. These changes transformed NECY into a holding company in which Kidder, Peabody was the dominant influence. The firm, together with the Barings, held large blocks of NECY securities; Kidder, Peabody partners and officers were represented on the board.

In view of its new status and functions NECY altered its charter in 1918 and changed its name to New England Investment Company (NEIC). Then in 1921, in anticipation of adding to its functions and scale of operations, NEIC was reincorporated with increased authorized stock plus a new assortment of securities, some to be marketed for new money. The name also was altered slightly, the word company being replaced with corporation. Within a few months and before these latest changes were effected, NEIC's name was changed again, this time to The Kidder, Peabody Acceptance Corporation.[37]

Capitalized at slightly more than $10 million, the securities of the Acceptance Corporation were designed to serve several purposes. Two classes of preferred stock were issued: Class A was used in exchange for the common shares of the predecessor company (NEIC), and Class B was sold to raise new capital. Both were nonvoting. Only the common stock had this right, all of which was held for the purpose of control by Kidder, Peabody and Baring Brothers.

Kidder, Peabody served the Acceptance Corporation in several ways. All its directors as well as the president and treasurer were partners in the firm. Kidder, Peabody distributed and dealt in the corporation's preferred stock, negotiated exchanges of issues, and served as transfer agent. In several instances the firm arranged exchanges of Acceptance Corporation shares for stocks in other companies Kidder, Peabody was financing.

For all practical purposes the Acceptance Corporation was a branch of the firm with the additional advantages of incorporation. Kidder, Peabody gained considerably by the relationship. By specializing in the letter of credit and acceptance business, the corporation extended and diversified Kidder, Peabody's activities in these areas. In addition it became a means through which the firm could enlarge its underwritings, for the corporation proved to be both a source of funds as well as a market for securities.

Originally the corporation functioned primarily as an acceptance bank. Prior to World War I Kidder, Peabody had financed American overseas trade with foreign currencies, chiefly sterling. Use of dollar acceptances at the time was slight. After the war demand for the latter increased so markedly that in 1919 the Federal Reserve Act was amended to facilitate the formation of corporations to engage in international banking. The Edge Act, as this amendment came to be known, encouraged the use of dollar acceptances still further. At the time the Acceptance Corporation was organized the volume of dollar acceptances outstanding stood at about $600 million; by the end of 1929 it had reached a peak of more than $1.7 billion.[38]

The Acceptance Corporation shared in the booming business. The volume of its outstanding acceptances, which increased from some $4 million in 1922 to nearly $40 million in 1929, made it one of the most important companies in the business. It stood second in the country among specialized acceptance houses and about twelfth among all banks issuing these instruments. Needless to say, the corporation's acceptances enjoyed prime status among brokers and dealers.[39]

But the Acceptance Corporation was more than a source of profits; it also aided and benefited the firm as an underwriter of and investor in its promotions. This was particularly true in 1928 and 1929 when the corporation's participation in Kidder, Peabody's underwritings increased significantly. The corporation's augmented operations in the new issues business altered both its liquidity and character. In the early 1920s most of its investments were in federal government bonds; by the end of the decade these had been replaced with securities of companies promoted by Kidder, Peabody. And while the corporation continued to function as an acceptance bank, it also took on many characteristics of an investment trust.[40]

At the time Kidder, Peabody widened the functions of the Acceptance Corporation, the firm strayed still further from its conservative principles by sponsoring its own investment trusts. Fewer than 200 of these companies had been organized in the United States by the end of 1926. Then a rising stock market and growing public demand for equities led to the formation of more. In 1927, the year Kidder, Peabody organized its first investment trust (Kidder Participations, Inc., No. 1), 140 such companies were set up and the movement had just begun to pick up momentum. By 1929 the number of investment trusts in operation stood at 770, more than four times as many as had been organized in the nation's entire history.[41] Kidder, Peabody contributed to that total with two of its own—Kidder Participations, Inc., No. 2 organized in 1928, and Kidder Participations, Inc., No. 3 set up in 1929. All three were management trusts, their portfolios controlled by the companies' officers and directors, nearly all of whom were partners in the firm.

Various reasons prompted Kidder, Peabody to launch these corporations. The announced purpose was to satisfy the demands of its clients and friends "to devise some means whereby they could acquire a stock interest in our business." Stockholders in the trusts found the prospect of sharing in the firm's underwriting profits highly attractive. Kidder, Peabody explained the organization of Participations No. 2 by saying that No. 1 was so successful and "the demand for its shares so insistent that it seemed wise to repeat the undertaking." Similar words were employed at the time No. 3 was established.[42]

Investment houses, of course, appreciated the profits to be made from organizing these corporations. Flotation of investment trust securities was a profitable business. But an equally important motive was the additional working capital such companies made available to the firms that sponsored them. This reason, probably more than any other, accounted for Kidder, Peabody's decision to launch its own investment trusts.[43] Also important was the fact that these affiliates provided the banking house that organized them with a market for the securities it sponsored. William Holway Hill, who was made a Kidder, Peabody partner in November 1926 and served as a director of all three of the firm's investment trusts, subsequently testified that almost all of the Participations' holdings were in "securities of companies [with] which Kidder, Peabody & Co. had banking relations."[44]

This was the declared objective of the Participations. Their function, as stated in a circular dated January 1929, consisted of "underwritings, participations, purchasing of blocks of securities and trading." While these activities would be conducted "with due regard to the reasonable safety of the Preferred stocks," the corporations' funds would be invested "with a view to the probable increase from year to year in security values." Investment in growth stocks, in other words, was the clearly stated purpose of the Participations.

The directors were given a free hand to choose securities as they deemed best. "The only limitation upon the absolute discretion of the Board of Directors in the choice of investments," Kidder, Peabody declared, was that not more than 10 percent of No. 1's "outstanding capital shall be invested in the securities of one corporation." This restriction was raised to 20 percent in the case of Participations No. 2 and No. 3.[45]

There were few significant differences between the investment policies of the Participations and the Acceptance Corporation. All held both stocks and bonds, but not in the same proportions. The Participations invested more in stocks than bonds; the reverse was true of the Acceptance Corporation. All four participated equally in Kidder, Peabody's offerings, both as underwriters and investors.

Kidder, Peabody charged no fee for its services in organizing the Participations. The firm paid itself in the companies' common stock, taking one-fourth of the total in the case of No. 1 and No. 2, and one-half in the case of No. 3.

Management of the three trusts was vested in Kidder, Peabody. Any conflict of interest was obviated by a statement to that effect in the agreements setting up the trusts. Each gave the directors and officers, all of whom were associated with the banking house, authority "to buy or sell to or otherwise deal with any firm, corporation or organization in which any one or more of the officers or directors of this corporation may be a member or in which he or they may be financially interested."[46]

All three Participations had similar capital structures. Each issued $5 million of preferred stock, and No. 1 and No. 2 issued 2.5 million shares of no par common. For No. 3 the amount of common was 100,000 shares. The preferred stock of all three trusts had complicated participating provisions and was convertible into common.

Kidder, Peabody sold the stock privately in blocks of one preferred and three-quarter share of common for Participations No. 1 and No. 2, and one of each in the case of No. 3. The blocks were offered at $102, $103.50 and $103.50, respectively, for the three trusts. The common stock not thus distributed was Kidder, Peabody's bonus. Sales went well, so that by December

1929 there were 1,300 preferred shareholders and 1,200 owners of common in No. 1; about 1,500 preferred and common holders in No. 2; and by December 1930 approximately 1,700 preferred and common holders in No. 3.[47]

Two additional investment trusts were launched in 1927 and 1929, both with Kidder, Peabody's cooperation and assistance. They bore the name of the investment firm that co-sponsored them, Mitchum, Tulley & Co., a San Francisco house and long-time correspondent and underwriting partner of Kidder, Peabody. The two trusts (Mitchum Tulley Participations No. 1 and No. 2) were organized and functioned like the Kidder Participations. Two Kidder, Peabody officials were on the directorates of the Mitchum Tulley trusts, with their other officers all recruited from the San Francisco banking house. Size was the only significant difference between the Kidder, Peabody and the Mitchum, Tulley companies, the latter being considerably smaller. Total capital stock of Mitchum, Tulley No. 1 had a nominal value of about $1 million. In all other respects, such as the various complicated provisions of the preferred stock and unit sales of preferred with common shares, they were similar to the three Kidder Participations.[48]

Still another of Kidder, Peabody's ventures into new financial areas was its organization of The Peabody Trust Company of Boston, incorporated under the laws of Massachusetts in August 1927. The stated reason for this addition to the Kidder, Peabody group of companies was to provide the firm's clients with "complete financial services," an objective widely acclaimed and pursued by financiers in the 1920s. The trust company was organized to function as a bank, but its chief purpose was to manage estates and trusts. To do this successfully, as Kidder, Peabody stressed in a circular announcing the formation of the company, required "integrity, ability, experience, and sound judgment." The trust company possessed all these qualities by virtue of the fact that its directors and officers were "either partners of Kidder, Peabody & Company or men . . . long associated with that firm."[49]

Within a few months of its organization, the trust company increased its original capital from $200,000 to $500,000. Compared to the capitalization of other similar Boston institutions at the time, The Peabody Trust Company was a relatively small organization. But the fact that it was so closely tied to Kidder, Peabody gave it a prestige and status far beyond its actual resources. *The Commercial & Financial Chronicle,* commenting on its establishment, said that it was "the first important charter granted in Boston in a great many years."[50] An even more important indication of its respected position among Boston financial institutions was the extent of its success in attracting clients. By the end of 1929 capital, surplus, and demand deposits exceeded $5.7 million, while trust accounts amounted to $10.4 million.

Kidder, Peabody and its various affiliates held most of the trust company's stock. Apart from these institutions, shareholders in The Kidder Peabody Trust Company, as it was renamed in 1929, numbered fewer than fifty.[51]

So long as the stock market continued to boom, affiliates added to the prosperity of the sponsor. Such was the case with Kidder, Peabody's investment trusts. Participations No. 1, for instance, started paying preferred dividends in 1926, the year it was organized, and participating dividends in 1928. Both continued through 1930, though in the latter year they were not earned. Between 1927 and 1929 the price for No. 1 preferred ranged between a high of $100 and a low of $93 a share. By 1931 it was down to $15. Similar results were shown by No. 2; the performance of No. 3 was somewhat less satisfactory.

Values of the Participations' stocks fell precipitously after the October 1929 crash. The earnings of No. 1 illustrate the extent of the decline. Within a year net income fell from $446,000 (1929) to $195,000 (1930). Loss of earnings and liquidation of assets had resulted in a decrease in its investment account from $5.5 million in 1929 to slightly less than $2.5 million in 1932, with a capital deficit of almost $1.4 million.[52] O. Kelley Anderson, president of the Consolidated Investment Trust into which the

Participations and the Acceptance Corporation had been merged, testified that some 75 percent of the three Participations' remaining funds "were tied up in unmarketable securities of local New England industries."[53]

The stock market debacle did much more than jeopardize the solvency of Kidder, Peabody's affiliates. It dealt an almost mortal blow to the firm itself. Not all its difficulties, however, were attributable to Kidder, Peabody's more recent ventures. These served only to aggravate a bad situation.

The sources of Kidder, Peabody's troubles were varied and deep-rooted. Its inability in the 1920s to hold on to its prewar position as a leading originator of prime new issues was the result, in part, of Boston's decline as a national and international capital market. Large corporations and governments looked to Wall Street not State Street for the funds they required, a development that had been in the making since the turn-of-the-century. Winsor's decision to enlist Morgan's assistance in financing AT&T's $100 million loan of March 1906 was an indication of Boston's slipping financial primacy.

Kidder, Peabody's difficulties, obviously, also stemmed from deficiencies within the firm. And among these none was more important in the 1920s than lack of initiative and ineffective leadership. Responsibility for these shortcomings rested with the partners, particularly Winsor, the undisputed head of the house. Though still only in his early sixties at the beginning of the decade, Winsor no longer was the effective, enterprising financier of earlier years. At a time when nearly all the new issues originated in New York, he continued to visit the firm's Wall Street branch only one day a week and even less frequently toward the end of the decade, leaving a partner, Sargent, to manage and supervise affairs there. Nor was Winsor as attentive to the firm's Boston business as he once had been.[54]

There were several reasons why Winsor failed to provide the kind of leadership of which he had been capable. His wife, a semi-invalid for much of her life, occupied his time and after her death his own deteriorating health led him to withdraw almost entirely from active participation in the firm's affairs. Adding to his distress, Winsor was deeply hurt by a prolonged court suit that charged him, Kidder, Peabody, and three other bankers with conspiracy to defraud Willett, Sears & Co. of its corporate interests in some twenty New England companies. The suit, which dragged through the Massachusetts courts for six years and received wide newspaper coverage, grew out of the bankers' activities in reorganizing various floundering properties in which Willett, Sears owned stock. The first verdict, in December 1924, found the bankers guilty of fraud and ordered them to pay Willett, Sears $10.5 million damages, but on appeal the Massachusetts Supreme Court set aside the lower court's verdict.[55] Despite the subsequent dismissal of all charges against him and the other bankers, Winsor never recovered from the ordeal of the prolonged trial, which finally came to an end in March 1927. The Willett, Sears case made him reluctant to assume any new responsibilities.

But it was not only the court trial and family and health reasons, important as they were, that account for Winsor's unwillingness to go after new business. Equally compelling was the fact that he considered it undignified, if not improper, for a banker to solicit business. At a time when the security affiliates of commercial banks and sales-oriented investment firms competed vigorously to underwrite new issues or to secure an appealing position in a syndicate managed by a prestigious house, neither Winsor nor Sargent deemed it appropriate to appear to be looking for clients. Like Morgan and Kuhn, Loeb's Otto Kahn, Winsor believed that Kidder, Peabody's name, reputation, and tradition were sufficient in themselves to attract corporate accounts and individuals in need of the firm's services.[56]

Though no longer as active in the firm as he had been previously, Winsor remained its dominant partner. No one questioned his decisions. Walter H. Trumbull, his son-in-law and partner, said Winsor was "an autocrat" who "snapped the whip" and "frightened the younger people at the office," clerks and junior partners alike. "It had reached a point," one of these young men recalled, "that one had to approach [Winsor] on *bended knees* to converse with him." And Albert H. Gordon, the subsequent head of the firm, testified: "Practically nothing was done in Kidder, Peabody & Co. without Mr. Winsor's full knowledge and approval."[57] Winsor's dominance over the firm need not in itself have been disastrous. At different times both Morgan & Co. and Kuhn, Loeb had been dominated by powerful, autocratic figures and survived the experience. Kidder, Peabody might have done so also had it not been for the crash. That event and the severe contraction that followed it not only exposed the firm's weaknesses but made it impossible to rectify them. Winsor and the firm's close ties with New England enterprises, for instance, had resulted in tying up a substantial part of Kidder, Peabody's capital in the securities of companies in that region. Some of these had been difficult to sell in the boom years; after the stock market collapse many of them became unmarketable at any price while others could be sold only at a considerable loss.[58]

Kidder, Peabody's difficulties also were made worse by the failure of Caldwell & Co., the Nashville, Tennessee, investment house founded in 1917. Starting as a specialist in Southern municipal bonds, the firm soon expanded its operations and by the mid-1920s had developed a thriving brokerage and underwriting business much of which was conducted through Kidder, Peabody's Wall Street branch. The New York office often carried Caldwell's underwriting participations until the Tennessee house had found a market for them. During the 1920s Kidder, Peabody also had advanced Caldwell & Co. substantial sums and guaranteed stocks it had pledged for loans with various Tennessee banks, among them the Bank of Tennessee, founded and controlled by the Southern investment firm. Caldwell's bankruptcy compounded Kidder, Peabody's troubles.[59]

As if all this were not enough, Kidder, Peabody also endured large losses of capital brought about by the death and retirement of five partners within the short span of five years, from

1926 through 1930. Remick died in October 1926, taking some $750,000 out of the firm; Webster and Winsor died in January 1930, within ten days of each other; and Benedict and Endicott retired in January 1928 and August 1929, respectively. The eleven partners added to the firm in that five-year period—two in 1926, five in 1928, and four in 1929—were admitted without requiring them to contribute any capital, a policy that with few exceptions had prevailed since the beginning of the house. A carefully drafted partnership agreement designed to protect the firm's capital might have prevented and certainly would have eased Kidder, Peabody's problems, but no such document existed. These matters, like most others among the partners, were decided privately and informally as had been the custom in the past.[60]

The final blow to Kidder, Peabody's solvency came when depositors, apprehensive about the firm's condition, started to withdraw their funds. Early in 1930 the Italian government closed its account, taking out more than $8 million. This huge withdrawal, together with others, made it impossible for Kidder, Peabody to meet its current liabilities. By November 1930, faced with the possibility of having to close, the partners appealed for assistance to the house of Morgan.[61]

The stock market crash, faulty leadership, poor management, and inadequate capital had brought Kidder, Peabody, one of the nation's most respected banking houses, to its knees. Strong leadership and careful planning together with utmost attention to protecting the firm's capital and maintaining its liquidity had allowed the firm to weather the great panics and long contractions of the 1870s and 1890s. No one can say that adherence to those principles would have saved Kidder, Peabody in 1930; on the other hand, no one can deny that failure to do so made it difficult, if not impossible, for the firm to survive the 1929 crisis without outside assistance.

CHAPTER
FOUR

Reorganization

It was only natural that Kidder, Peabody should turn to J. P. Morgan & Co. for assistance. The two houses had enjoyed long and friendly relations. Both had been associates in many successful flotations, most notably the financing of the American Telephone & Telegraph Company and its subsidiaries, as well as such other corporate giants as United States Steel and the New York Central. Together they had helped finance several foreign governments, among them Austria, Australia, Belgium, Czechoslovakia, Germany, and Italy. Close personal ties also existed among the partners of the two houses. Winsor had been a friend and business partner of both the elder Morgan and his son J. P. (Jack) Morgan. When Winsor died Morgan, in plug hat and black frock coat, walked across the street from his office at 23 Wall Street to express his condolences to Sargent and the other partners. And George Whitney, a Morgan partner who was to play a leading role in salvaging the Boston firm, had started on his career in finance as a clerk in Kidder, Peabody's

Devonshire Street office in 1907. All these considerations, as well as the very practical one of trying to avoid the calamitous consequences that might follow from the failure at a critical time of a house with Kidder, Peabody's traditions, persuaded the Morgan firm to intervene.

Negotiations lasted some four months, from December 1930 to March 1931. The first step was to provide Kidder, Peabody with some much needed cash. For this Morgan & Co. organized a revolving credit of $10 million, to which it and the Chase National Bank contributed $2.5 million each. The balance came from three other New York City banks and four in Boston.[1] To secure the loan Kidder, Peabody's partners had to raise an additional $5 million themselves, which they did by borrowing from a group of eight wealthy individuals and seven banking firms, all but two from Boston and all with close personal or business ties with the financially hard-pressed banking house. The largest contributor ($950,000) was Frederic C. Dumaine, a close personal and business friend of the late Winsor and a widely respected New England businessman, president of the Amoskeag Manufacturing Company, the world's leading fully integrated cotton plant. Since 1923 and largely because of Winsor, Dumaine also was the head of the Waltham Watch Company. The next three largest contributors who together with Dumaine put up 58 percent of the required $5 million were Edwin S. Webster, Sr. ($750,000), the son of Frank G. Webster, who died at the age of eighty-nine after sixty-five years with Kidder, Peabody; William Endicott ($600,000), a recently retired partner; and Baring Brothers ($600,000). The balance ($2.1 million) was contributed by six Boston investment and commercial banks and five individuals, one of whom, Mortimer L. Schiff, was a partner in Kuhn, Loeb & Co. The entire group subsequently organized itself as the Commonwealth Corporation, with Dumaine as its president.[2]

Within a month of the $15 million loan Kidder, Peabody was in need of cash again. Even worse, an audit by outside public accountants disclosed that its assets "had been so optimistically stated that the firm did not have enough funds with which to conduct its business." Not only had the value of the securities it held declined precipitously (the auditors estimated the loss at $6.5 million), but business was so poor that the firm was losing over $2,000 a day and there was no indication that the situation would improve in the near future. Indeed, every indication was that conditions would worsen.[3]

Despite the grim prospects, Morgan & Co. considered Kidder, Peabody salvageable. Its greatest assets were its name and reputation, but it also possessed others. Some of the securities it held would—and subsequently did—regain value, and the firm continued to enjoy the confidence of its clients.

Several solutions were considered. The one finally adopted was to ask Edwin S. Webster, Sr. to reorganize Kidder, Peabody. He had started in business with the house under his father's supervision, leaving it in 1889 to organize, with Charles A. Stone, the engineering, construction, and consulting firm of Stone & Webster. Webster already had shown his interest in saving Kidder, Peabody by responding generously to the partners' earlier appeal for assistance. He possessed the capital, ability, and experience to rehabilitate the firm, as well as the business contacts necessary to assure its success. Because of his age and responsibilities, Webster refused to do so. He was then in his early sixties and one of the two senior officers of Stone & Webster, as well as its principal stockholder. But his son Edwin S. Webster, Jr., who was then thirty-one years old and a vice president of Stone & Webster, had been considering going into business for himself. The opportunity to restore Kidder, Peabody, an old and reputable house with which his family long had been closely associated, appealed to him strongly. His father shared the son's enthusiasm and agreed to help him, not only financially but in negotiating the reorganization as well, since at the time young Webster was in the hospital recovering from a serious accident.[4]

Participating in the negotiations were Chandler Hovey and Albert H. Gordon. Together with young Webster, they were to become the three founding partners of the reorganized Kidder, Peabody. Whitney, the Morgan partner most directly concerned, though not involved in the actual negotiations always stood ready to help and was consulted frequently.

Hovey, the senior Webster's son-in-law, was fifty-one years old at the time and some twenty years older than his prospective partners Webster and Gordon. Hovey came from an old, moneyed Boston business and newspaper family. His grandfather, C. F. Hovey, had been the founder, in 1833, of a dry goods firm that continued in business under his name for more than a century, and his father, William A. Hovey, had been a longtime editor of the *Boston Evening Transcript*. Hovey himself brought to Kidder, Peabody thirty years of experience in finance, mostly in the brokerage business. He had been with Kidder, Peabody early in the century, starting as a messenger in 1900 and, after nine years, rising to order clerk at $35 a week. In 1909 Hovey left Kidder, Peabody and joined the brokerage house of Bradley & Cutler, leaving it the next year to organize his own stock commission firm, Chandler Hovey & Co., which he operated until 1931 when he withdrew to become a partner in the newly reorganized Kidder, Peabody.[5]

Gordon, the youngest of the three at age thirty, was born in North Scituate, Massachusetts, the son of a prominent Boston leather merchant. Gordon and young Webster were classmates at Harvard College and the Harvard Graduate School of Business Administration. Upon completing his business degree in 1925, Gordon, taking his father's advice—go "to New York where the pot boils the fastest"—accepted a job selling commercial paper for Goldman, Sachs & Co. Like Webster, Gordon too was anxious to go into business for himself. The opportunity to participate in salvaging Kidder, Peabody appealed to him. The firm's name, he recalled later, appeared to offer "excellent opportunities."[6]

Gordon, Hovey, and the elder Webster acting for his hospitalized son settled the numerous questions that led to their purchase of Kidder, Peabody. One of the first decisions agreed upon was that the main office of the new firm would be in New York City, not in Boston. Gordon was convinced that if Kidder, Peabody was to reestablish itself as a leading national investment house its main office had to be at the financial center of the country. Had it been there in the 1920s, where he believed it belonged, instead of in Boston, where Winsor insisted on keeping it, the problems and difficulties Kidder, Peabody faced might have been averted, certainly prevented from deteriorating to the point where they threatened the firm's very survival.

It required considerably more deliberation—and still greater daring, considering how starved Kidder, Peabody was for capital—to decide not to invite anyone else to become a partner. Hovey had suggested bringing in an older, well-known banker to give the firm added stature and wider contacts in the financial community. He had proposed inviting E. V. R. Thayer, the head of Chicago's Central Trust Company. Thayer had all the business and financial qualifications Hovey considered desirable, and he was also the grandson of Nathaniel Thayer, the later head of J. E. Thayer & Brother, the predecessor firm to Kidder, Peabody. Thayer was interested, but when he made it known he intended to alter the firm's name to include his own, the plan was dropped. No one was prepared to make such a concession, neither the new partners nor the members of the revolving credit.[7]

Nor was it considered wise or practicable to invite into the new firm any of the partners from the old one. Such a move would have meant asking established bankers to accept a lesser interest than the one they then held. No one wanted to do this. Even more important, it would have defeated the very purposes for which the reorganization was intended: to spearate the new firm completely from the old one. "We were fearful that undisclosed liabilities would rise up to haunt us," Gordon said.[8]

By early March 1931 the final terms of the sale had been arranged. The new partnership assumed the deposits of the old one, which amounted to some $8 million, and purchased its name, goodwill, accounts receivable, and the former partners' seats on the New York and Boston stock exchanges, as well as certain securities "with readily marketable value." Special care was taken, Gordon declared, to purchase "only those assets we considered current and liquid."[9]

No cash was paid at the time of the sale. The new firm agreed to pay the old partners, who organized themselves into a corporation named Devonstreet & Co., 25 percent of net earnings up to $2 million. The new firm also agreed that once this amount had been paid it would turn over 10 percent of its net earnings for five years to the old Kidder, Peabody's creditors, the Commonwealth Corporation. Both these obligations were subsequently reduced considerably. The $2 million payment to the old partners was cut to $700,000, all of which went to satisfy the deficit of the revolving credit, and the new firm's obligations to the Commonwealth Corporation were trimmed substantially by buying a sizable block of its common stock.[10]

On March 16, 1931, the new Kidder, Peabody opened officially for business, with Gordon the active partner in New York and Hovey in charge in Boston. Some 90 percent of its $5.35 million capital came from the elder Webster in the form of cash ($1.26 million) and securities ($3.56 million), with nearly 76 percent of the latter being Stone & Webster capital stock (58,500 shares). The balance was made up by Hovey ($425,000) and Gordon ($100,000). The former's share was composed of cash ($106,000) and his seats on the New York and Boston stock exchanges which were valued at $300,000 and $19,000, respectively; and the latter's contribution was entirely in cash.[11]

At the time the new Kidder, Peabody started in business, the firm's daily expenses amounted to some $5,000; its income, earned mostly from brokerage commissions, averaged $1,500 a day. Cutting expenses became the first order of business, and the job of doing so fell largely upon Hovey, known in the office as "the east wind" because of his sailing interests. The staff of the Boston office, which had numbered about 170 in September 1929, was reduced to 100, and in New York City more than half of the 300 employees were discharged. Without these and other drastic economies, "Kidder, Peabody would have folded," Hovey observed.[12]

That it did not fail is a tribute to the new partners' determination and skills as business executives. The year 1931 was a grim one, not only on Wall Street but throughout the country. Every economic indicator registered the extent of the decline from the dizzy heights of the boom years. The Dow Jones averages, which had peaked at 354.3 in the third quarter of 1929, were down to 176.3 by the end of the first quarter of 1931 when Gordon and Hovey were struggling to keep Kidder, Peabody afloat. Gross national income had fallen from $87.8 billion in 1929 to $75.7 billion in 1930. Other indexes registered equally frightening declines. Unemployment almost tripled between 1929 and 1930, going from 1.6 million to 4.3 million. Every minor recovery was followed by a steeper decline. This was to be the pattern for another two years.[13]

Some of Kidder, Peabody's most crucial long-term decisions were made during these dismal times. Several of them altered significantly the character of the firm. Before the reorganization Kidder, Peabody had been chiefly a banking and foreign exchange house. By the time the new firm was organized both these functions, as well as the letter of credit business, had been taken over by the large metropolitan banks. The new partners, Gordon especially, concluded that the firm's future lay in the securities business rather than general or foreign banking. The decision to deemphasize these services did not mean abandoning the firm's foreign connections, particularly those with the Barings. These were to be continued and used to strengthen Kidder, Peabody's principal functions: the underwriting and distribution of high-grade securities.[14]

Late in December 1931 the partners made another decision designed to increase Kidder, Peabody's investment banking capabilities. Kissell, Kinnicutt & Co., a New York City banking and brokerage house established in 1906, found itself in financial difficulty. The crash and depression had wiped out many of its assets and its remaining capital was being drained rapidly.

To prevent its liquidation, Whitney, the Morgan partner who had supervised Kidder, Peabody's reorganization, suggested to Gordon and the elder Webster that they absorb Kissell, Kinnicutt into their own firm. Such a merger, Whitney explained, would be advantageous to all concerned. It would prevent Kissell, Kinnicutt's failure, a firm with which Morgan & Co. long had been associated. G. Herman Kinnicutt, the senior partner, had been a Morgan employee for several years, beginning in 1898. He was a mature and experienced, widely known and respected financier, the type of individual Whitney and other Wall Street leaders believed would add prestige and some needed seniority to the new Kidder, Peabody. Gordon agreed and also saw other advantages in Whitney's proposal. The merger would bring Kidder, Peabody additional business which the firm desperately needed to cover its overhead. "From the start through October 15, 1931," Gordon wrote Hovey, "we have lost $233,000," and "this overhead, as you know, does not allow anything for your and my services." The proposed merger, Gordon continued, also would yield Kidder, Peabody "certain connections which should prove valuable and enable us to get positions in sound syndicates"; and the admission of Kinnicutt, who was then in his sixties, would free Gordon from routine office details and allow him to concentrate on developing new business. "To the extent that I am handicapped in building up my outside relations," Gordon explained, "we must of course expect to have our syndicate profits cut down." And lastly, not the least of the advantages to be gained was the capital that Kinnicutt's admission would add to the firm, particularly since the shrinkage in security values between early March and mid-October 1931 had reduced Kidder, Peabody's original $5.35 million to about $3.4 million, a drop of almost 35 percent. Gordon saw in the proposed merger a way to "add $365,000 of net income to our business which will put us in the black instead of in the red," and "with any pick-up in business at all, with Kinnicutt's connections added to our own, we should be in a fair way to make some profits." After considerable discussion the merger was arranged and went into effect on January 2, 1932. Kidder, Peabody agreed to accept some of Kissell, Kinnicutt's brokerage accounts, to employ four of its partners and certain other personnel, and to admit Kinnicutt as a general partner.[15]

By the end of 1931 Kidder, Peabody's reorganization had been completed and the first basic guidelines for its recovery defined. The firm's headquarters were to be on Wall Street with Boston officially becoming the branch late in 1933 when Edwin Webster, Jr. moved permanently to New York City. The primary activity—investment banking—also was clearly fixed, and the partnership agreement specified, more precisely than before, the interests of the individual partners, the assignment of profits or losses, how the business' capital was to be increased, and in the event of a partner's death or retirement, the way the capital was to be distributed so as not to jeopardize the firm's liquidity. The basis had been set for "a strong future under active young men" aided by "older, experienced heads," as one of the firm's employees later recalled the new Kidder, Peabody's beginning.[16] Much had been done to rehabilitate the old house from its "quiet failure," but much more remained to be accomplished to restore Kidder, Peabody to its formerly proud position in the investment banking community.

PART
TWO

Investment Bankers

CHAPTER
FIVE

New Leaders for a New Era

The task of rebuilding Kidder, Peabody occurred during the worst depression in American history and at a time when the financial community generally and investment bankers particularly were under widespread attack. The stock market crash and the failure of hundreds of brokerage and investment houses dealt a heavy blow to the reputation of Wall Street's leaders. Not only had events proven them false prophets, but it appeared as if the great financiers were as incompetent in managing their own affairs as they were in advising their clients. Neither the collapse of the security markets nor the disclosure of poor business judgment blasted the image of the investment banker as much as did the exposure of irresponsibility, negligence, and deception in the world of high finance.

Week after week throughout the early 1930s a seemingly endless procession of bankers appeared in Washington, D.C., to testify before various congressional committees and federal agencies to explain their conduct and actions during the halcyon days preceding the stock market crash. The Federal Trade Commission, which had begun its probe into the practices of utility corporations more than a year before the panic, uncovered numerous abuses, many of them involving prominent financiers. Its findings were pushed off the front pages of the daily press by the more startling disclosures that came out of the Senate Finance Committee's inquiry into the sale of foreign bonds, and the alleged connections between the bankers who distributed these issues and America's entry into World War I. A few days after the start of these hearings, the Senate Banking and Currency Committee launched its probe of short sales on the New York Stock Exchange.

Not satisfied with such a limited mandate, the Senate expanded the committee's authority and assigned the task of conducting the investigation to a special subcommittee. The probe started late in April 1932 and lasted until May 1934. Its findings revealed gross abuses on the part of stock market operators who had enticed innocent investors to buy securities that were being manipulated for the benefit of a few insiders. Other, more lurid, aspects of high finance in the 1920s disclosed by the subcommittee included the profiteering that accompanied the launching of several investment trusts, the deceptions perpetrated by Ivar Kreuger, the once highly respected Swedish financier, and the many questionable practices employed by some of Wall Street's most eminent figures. All this proved to be only a prologue to the still more shocking revelations that came out after January 1933, when the New York City attorney Ferdinand Pecora was appointed the subcommittee's counsel. Through him the public learned of the misdeeds of other prominent bankers and the heavy losses they inflicted on investors. No other investigation accomplished more to shatter Wall Street's reputation than this one. Its findings, together with those of several other House and Senate committee probes, played a decisive role in bringing about a new era in American finance, in which the investment banker would become more closely regulated than most other business executives.[1]

Kidder, Peabody's partners escaped Pecora's wrathful questioning, and the firm also was spared a searching examination of its record by other congressional investigators. During the 1920s Kidder, Peabody had not employed any of the selling practices that, though legal and acceptable during the days of the great bull market, came under attack and censure during the grim days of the depression. The firm had not engaged in the kind of speculative operations that so disfigured the records of other houses, nor had it abused the confidence of investors or violated its fiduciary responsibilities. And while the Kidder Participations had not performed as successfully as their sponsors had hoped, the firm had not misused its investment trusts. William Holway Hill, a partner in the old firm, testified that while the Participations were intended for "the benefit of all concerned," they had not "worked out" that way, and the recent disclosure of abuses had led him to conclude that the kind of close relations that had existed between Kidder, Peabody and its investment trusts should be avoided in the future. Such ties, he said, provided "too much possibility of misuse of power."[2] The new partners not only concurred fully with this view, but moved immediately to disassociate the reorganized firm entirely from these earlier ventures.

By the time Pecora concluded his probe, Congress already had established the basic framework for federal regulation of the securities industry. The first of several statutes designed to reform Wall Street practices was the Securities Act of May 1933. With certain exceptions, among them federal, state, and local government bonds, the law required the registration of all new issues in excess of $100,000 that were to be sold in interstate commerce or through the mails. To prevent the kinds of deception that had been perpetrated in the 1920s the law also required that a detailed prospectus, disclosing all pertinent information relating to the securities, accompany the offering. Originally the Federal Trade Commission was authorized to enforce the law, but in 1934 this task was assigned to the newly created Securities and Exchange Commission.[3]

Three weeks after President Franklin D. Roosevelt signed the Securities Act, Congress passed the Glass-Steagall Banking Act. One of its provisions required the complete separation of commercial and investment banking. Its effect upon the financial community was far more drastic than the Securities Act. The latter, despite the pained outcry from Wall Street, required investment houses to revise their underwriting and distribution practices, while the 1933 Banking Act brought about fundamental structural changes in the securities business. The law's divorcement provision outlawed the security affiliates of commercial banks, and forced private banking partnerships, like Kidder, Peabody, to choose between deposit and investment banking. More than two-thirds of the nation's private banks opted for investment banking. Since Kidder, Peabody already had decided to de-emphasize its deposit business, the law, which went into effect in June 1934, only served to expedite the firm's transition from a private to an investment banking house.

Compliance with the Banking Act brought widespread changes in the makeup of the investment banking community. Old, established firms had to revise their operations, dropping some services and adding others. The law also was responsible for the organization of new firms to replace the defunct security affiliates. These and other changes resulted in a major reshuffling of personnel, as former officers of security affiliates and partners in private banks that chose to stay in the deposit business moved to various security houses, both old and newly organized firms.[4]

Kidder, Peabody was not immune to the consequences of the Banking Act. The reorganization of the securities business that occurred in the year following the passage of that law provided Kidder, Peabody the opportunity to recruit some of the experienced personnel necessary to strengthen the firm's investment banking capability. Early in 1933, when the Chase Harris Forbes Corporation was dissolved, Kidder, Peabody added to its staff a group of salesmen from that organization. And the next year Fred Moore, who had himself just joined Kidder,

Peabody, initiated the move that led to the firm's takeover of the offices and most of the staff of the Philadelphia National Company, the security affiliate of the Philadelphia National Bank, then the second largest commercial bank in Pennsylvania. The affiliate's president, Orus J. Matthews, was made manager of Kidder, Peabody's new Philadelphia branch, and two of his vice presidents (Erwin A. Stuebner and Alfred Rauch) became his assistant managers. The addition of new sales personnel and the acquisition of a Philadelphia office, at a time when retrenchment was the order of the day on Wall Street, fitted perfectly the new Kidder, Peabody partners' long-term plans for the firm: to strengthen and widen its ability to distribute securities.[5]

On June 6, 1934, ten days before the Banking Act's divorcement provision went into effect, Congress approved the Securities Exchange Act, the last of the early New Deal's major securities statutes. This lengthy and detailed measure extended the full disclosure principle of the Securities Act to issues listed on national exchanges, prohibited various practices considered inimical to the public interest, and regulated others subject to abuse. The law created an independent five-member Securities and Exchange Commission (SEC) to police the securities markets.[6]

Many of the law's provisions did not affect investment bankers directly, and several of the reforms it incorporated were strongly endorsed by prominent Wall Streeters. G. Hermann Kinnicutt of Kidder, Peabody, for example, had been among the financiers who appeared before the Senate Banking and Currency Committee to urge that enforcement of the securities laws be entrusted to an independent agency, rather than kept with the Federal Trade Commission, as the House version of the SEC bill originally had recommended.[7]

During the half-dozen years following the passage of the SEC law, Congress enacted several other statutes limiting and regulating still further the activities of investment bankers. In August 1935 the Public Utility Holding Company Act authorized the SEC to review new security issues of electric and gas utility holding companies and their subsidiaries providing interstate service. The law also required that the SEC approve the types of securities these companies issued and their price and method of offering, as well as supervise the relations between these corporations and the investment houses that financed them. Three years later, the Chandler Act limited the activities of investment bankers in reorganizing publicly held corporations.

Still other restrictions followed in rapid succession. The Trust Indenture Act of 1939, the Investment Company Act, and the Investment Advisers Act, the last two of which were approved in 1940, extended still further the SEC's regulatory authority over investment houses. By the time the last of these laws went into effect few, if any, of the investment bankers' traditional functions and services fell outside the SEC's purview.

Meanwhile, the industry itself also had moved toward greater and more effective self-regulation. In June 1938 Congress added the Maloney Amendment to the SEC law, creating the National Association of Securities Dealers, Inc. This organization, designed to regulate the over-the-counter brokers and dealers under SEC supervision, grew out of the industry's 1933 Blue Eagle code under the National Industrial Recovery Act.[8]

While the federal government was busy enacting legislation to prevent a recurrence of the abuses that had so disfigured American finance in the 1920s, investment bankers were undergoing a difficult period of readjustment. The protracted depression and continued suspicion of Wall Street, even more than federal regulation, made the 1930s an especially difficult decade for investment bankers. Recovery was slow and irregular. The volume of new corporate issues stayed at depression levels throughout most of the decade, rising from $380 million in 1933 to $4.4 billion in 1936, only to drop back to $2.1 billion in 1939 (see Table 5.1). The latter figure was not exceeded again until 1940, when new corporate offerings that year amounted to slightly more than $2.6 billion. Brokerage commissions also fell precipitously as the volume of shares traded on the New York Stock Exchange tumbled from 1.1 billion shares in 1929 to 425

TABLE 5.1 *Security Issues, 1929–1945* (in millions of dollars)

	Total corporate	Total state and municipal
1929	9,376	1,431
1930	4,957	1,487
1931	2,372	1,256
1932	644	849
1933	380	520
1934	490	939
1935	2,266	1,232
1936	4,431	1,121
1937	2,239	908
1938	2,110	1,108
1939	2,115	1,126
1940	2,615	1,238
1941	2,623	956
1942	1,043	524
1943	1,147	435
1944	3,142	661
1945	5,902	795

SOURCE: *Historical Statistics of the United States Colonial Times to 1957*, p. 658.

million in 1932, climbed back to 655 million shares in 1933, dropped to 324 million the next year, recovered to 496 million in 1936, then started on a plunge that lasted through 1942. That year trading on the New York Stock Exchange reached a twenty-eight-year low of 126 million shares (see Table 5.2).[9]

TABLE 5.2 *Volume of Sales on the New York Stock Exchange, 1929–1945* (in millions of shares)

1929	1,125	1938	297
1930	810	1939	262
1931	577	1940	208
1932	425	1941	171
1933	655	1942	126
1934	324	1943	279
1935	382	1944	263
1936	496	1945	378
1937	409		

SOURCE: *Historical Statistics of the United States Colonial Times to 1957*, p. 659.

It was during these years of deep depression and widespread political, social, and economic change that Kidder, Peabody's partners laid the foundations for the firm's recovery and growth. All had agreed that Kidder, Peabody would emphasize the underwriting and distribution of securities, the business the partners considered themselves most competent to conduct. The firm also decided to develop its commission and bond trading business, activities that would allow it to offer the public a diversified range of investment services. The partners decided not to deal in commercial paper, trade in commodities, or manage investment trusts. The decision to avoid these operations was dictated partly by the need to conserve the firm's limited capital, but also by the fact that the partners, particularly Gordon, did not want to be distracted from their primary objective, investment banking.

All four partners also agreed on several other basic policies. Though Gordon was assigned and did take on the major responsibility for recruiting new business, the other partners also were expected to contribute significantly to this effort, as well as fill other jobs. Webster, for example, not only provided most of the capital that kept the firm functioning, but he also used his Stone & Webster ties to widen Kidder, Peabody's corporate connections, particularly among the country's electric and gas utility companies, enterprises with which his father's firm was closely associated. Hovey and Kinnicutt, on the other hand, devoted themselves almost entirely to supervising the firm's internal operations, the former in Boston and the latter in New York City.

But it was Gordon who made the greatest contribution to Kidder, Peabody's revival. He "picked up a firm in shambles and built it up from scratch," one of the firm's employees recalled later. Gordon not only was the principal recruiter of new business, but he was also the chief policymaker; his energy and drive were felt throughout the firm. He set the pace and established the pattern of operation. Frederick L. Moore, who left the Guaranty Company, the security affiliate of the Guaranty Trust Company, to join Kidder, Peabody in March 1934, stated that Gordon "was operating a one-man show."[10] But unlike the autocratic and unapproachable Winsor, Gordon was a "tough but fair boss," friendly and courteous with everyone. "His office door always was open; the junior men felt free to go and speak with him, to complain or offer advice." Gordon "not only listened, but if someone's suggestion was good, he took it and gave credit for it."[11]

Gordon's primary purpose was to reestablish Kidder, Peabody's reputation and restore the firm to its once prestigious position in the nation's capital markets. The best way to achieve this dual objective, Gordon believed, was to build a record of demonstrated achievement in distributing quality securities. Efficient nationwide distribution, he maintained, was the only certain route to increased underwriting participations. His ultimate goal was to make Kidder, Peabody a major originator, underwriter, and distributor, the kind of house that was able and competent to provide issuers with complete investment banking services, from the conception of a new offering to the final sale of the security.

The decision to build Kidder, Peabody into a national distributor or, as a contemporary observer once said, the policy of "selling your way to success," was implemented at once. The addition of the Chase Harris Forbes and Philadelphia Company's sales personnel was a move in the direction of making Kidder, Peabody a firm that the leading houses of issue would consider to be essential to include in their syndicates to help sell their underwritings. The old firm also had tried to tap a national market, relying on correspondents across the country to distribute the securities it sponsored. Gordon continued the practice, but because he wanted to develop Kidder, Peabody's own independent sales capacity, he also started opening branches in key cities. When a branch's sales had increased sufficiently and the prospects for other business appeared promising, it was turned into a regional office. The first of these, Philadelphia, was opened in June 1934, at the time Kidder, Peabody took over the Philadelphia Company. Acquisition of this organization gave Kidder, Peabody increased sales strength throughout Pennsylvania, southern New Jersey, and Delaware. The next regional office, Chicago, opened in August 1937, was designed to give Kidder, Peabody access to an increasingly important capital market, one which the partners believed would add not only to the firm's sales capacity but, in time, also bring it new corporate clients.[12]

Strong sales depended, of course, upon winning and holding the confidence of investors, both large and small. And this the partners agreed could be accomplished only by carefully selecting the securities sold. Kidder, Peabody had earned much of its reputation as a distributor of American Telephone & Telegraph (AT&T) bonds and stocks, securities that had weathered the depression as well as any and had continued to pay their owners interest and dividends regularly. The goodwill the firm had gained from the sale of these issues had been partly dissipated. Some of the securities Kidder, Peabody had sponsored in the 1920s, like those of so many other houses, had suffered serious declines, and dissatisfied clients blamed the firm for their losses. The most effective way to restore Kidder, Peabody's reputation, win back disgruntled clients, and attract new ones, the partners maintained, was by distributing only high-grade securities. "By accenting quality," a later partner explained, "we hoped to boost sales, earn enough to stay in business, and attract underwritings."[13]

To restore Kidder, Peabody to its former position as a leading underwriter proved to be no easy task. The firm's once eminent reputation as an underwriter and its close and influential contacts with prime issuers had deteriorated badly in the 1920s. Even its ranking as a top underwriter and distributor of AT&T issues had declined. Before World War I the firm had sold approximately 47.5 percent of this company's offerings; in the 1920s Kidder, Peabody's share of this business had dropped to 31.5 percent.[14]

The likelihood that Kidder, Peabody would inherit some of

the old firm's underwriting accounts, including its former position in AT&T bond syndicates, was slight at best. Some of the new firm's partners sometimes spoke as if they would regain some of the old Kidder, Peabody's underwriting business. Gordon never did so. He was too much of a realist to expect that this would occur. George Whitney of Morgan & Co. told him as much. In a conversation concerning new AT&T offerings, Whitney told Gordon that Kidder, Peabody's participation in any future syndicates managed by the Morgan firm would be determined strictly on the merits, without any reference to the old firm's previous position.[15]

The task of rebuilding Kidder, Peabody's underwriting business was made more difficult by the depression, which reached its depth in the months between Roosevelt's election and his inauguaration. The deepening crisis virtually eliminated the need for corporations to raise new capital to expand and improve idle plants. As though the depression was not enough to deter business executives from planning new financings, the uncertainties created by the United States going off the gold standard, Roosevelt's scuttling of the London Economic Conference in June 1933, and Wall Street's fears concerning the New Deal's banking and securities statutes made corporations all the more reluctant to seek new funds. The result was a near cessation of new capital issues, with the volume of these offerings dropping from nearly $1.6 billion in 1931 to $152 million in 1934. That year Kidder, Peabody managed one new offering, the first public sale under the new SEC's rules. The firm developed and sold $8 million of privately held bonds of the Scovill Manufacturing Company.[16]

But if the depression produced a sharp decline in new capital issues, the fall in interest rates that accompanied the contraction led many businesses to take advantage of cheaper money to refund their bonded debt. In 1934 refundings accounted for nearly 60.2 percent of all corporate offerings, and the next year these issues represented 80.2 percent of the total. Between 1934 and 1939 refundings never amounted to less than 49.1 percent of all corporate offerings.[17] Kidder, Peabody participated in some of these underwritings, but most of these offerings were managed by the banking houses that had brought out the original offerings.

Realizing that refundings, like the underwriting accounts of most large corporations, were as Gordon put it, "sewed up," he decided to rebuild Kidder, Peabody as an originator of new issues by recruiting sound smaller companies with potential for growth, a group usually neglected by the more prestigious houses of issue. This was the policy that Lehman Brothers and Goldman, Sachs & Co. had employed early in the twentieth century when these two firms first became underwriters. Gordon's strategy, to help young companies and grow with them, became a fixed policy, one that Kidder, Peabody has continued to follow to the present day. Not all the corporations the firm financed in the 1930s remained with Kidder, Peabody, but enough of them did so to confirm the wisdom of the policy.

To hold on to its issuer-clients, Kidder, Peabody not only had to provide them with top quality service but also had to make it financially attractive to corporations to employ the firm as the originator and underwriter of their securities. Gordon's decision to build a strong national distribution system made it possible for Kidder, Peabody to secure up-to-date information on market conditions across the country, to gauge the likely reception for a new issue, and to determine the best possible price at which it could be marketed successfully. Gordon's reputation as an "expert pricer," one of the "toughest on the Street," grew out of his close, intimate knowledge of the new issues market, most of which he gained from the firm's sales and corporate trading personnel. "The secret of correct pricing is direct contact with the market," Gordon said repeatedly, "not to be dependent on other houses for the information you need, to develop your own through your own sources." Gordon made "good pricing" a Kidder, Peabody trademark, one which he used to attract business. "He always tried to get a little better price than the market seemed to dictate," said one of the firm's longtime employees.[18] Gordon's loyalty to issuers and his conservatism in spending other people's money made the firm "sweat" for its profits, but impressed corporate executives and attracted new accounts.

Service and sales capacity became two of Kidder, Peabody's most effective arguments in competing for new business. The firm went after any account it believed there was a chance of winning. Unlike Winsor, who had considered it undignified for a banker to solicit business, Gordon and his partners "went out and rang door bells," as one of them later recalled. They tried to learn of companies planning new issues, wrote to or made personal calls upon the officers, board members, or anyone who might help get Kidder, Peabody an underwriting position.[19] A typical letter to win an account or participation included a review of the firm's recent record in distributing securities and concluded with a statement similar to the one Gordon used in writing to a vice president of Western Cartridge Company in November 1939. "If now or in the future you have need for an investment banker, we hereby apply. Our experience, our position in the business, and the reputation we believe we have in financial circles throughout the country make us confident that we can do whatever you wish better than any other concern."[20]

Kidder, Peabody also worked to develop close ties with the major houses of issue, the ones that managed most of the large syndicates. The firm's partners sought to impress upon the heads of these firms Kidder, Peabody's record as a distributor and the advantages of including Kidder, Peabody in their underwriting groups. In September 1935 when Morgan Stanley & Co. was organized as a wholesaler of securities and AT&T turned to this firm to finance one of its subsidiaries, Gordon immediately called on Harold Stanley, a top officer in the new house, to seek a participation in the proposed syndicate. "I used every argument at my command to get as large a position as possible for my firm," Gordon testified later. "The matter was of very great importance to us, obviously."[21] Kidder, Peabody secured a position in the syndicate, but its underwriting percentage in Bell System bond offerings, which had been 31.5 percent in the 1920s, fell to 12 percent in this issue, then to 6 percent in subsequent ones. "The 6 percent hasn't been taken from us because we haven't built up our distribution or because we have failed," Gordon explained, "it has been taken from everybody in order to get more people into the business, in order to do the job more and more effectively." Gordon also understood that the only way Kidder, Peabody could hold on to its 6 percent was by demonstrated ability to distribute telephone securities. "If we ever fall down on our distribution, then we would expect to be reduced."[22]

Gordon's approach to Morgan Stanley was not unique. Other partners used similar tactics with other major houses of issue. Orus Matthews, the head of Kidder, Peabody's Philadelphia office since June 1934 who became a partner in January 1935, used his former connections with the Philadelphia National Company to develop friendly ties with the newly organized Mellon Securities Corporation of Pittsburgh. "In my opinion, outside of Morgan Stanley," Matthews wrote his partners and senior associates in September 1936, "the Mellon Securities Company represents the best prospect for participations in excellent business." Matthews suggested that "one or more of the partners arrange to go to Pittsburgh from time to time during the next few months . . . for I believe now is the time to actively develop this contact."[23]

The partners did not limit themselves to rebuilding the firm's traditional investment banking services. They also developed, expanded, and adapted to the needs of the times the old but until then little used method of selling a corporation's securities directly to a few buyers, usually institutions—life insurance, trust companies, investment trusts, and pension funds. Before 1933 direct sales of this type, commonly called private placements, had accounted for less than 3 percent of all security offerings; between 1934 and 1939 direct sales of corporate bonds and notes averaged 23.3 percent a year, and their volume, both in number and dollar value, grew still further after World War II.[24]

Several factors contributed to the increase in private placements. The Revenue Act of August 1935, by hiking the rates on personal income particularly in the higher brackets of $50,000 and above, drove many wealthy individuals out of the corporate bond market, leaving it largely to institutions such as life insurance, casualty, and trust companies, savings banks, and loan societies. The funds these institutions had available for investments grew significantly in the 1930s. The total income of life insurance companies grew by about a billion dollars, from $4.62 billion to $5.65 billion; during the same period total savings and other time deposits increased by some $4.7 billion, from a 1933 low of $21.1 billion to nearly $25.8 billion in 1940.[25]

Federal regulation of the security markets also contributed to the growth of private placements. The Securities Act, by imposing new responsibilities on both issuers and investment houses, increased the cost of a public offering and lengthened the time to prepare it for SEC registration and approval. Private sales not only were less expensive than public offerings, sometimes substantially so, but they also were easier and quicker to arrange—often the entire transaction was completed in a week or two—and they allowed the investment banker greater flexibility in arranging terms that were satisfactory to all parties. Institutional buyers, particularly the life insurance companies, liked direct sales because they could influence terms, such as fixing the life span of the bonds or notes, an important consideration in their financial planning. Issuers found private placements attractive because they eliminated the delay and uncertainty accompanying a public offering.[26]

Kidder, Peabody recognized the trend and cultivated it assiduously. At first private placements were assigned to the corporate finance department, organized by Moore when he joined the firm in 1934. He, together with Willard T. Grimm and Joseph W. Hibben, the resident manager and assistant manager, respectively, of the Chicago office, stressed the advantages of direct sales to issuers and institutional investors, large and small, across the country. They and the partners sought out companies in need of financing and, if practicable, tried to convince them to accept a private placement. Direct sales usually were planned and set up in the firm's New York office, but the representative and branch offices were expected not only to develop the business but also to help find the institutions that would buy the securities. The firm's commitment to national distribution was applied to generate a nationwide private placement capability. This, as much as anything else, made Kidder, Peabody a leader in this business. Its first private placement, $3.0 million of debentures, was for the Freeport Sulphur Company, a corporation that Kidder, Peabody had served previously. In January 1933 the firm had originated and managed a $2.5 million offering of convertible preferred for the Sulphur Company's wholly-owned subsidiary, Freeport Texas. This was Kidder, Peabody's last pre-SEC offering.[27] The firm also arranged two other private placements in 1939, all three totaling $4.2 million. Kidder, Peabody continued to emphasize these sales, and between 1940 and 1945 it negotiated fourteen private sales amounting to nearly $68.4 million.[28]

The firm also pioneered the use of direct sales to dispose of large blocks of common stock. "The passage of the Securities and Exchange Act convinced us," Gordon wrote a prospective client late in 1939, "that the distribution of large blocks of investment securities could be more advantageously sold by direct placing rather than by the auction method provided by the Stock Exchange." To facilitate such sales the firm developed close ties with several investment trusts in New York and Boston. "The first large block of shares handled off the Stock Exchange," Gordon said, "was the sale by us of 88,000 shares of F. W. Woolworth Company stock." Other similar transactions followed, with the annual number growing from two a year in 1939, 1941, and 1942 to four in 1943 and eight in both 1944 and 1945. Most of these sales were negotiated entirely by Kidder,

Peabody; a few, such as the 1943 secondary offering of 100,000 shares of Bank of America NT&SA common, was arranged in collaboration with two other investment houses. By then the firm had made a specialty of this type of distribution.[29]

During the late 1930s government officials, pressed by a few interested bankers and reformers still convinced of the existence of a money trust, urged the SEC and other regulatory bodies to require corporations they supervised to sell their securities at competitive bids as a means of destroying the alleged monopoly of the new issues business by a few New York City investment banking houses. Charges of the existence of a Wall Street banking monopoly were not dissimilar to those expressed a generation earlier by the Pujo subcommittee and revived during the Senate's investigation of stock exchange practices in the early 1930s. The topic was taken up again at the close of the decade by the Temporary National Economic Committee.

Competitive bidding, that is, the sale of securities at auction, was an old practice going back to the early years of the nineteenth century, one which had been debated periodically since then. This type of sale was favored by all who believed a few Wall Street bankers monopolized the marketing of new bonds and stocks, particularly the top-quality issues of the prime borrowers.[30] Kidder, Peabody, like the vast majority of investment firms, opposed competitive sales. Matthews, the partner who headed the firm's Philadelphia office, urged his New York partners against joining any competitive groups. To do so, he wrote, "would seem to be absolutely contrary to our best interests." Competitive bidding, Matthews continued, "would serve to encourage cut-throat competition and, in my opinion, would result in many cases of unsound issues."[31] Gordon, one of the industry's most vigorous competers, also argued very strongly against competitive bidding, particularly for equities, and he added that the system deprived issuers and their bankers of the opportunity to work together in planning and marketing new offerings. But as much as he and the other partners opposed auction sales, they adjusted quickly to the SEC's ruling of June

1941 requiring competitive bidding for most issues of public utility holding companies and their subsidiaries under the federal agency's jurisdiction. Even before the SEC's ruling went into effect, Kidder, Peabody had accepted underwriting participations in some competitive syndicates. After 1941 it started to manage and comanage bidding groups of its own. Some of the firm's earliest winning tenders included a $4 million offering for Minnesota Rural Credit Deficiency Fund (1943), a $4.3 million issue of Central Ohio Light & Power Co. bonds (1944), and $16.5 million of first mortgage bonds for the Florida Power Corporation (1944), as well as others.[32]

By the beginning of the 1940s the partners' decision to remake Kidder, Peabody into a national diversified investment banking house, capable of meeting the changing needs of borrowers and lenders, seemed on the verge of accomplishment. The firm had survived near-bankruptcy and had adjusted to the new era of federal regulation of the securities industry. Except for the first year (1931) when "we were putting the business on a realistic basis," to use Gordon's words, the firm showed steady annual profits with net earnings reaching over $250,000 in 1933 and over $750,000 in 1936.[33] As much as 40 percent of Kidder, Peabody's annual profits, particularly during the first half-dozen or so years, came from brokerage commissions. Total annual dollar volume from this source, the "bread and butter" of the firm's business, rose from $671,000 in 1934, the low for the decade, to $1.13 million in 1936, after which it fell to $745,000 in 1938, rose to $805,000 in 1939, dropped to $581,000 in 1941, then started moving up again, reaching $1.68 million in 1945.[34]

Substantial progress also was registered in the number and dollar volume of syndicate managements and underwriting participations. Between 1932, the year the new firm cosponsored its first issue ($1.15 million of Milwaukee Gas Light bonds), and 1945, Kidder, Peabody managed or comanaged seventy-nine syndicates offering nearly $6.43 billion of corporate securities, with nearly 38.6 percent of the total dollar value for the entire fourteen-year period brought out in 1945. During these years the firm also was allotted eighty-six underwriting participations of $1 million or more, some 20 percent of which were in syndicates led by Morgan Stanley and another 10 percent in groups headed by Kuhn, Loeb. In addition Kidder, Peabody accepted numerous smaller participations in which the firm's name did not appear in public announcements advertising the offerings. Some of the firm's managements and underwritings were for corporations that had turned to Kidder, Peabody on the recommendation of Morgan Stanley and, with the notable exception of issues for AT&T and its subsidiaries, nearly all the other offerings the firm sponsored were for companies with which it had not been associated previously. Gordon credited the firm's growing volume of underwritings in the mid- and later 1930s, as compared with its poor record in the 1920s, to its "active and aggressive . . . solicitation" of new business, a view that was confirmed by the SEC in 1936.[35] Between July 1 and December 31 of that year Kidder, Peabody, according to the SEC, ranked fourth among the country's investment houses in terms of the number of underwriting participations in offerings registered under the Securities Act. Gordon's claim that the firm's "real progress since 1931" was the result of its forceful "solicitation of underwritings" was substantiated still further by Circuit Judge Harold R. Medina. After reviewing Kidder, Peabody's underwriting business between 1935 and 1949, Medina concluded his appraisal of the evidence by saying: "The partners and employees went after everything, from managerships, if they could be secured, if not for participations and even selling positions. No issue was too small, no participation too insignificant."[36]

Not all the firm's underwritings proved successful or profitable. Two of its worst failures occurred early in September 1937, one month after the onset of the acute ten-month recession that brought sharp declines in stock and bond values, forced about 12,800 businesses to close their doors—an increase of some 3,300 over the previous year—and swelled the unemployment and relief rolls. Kidder, Peabody's losses in these two underwritings amounted to some $750,000, wiping out nearly all the firm's 1936 earnings. The first of these costly transactions, a $44.2 million offering of Pure Oil Company convertible preferreds managed by Edward B. Smith & Co. with forty-two underwriters, was negotiated at $100 a share; the stock found so few buyers by the time the registration statement had become effective that it immediately fell to $70 a share. The second, equally unsuccessful issue—$48 million of Bethlehem Steel Corporation convertible debentures offered to the company's shareholders—was brought out by a group of twenty-five underwriters headed by Kuhn, Loeb and Mellon Securities Corporation. When sales of the Pure Oil stock in the United States proved badly disappointing, Kidder, Peabody tried to distribute some of its 200,000-share commitment in Europe. Moore left for England and Holland hoping to find buyers among the officers of several Scottish investment trusts and the firm's Dutch clients, only to learn that the Europeans were as uninterested in the issue as Kidder, Peabody's American customers. Moore returned to New York without having sold a single share. The "two deals," he recalled later, "were a body blow and a lesson to us," as they were to much of the investment banking community. Edward B. Smith & Co., with much of its capital tied up in the two issues, merged with Chas. D. Barney & Co. at the end of the year to form the new firm of Smith, Barney & Co. Other managing houses, alarmed at the number of firms embarrassed by these two transactions, sought to insure themselves against similar misfortunes in the future by increasing substantially the number of participating underwriters in their syndicates. And Kidder, Peabody, which had to borrow from commercial banks to carry the unsold securities, established a commitment committee to make certain no single partner ever again could commit the firm to an underwriting participation on his own authority, as had occurred in these two instances.[37]

The decision to set up a commitment committee, like the one to reorganize and expand the corporate finance department in

1935, was part of an ongoing effort to strengthen every area of the firm's operations. From the start the partners, and Gordon in particular, recognized the firm's shortcomings and capabilities, and while they sought to correct the former and develop the latter, they realized that a successful, diversified investment house needed strength in all departments—brokerage, trading, underwriting, research, and new business, as well as effective internal management—and that each area depended upon all the others. In April 1931, a month after the new firm had opened for business, Gordon wrote Baring Brothers to inform the London house that the "numerous changes and consolidations in departments" being instituted were designed to permit the firm to transact its affairs "more expeditiously and with less confusion than was previously the case." Since the brokerage business had to "carry the greater part of our overhead," Gordon wrote, this was the area of operations that had received top priority, and the one that continued to occupy the partners' chief attention.[38] Turnover among salespeople was large and rapid, with only those who produced being kept and rewarded.

By 1935 the entire sales department had been reorganized, its operating costs reduced substantially, and its productivity increased. Amyas Ames, who had started on his investment banking career in 1931 as a salesman and analyst at Kidder, Peabody's Boston office, moved to New York as assistant sales manager in 1934, where he helped guide the reorganization. The next year, while still only in his late twenties, Ames was made sales manager. A similar revamping occurred in Boston where John C. Flint, the sales manager since 1931, undertook to revitalize the firm's merchandising capability in New England.

Other changes aimed at making Kidder, Peabody more efficient and attractive to a diverse clientele of individual and institutional clients included the expansion of the municipal bond department. Frank Gallagher, brought to Kidder, Peabody by Fred Moore, was a former employee of George Gibbons & Co., a house specializing in the sale of New York state and municipal bonds. In March 1938 he was put in charge of the firm's municipal department. The partners also approved a marked increase in the size and budget of the research staff which had been cut to two statisticians in the great "blood-letting" of 1931, when the business, in Gordon's words, was "being put on a paying basis."[39] He saw research as an essential staff function, one that would give strength to both the sales and underwriting departments by providing each with a wide range of detailed, in-depth information that kept the firm abreast of technological innovations in industry and other changes in the economy that might affect the needs of both lenders and borrowers.

None of the policies adopted to rehabilitate Kidder, Peabody was more important than the decision to strengthen the firm's internal operations—accounting, stock and bond transfers, and the myriad of other administrative and clerical details required to support the house's various operations. Poor accounting practices had contributed to the old firm's difficulties; the new partners were determined to avoid a similar experience. That they did so is in no small measure the accomplishment of William N. Loverd, whom Moore called the "hero in our midst." A high school graduate who had started on his Wall Street career as an accountant with Kissel, Kinnicutt & Co., Loverd joined Kidder, Peabody in December 1931 at the time it took over the former house. Starting as assistant to Kidder, Peabody's head accountant, Loverd helped establish an efficient system of accounting controls and, more important, implemented Gordon's policy of creating reserves against inventory losses and a general reserve fund that by the close of the 1930s gave the firm a stronger financial base than it had enjoyed since the immediate post-World War I era.[40]

Responsibility for the firm's total operations, of course, rested with the partners. They were the firm; they set its course, tempo, and image. The three founders—Webster, Gordon, and Hovey—were active, dynamic individuals who got along well with each other and enjoyed the challenge of remaking an aging firm; as the business grew they sought associates who shared their views and objectives. The three partners added in the mid-1930s—Matthews (1935) and Moore and Flint (1936)—were men who had contributed significantly to rebuilding Kidder, Peabody and promised to contribute still more to its development in the future.

By the end of the 1930s, despite Kidder, Peabody's impressive recovery, the partners did not consider its rehabilitation complete. Neither their own nor the firm's reputation among the country's top business and financial leaders had been fully established. In part this stemmed from the partners' relative youth; Gordon, the most active senior member, was only thirty-eight years old in 1939 and, except for Kinnicutt and Hovey, most of the firm's top officials were not much older. Also contributing to Kidder, Peabody's still modest reputation was the fact that the partners' achievements in taking over a nearly bankrupt firm and turning it into a profitable and growing business were as yet not widely known. The firm had established itself as a distributor; it still had to earn its reputation as an originator and underwriter of securities. The partners were aware of this. "We tried to keep a realistic sense of our importance and ability," Gordon said.[41] America's entry into World War II delayed Kidder, Peabody's recognition still further.

Gordon's chief concern during the war years was to hold the firm together and preserve its capital. And though investment banking did not experience the same wartime boom enjoyed by most other sectors of the economy, the years 1942 through 1945 proved to be considerably less disastrous than some Wall Street leaders had anticipated at the time of the Pearl Harbor attack. Total corporate offerings fell from $2.6 billion in 1941 to $1 billion in 1942, rose slightly to $1.1 billion the next year, then jumped to $3.1 billion in 1944 and to $5.9 billion in 1945; new state and municipal issues declined from $956 million in 1941 to $524 million in 1942, fell to $435 million the next year, and then started upward to $661 million in 1944 anf $795 million in 1945. As in World War I, the Treasury requested that new issues be timed not to interfere with its own bond drives. Trading on the

New York Stock Exchange followed the trend set by the new issues market, with a drop from 171 million shares in 1941 to 126 million in 1942, then a steady increase to 179 million in 1943, 263 million in 1944, and 378 million in 1945.[42]

Unlike the securities industry generally, which suffered its worst decline in 1942, the first full year of war, Kidder, Peabody ended the twelve months showing a slight improvement over 1941. The firm managed or comanaged three underwriting groups in both 1941 and 1942 with the total dollar value somewhat higher in the latter year ($25.4 million) than in the former one ($23.3 million). The same was true of its private placement record—a single $5 million sale in 1941 as compared with two amounting to almost $6.1 million in 1942. The next year the firm registered a significant recovery that was maintained through the end of the war. The total number and dollar value of issues managed or comanaged rose from seven ($52.7 million) in 1943 to ten ($83.8 million) in 1944, then soared to thirty-two ($290.0 million) in 1945. The number of Kidder, Peabody's managements or comanagements in 1945 represented some 40.5 percent of all those it had headed in the previous fourteen years, and their value constituted about 45 percent of the total since the start of the new firm in 1931. Private placements also peaked in 1945, with eight sales totaling $47.6 million. The marked increase in underwritings, together with a substantial increase in stock exchange transactions that lifted total brokerage commissions from slightly more than $642,000 in 1942 to nearly $1.7 million 1945, boosted the firm's total earnings for the year that the war ended to above 1 million dollars.[43]

Together with other investment houses, Kidder, Peabody also participated actively in selling the Treasury's seven war loans and the 1945 victory drive. Among the 450 or more investment houses selling government bonds the firm stood in first place in every Treasury drive save one, when it dropped to second place, and the Boston office also scored high, being awarded a citation for leading all that city's firms in total individual sales. Kidder, Peabody, like all businesses, also contributed some of its personnel to the war effort. Ames, who had been made a partner in January 1941, served as an administrative officer of the War Shipping Administration in Washington, and seventy-three other employees, almost a fifth of the staff, joined the armed forces.[44]

Like some other Wall Street leaders, Gordon believed investment bankers had more to contribute to the war effort than selling the Treasury's bonds. Speaking before the National Association of Securities Commissioners meeting in St. Louis in September 1942, he called for more effective use of the country's investment houses in helping the government finance the war expansion. He urged that Washington make it easier for corporations who were able to finance themselves by simplifying regulatory practices, thus relieving the government of some of its responsibilities and the taxpayers of some of the cost of new construction. The appeal brought few results. Washington continued to finance most of the industrial expansion, much of it through the Defense Plant Corporation, a subsidiary of the Reconstruction Finance Corporation.[45]

Despite Gordon's failure to convince the government to make greater use of investment houses, his own firm's impressive increase in business led to the first large additions to the partnership. Between 1941 and 1945 Kidder, Peabody admitted eight regular partners, all of whom were recruited from within the firm. Each fulfilled Gordon's chief criterion for a partnership—demonstrated ability and productivity.[46] In January 1945 the firm also added its first limited partner, Randolph P. Compton, a former executive of the Republic Aviation Corporation who had begun his business career in his father's Kansas City investment firm.[47] A man of substantial wealth, Compton brought to Kidder, Peabody additional capital and several important corporate accounts. His appointment together with the eight other recent admissions gave Kidder, Peabody a total of fifteen partners, five times as many as there had been in 1931. Kinnicutt, the first new partner to be added, died in December 1943.

Kidder, Peabody's wartime record was marred by the firm's first publicly announced violation of the Securities Exchange Act. The incident occurred on September 23, 1942, and involved a $963,000 secondary distribution of 4 percent first mortgage bonds of the Jamestown, Franklin & Clearfield Railroad Co., a subsidiary of the New York Central System. The bonds, which Kidder, Peabody had purchased from a life insurance company at 49 and reoffered to the public at 50¼, less a point to dealers, were listed on the New York Stock Exchange and selling at 49¾ asked and 49½ bid. The SEC charged Kidder, Peabody with unlawful "manipulation of the market" ("rigging") which according to the Commission "created active and apparent trading and raised the price of the security." Kidder, Peabody's efforts at stabilizing the price at 50¼ instead of 49¾, the one at the last sale, was designed, the SEC charged, to attract buyers at the allegedly rigged price. Kidder, Peabody denied the charge it had willfully violated the rules, saying the difficulty "arose over a net change of a ½ point and revolved around a highly technical interpretation of the stabilization provisions of the Securities Exchange Act . . . on which there might well be a difference of opinion, but with respect to which the firm believed that it had acted correctly and in entire good faith." After a careful review of the evidence the SEC agreed that Kidder, Peabody had acted in "good faith" and dropped the reportedly stiff penalties it originally had considered imposing on the firm. The violation, the SEC finally determined, had stemmed from the firm's "relative inefficiency in supervising the distribution" which, in turn, was due "in part" to wartime conditions. The Commission concluded the proceedings by ordering the firm suspended for ten days from membership in the National Association of Securities Dealers, the industry's self-regulatory body; and it also ordered Clifford suspended from membership on the New York Stock Exchange for the same period of time, both rulings to take effect beginning May 17, 1945. Kidder, Peabody had erred unknowingly and had to suffer the embarrassment of official censure and the loss of business that came from being denied for a two-week period the privileges of membership in two essential organizations.[48]

Early in June 1945, when the SEC's restrictions on Kidder, Peabody's activities came to an end, the country was celebrating the defeat and occupation of Nazi Germany. And though the war against Japan still raged on, the final outcome of that conflict also ceased to be in doubt. The future looked good both for the country and for Kidder, Peabody. Gordon's concern at the time of Pearl Harbor about the firm's ability to hold together during the war had proved ill-founded. Not only had Kidder, Peabody survived, but it had emerged from four years of war in a stronger financial condition and with greater prestige than it had enjoyed at any time since the reorganization. The firm had established itself as an effective national distributor; it still had to win the financial community's recognition as an undisputed major underwriter, a full-fledged member of that small group of houses at the top of the industry's power structure.

CHAPTER SIX

Growth, Expansion, and Diversification

Kidder, Peabody, like most other investment houses, shared in the economy's spectacular expansion that followed the surrender of Japan in August 1945. For almost a quarter of a century, from 1945 through the early months of 1969, the economy registered impressive gains. The sustained advance, interrupted only by a few brief, mild setbacks, stemmed from many sources: an increase in population (from 140.1 million in 1945 to 205.0 million in 1950 with the largest gains registered in the West); the accelerated pace of urbanization, particularly in the Southwest and Far West, with the greatest growth everywhere occurring in the suburbs rather than in the central cities; and an equally striking increase in income.

Seldom before had the country enjoyed so long a period of virtually uninterrupted prosperity. Gross national product expressed in 1958 dollars more than doubled between 1945 ($355.2 billion) and 1970 ($722.5 billion), and during the same period per capita disposable personal income (also measured in 1958 dollars) increased from $1,642 to $2,610, a rise of almost 59 percent. The advance in income owed much to the striking gains in productivity—output per person-hour in private industry more than doubled between 1947 and 1970—and this advance, in turn, rested heavily on the expanded use of new and improved technological processes, the most dramatic of which was the mechanized regulation achieved with computers. To meet the demands of a growing and increasingly affluent people, and at the same time to supply Europeans with the massive quantities of goods necessary to reconstruct their war-torn countries—mostly financed through the Marshall Plan and other similar aid programs—American business executives increased their expenditures for new plant and equipment by more than four times, from some $19.3 billion in 1947 to over $79.7 billion in 1970.[1] Investment houses like Kidder, Peabody occupied a decisive position in helping corporations and governments raise the vast amounts of capital necessary to finance the economic expansion of the post-World War II era. Total corporate issues soared from $5.9 billion in 1945 to $38.9 billion in 1970, and state and municipal offerings grew by an even greater amount, from $795 million to $24.3 billion.[2]

At the very time Kidder, Peabody was entering upon its most expansive years, the partners were forced to defend themselves against a prolonged and costly antitrust suit. The trial stemmed from some of the same old anti-Wall Street prejudices, fears, and suspicions that had sparked the Pujo money trust investigation of 1912 and that underlay many of the congressional probes of the 1930s.[3] In October 1947 the Justice Department accused Kidder, Peabody along with sixteen other top investment houses of having combined and conspired to monopolize, and in effect having monopolized, the securities business of the United States.[4]

The trial, one of the longest and costliest in the history of antitrust prosecutions, resulted in a total defeat for the government. Kidder, Peabody's record as an underwriter during the years 1935 through 1949, the period covered by the Justice Department's complaint, contributed significantly to shattering the government's charge of lack of competition in the investment banking business. The defense repeatedly cited the firm's record as syndicate managers and underwriting participants to refute some of the government's most important allegations. Nor did the government uncover any evidence to show that Kidder, Peabody used its representation on corporate directorates to dominate or influence issuers as charged in its complaint; and the Justice Department's attorneys also failed to prove, despite the hundreds of documents offered in evidence, that the firm refused to compete for business simply because some other investment house had sponsored a company's earlier issues or was represented on the corporation's board. Kidder, Peabody, Gordon testified, made it a practice to compete for every issue "we think we have much chance of getting."[5]

Proof of Kidder, Peabody's successful competitive practices was documented fully in detailed statistical tables. The data covering the years 1935 through 1949 disclosed the dollar amounts and number of participations of the seventy-five top investment houses, including the seventeen defendants, "in all underwritten new and registered secondary issues [in excess of $1 million] of domestic and foreign business corporations and foreign governments (excluding domestic railroad equipment trust certificates)." The tables included both negotiated and competitively sold offerings. Another set of exhibits, employing the same criteria of selection, provided quantitative evidence on the seventeen defendants' activities as "managers or agents" for securities sold at bids and by negotiation. Nonunderwritten public offerings and direct placements of $100,000 or more also were listed in the tables setting forth the data on negotiated issues.[6]

Analysis of the statistics laid bare Kidder, Peabody's remarkable recovery from the brink of bankruptcy and its impressive performance as manager or agent and underwriter. In the period 1938 through 1940 Kidder, Peabody ranked in twenty-eighth place in terms of its dollar volume of new negotiated underwritten managements of $1 million or more; in the three-year period between 1944 and 1946 it had shot up to ninth place, then declined to tenth place in the next three-year period. Even more impressive was the firm's progress in the dollar amount of its underwriting participations in offerings of the same type. The record showed that in this category of transactions Kidder, Peabody jumped from twelfth place in the years 1938 to 1940 to second place in the period 1947 to 1949. But the firm's greatest gains were registered in negotiated underwritten managements of smaller issues, those between $100,000 and $1 million. Its dollar position in this category soared from two-hundredth place—"no rank whatever," in Judge Harold R. Medina's words—to first place in the years 1947 to 1949.[7] The underwriting and management statistics, defense counsels stressed, not only disproved the government's charges against Kidder, Peabody but, together with other evidence and testimony, also undermined significantly the Justice Department's allegations against the other sixteen defendants. The inclusion of Kidder, Peabody in the trial, said the firm's attorneys, demonstrated the fundamental weaknesses of the government's entire case, a view with which Medina concurred when he dismissed "the complaint . . . on the merits and with prejudice."[8]

Costly and burdensome as it was, the antitrust trial yielded Kidder, Peabody some important benefits. It disclosed the extent of the firm's recovery and confirmed beyond dispute its position as one of the leading investment banking houses in the United States. No amount of skillfully prepared advertising copy could have done as much as its own unadorned record to establish Kidder, Peabody's status and reputation among business executives and financiers.

The antitrust trial began just as Kidder, Peabody's business, fed by the nation's postwar economic expansion, started to increase substantially. Between 1945 and 1969 Kidder, Peabody added, on an average, some thirty new corporate clients a year. Most of them were, as in the past, medium-sized companies with assets of less than a billion dollars but with potential for growth and likely to require additional financing. The firm, and Gordon in particular, made a concerted effort to recruit clients among the recently divested gas and electric utilities, companies which before the deadline imposed by the 1935 Public Utility Holding Company Act had been financed by the parent concerns of the systems to which they belonged. The law's divestiture provision, the so-called death sentence requirement, was intended to break up the huge utility empires built in the 1920s and return the industry to "local management and local regulation" by limiting these concerns to "a single, integrated . . . system." Holding companies that failed to meet this requirement by 1940 were to be dissolved. By 1952 some 750 electric and gas utilities had been set free from their parent companies. "These were companies that needed a banker," Gordon said, "and we wanted the opportunity to show how we could serve them effectively."[2]

Kidder, Peabody invested considerable time and money to secure electric and gas financings. The firm's underwriting staff was expanded to include several newly recruited utility experts, among them Henry Witt, a utility analyst formerly with the General Electrical Securities Company. Witt, the partners, and other employees with close ties to executives of the divested companies were assigned to assist the underwriting staff. To add still more strength to its utility operations, the firm also made extensive use of outside consultants. The partners continued to rely heavily on their Stone & Webster connections and developed others, one of the most important of which was with W. C. Gilman & Co., a firm of engineering consultants specializing in utility work. William C. Gilman, the head of this concern, was a McGill University graduate with an engineering degree from the Massachusetts Institute of Technology. Widely known among utility company executives throughout the country—he had served as the first chief of the Securities and Exchange Commission's public utility division before going into business for himself—Gilman provided Kidder, Peabody with information and detailed studies of companies seeking to raise capital, which the firm used to solicit business. The purpose of Kidder, Peabody's utilities group, which in 1963 was made independent of the underwriting department, was twofold: to seek new clients and service old ones. Alfred E. Borneman, who had joined Kidder, Peabody in 1928 after graduating from the Harvard Business School, was put in charge of the firm's utility department. Widely experienced—he had moved up from statistics and research through the advertising and sales departments to a partnership in January 1953—Borneman developed close ties with utility executives and gained the confidence of many of them.[10] Aided by the firm's research department, Borneman and the new group prepared detailed, long-term estimates of the industry's capital requirements, the projected costs of new plant and equipment to meet the energy needs of a growing population, and the probable terms upon which the financing could be accomplished. Similar studies were prepared for companies likely to need financing. Armed with this information, Gordon crisscrossed the country, calling personally on utility executives to solicit their business. Together with Borneman, Webster, and other members of the firm, Gordon appeared before federal and state regulatory agencies to testify on problems confronting the industry, as well as on specific rate and financial questions concerning Kidder, Peabody's actual or prospective clients.[11]

The firm's efforts to cultivate the utility business proved successful. Between 1947 and 1960 Kidder, Peabody managed or comanaged public offerings of nearly $2.3 billion of utility issues, an amount representing almost 58.7 percent of the firm's total corporate securities sold publicly. During the same period Kidder, Peabody's privately placed utility issues amounted to $721.1 million, or about 36.6 percent of its total direct sales (see Table 6.1). The marked increase in private placements owed much to the partners' efforts at trying to educate gas and electric company officials to alternative methods of raising capital. Speaking before the Edison Electric Institute in June 1968, Gor-

Henry P. Kidder, the firm's first senior partner, was forty-two years old at the time Kidder, Peabody & Co. opened for business in March 1865.

Francis H. Peabody, the son of a prominent Unitarian minister, with some eighteen years of business experience, was thirty-four years old when he, his younger brother Oliver, and Henry P. Kidder took over the stock and exchange business of J. E. Thayer & Brother.

Oliver W. Peabody, at thirty-one years of age the youngset of the three founding partners, brought to the newly organized Kidder, Peabody & Co. some thirteen years of business experience, all of it gained with J. E. Thayer & Brother.

Nathaniel Thayer headed J. E. Thayer & Brother, the firm founded by his brother, John Eliot Thayer, from the time of the latter's death in 1857 until he retired from active business in 1865, the year Kidder, Peabody & Co. was organized. (Courtesy of Mrs. Helen Thayer Storey.)

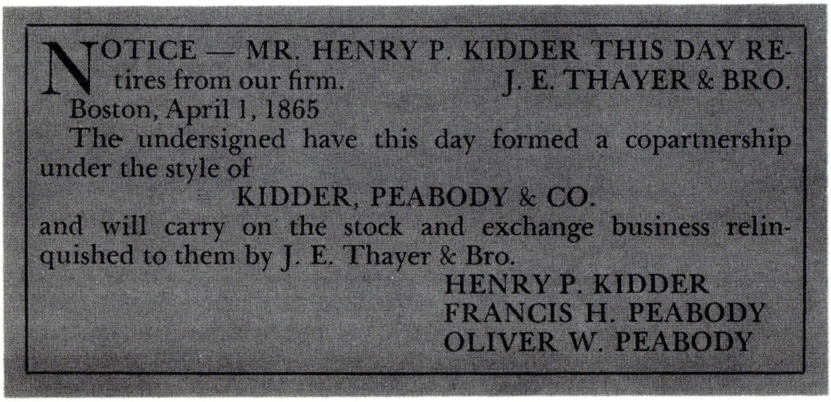

NOTICE — MR. HENRY P. KIDDER THIS DAY RE- tires from our firm. J. E. THAYER & BRO.

Boston, April 1, 1865

The undersigned have this day formed a copartnership under the style of

KIDDER, PEABODY & CO.

and will carry on the stock and exchange business relinquished to them by J. E. Thayer & Bro.

HENRY P. KIDDER
FRANCIS H. PEABODY
OLIVER W. PEABODY

Announcement of the organization of Kidder, Peabody & Co. as it appeared in The New York Herald *on April 6, 1865.*

TABLE 6.1 *Public Utility Financing by Kidder, Peabody, 1947–1960* (in millions of dollars)

	Public offerings			
Year	Negotiated	Competitive	Private sales	Total
1947	1.5	37.2	4.8	43.5
1948	57.0	20.3	11.7	89.0
1949	27.2	75.3	7.7	110.2
1950	142.8	88.2	49.0	280.0
1951	11.4	51.7	52.9	116.0
1952	18.9	75.0	31.4	125.3
1953	41.7	124.2	72.3	238.2
1954	68.4	161.4	77.5	307.3
1955	62.2	100.6	63.9	226.7
1956	16.5	145.8	17.4	179.7
1957	105.3	143.5	76.0	324.8
1958	108.0	259.3	107.5	474.8
1959	74.0	109.9	101.6	285.5
1960	26.6	138.8	47.4	212.8
Totals	761.5	1,531.2	721.1	3,013.8

SOURCE: Kidder, Peabody & Co., Records—New York City.

don advised utility leaders that the electric industry was "in a rugged competition for the savers' dollars," that they should follow the example of industrial corporations and "tailor make their securities to fit the changing [financial] markets," and he urged them to impress upon their regulators the need to allow them more flexibility in deciding upon the method to be used in raising capital, not only between public and private sales but also between competitive and negotiated transactions. Competitive bidding, Gordon said, was ordered "to reduce underwriting spreads and to cut the alleged historical ties to Wall Street firms," but "today," he emphasized, "the spreads on negotiated public offerings are substantially lower than for competitive bid offerings, and the differential for privately placed offerings is even greater."[12]

Kidder, Peabody was prepared to assist utilities in seeking exemptions from the compulsory competitive bidding requirement if a negotiated sale appeared to be more advantageous to the issuer. Gordon cited evidence from the firm's record to show issuers that in most cases a negotiated sale was preferable to a competitive one, not only because underwriting spreads often were smaller in a privately arranged offering than in one sold at bids, but because the former method allowed for greater flexibility in timing an issue and in planning a strong sales effort, both of which generally proved beneficial to the company. Effective nationwide distribution—the ability to sell—was Kidder, Peabody's greatest strength as an underwriter. It was the basis upon which Gordon had rebuilt the firm's reputation, and it also was the principal reason it could get an issuer a better price for its securities than could be obtained by a competitive sale. The combination of brokerage and underwriting strength, both carefully supervised by Gordon, proved beneficial to both the issuer and the firm; for the former it meant a lower cost of money, for the latter it served as an effective means of attracting new corporate clients.

The techniques employed to cultivate the utility business also were used to attract industrial and other corporate underwritings. During the years 1946 through 1969 Kidder, Peabody managed or comanaged 841 public offerings of corporations totaling slightly more than $11.1 billion (see Table 6.2). By the latter date the firm clearly had established itself as a major underwriter, one of the leading firms in the industry and among the top ten both in the number and dollar value of issues managed or comanaged.[13]

Kidder, Peabody's record in private placements was even more impressive. During the period 1946 through 1969 the firm arranged 1,342 private sales ranging in size from $95,000 to $100 million and totaling some $5.5 billion (see Table 6.2). Over $50 million of Kidder, Peabody's direct sales during the years 1951 through 1955 were for independent telephone companies. The firm's financing of these corporations helped establish their credit with institutional investors and brought Kidder, Peabody a group of new clients that, like many of its gas and electric utility customers, turned to the firm repeatedly for assistance in raising the growing volume of capital they required. Corporate

TABLE 6.2 *Corporate Public Offerings and Private Placements by Kidder, Peabody, 1946–69* (in millions of dollars)

	Public offerings managed or comanaged		Private placements	
Year	Total number	Total dollar volume	Total number	Total dollar volume
1946	26	275.6	7	34.8
1947	11	91.9	20	40.2
1948	18	117.3	23	50.5
1949	22	118.6	30	53.6
1950	36	274.2	46	132.2
1951	17	132.9	38	149.7
1952	35	252.4	40	125.1
1953	33	274.5	47	117.8
1954	38	296.7	58	160.2
1955	28	302.4	53	144.8
1956	34	436.3	44	170.1
1957	41	413.0	50	180.2
1958	33	498.6	61	202.6
1959	57	293.9	47	257.5
1960	43	404.5	60	184.7
1961	49	518.8	87	283.0
1962	28	445.1	73	268.9
1963	25	314.8	73	270.5
1964	28	420.0	69	447.7
1965	37	877.6	109	509.7
1966	31	573.8	72	482.8
1967	51	1,093.3	77	379.2
1968	46	984.3	78	415.3
1969	74	1,740.2	80	440.8
Totals	841	11,150.7	1,342	5,501.9

SOURCE: Kidder, Peabody & Co., Records—New York City.

finance—direct placements, managements, and underwriting participations—accounted for approximately 30 percent of Kidder, Peabody's gross annual revenues between 1945 and 1969, with the peak for the period (34 percent), reached in 1965.[14]

The postwar years also witnessed an increase in the number and dollar value of Kidder, Peabody's management and comanagement of state and municipal issues (see Table 6.3). Prior to World War II the firm's sponsorship and underwriting of tax-

TABLE 6.3 *State and Municipal Issues Managed and Comanaged by Kidder, Peabody, 1947–1969* (in millions of dollars)

Year	Number of issues	Dollar value
1947	7	112.4
1948	17	252.6
1949	15	102.9
1950	27	56.5
1951	27	54.9
1952	19	31.2
1953	28	61.5
1954	32	68.0
1955	19	102.8
1956	23	61.9
1957	38	192.1
1958	41	306.3
1959	34	183.0
1960	34	180.0
1961	26	194.7
1962	42	197.1
1963	34	586.4
1964	27	642.0
1965	30	385.6
1966	34	888.0
1967	59	902.8
1968	71	1,165.2
1969	47	1,456.8
Totals	731	8,184.7

SOURCE: Kidder, Peabody & Co., Records—New York City.

exempt securities had accounted for about 5 percent of its total annual gross revenues; in the years 1947 through 1969 its state and municipal business grew to a high of 17 percent in 1955 and averaged about 8.6 percent for the entire period. The annual number of tax-exempt issues headed by Kidder, Peabody exceeded forty for the first time in 1958, hit fifty-nine in 1967, and reached seventy-one in 1968, the all-time high until then.[15]

Kidder, Peabody's rise to a major position in the state and municipal bond business occurred at a time of intense competition which threatened to increase still further. During the early

1960s the nation's giant commercial banks, led by First National City Bank in New York and Bank of America in San Francisco, sought to expand their underwriting activities by getting Congress to lift the ban imposed on them by the Glass-Steagall Banking Act of 1933. That law, which separated commercial and investment banking, permitted banks of deposit to underwrite only general obligation bonds, those backed by the full faith, credit, and general taxing power of the state or municipality that issued them, but denied these institutions the right to sponsor revenue bonds, securities whose redemption generally depended upon the tax receipts of the government that sold them. Commercial banks argued that an amendment to the law allowing them to underwrite revenue bonds would help state and local authorities by reducing the cost of borrowing, a claim that was not substantiated by independent studies conducted by the Federal Reserve and Professor Bertrand Fox of the Harvard Graduate School of Business Administration, the investment banking expert responsible for compiling the statistical tables used in the antitrust trial. Both studies disclosed that the slight interest rate differential between general obligation and revenue bonds of comparable quality and maturity (about 0.12 percent) was "solely due to the difference between the lesser security of revenue bonds and the all-resources type security of general obligations."[16] The statistical evidence presented at the House Banking and Currency Committee hearings, combined with strong pressure from investment houses, kept the proposed bill stalled, but the threat remained and Kidder, Peabody's partners prepared to meet the challenge by strengthening still further the firm's state and municipal capacity.

Expansion of Kidder, Peabody's ability to underwrite and sell state and municipal issues began in the decade after the end of World War II, when the volume of securities offered by these authorities started to climb appreciably. In May 1958 Joseph Vostal succeeded Frank Gallagher as manager of the firm's municipal section. Vostal had started with Kidder, Peabody as a clerk in 1926, had worked closely with Gallagher and other members of the firm's municipal staff from 1934 until September 1946 when he left to open his own house. In May 1948 he returned to Kidder, Peabody's municipal department; ten years later he headed the group, expanding it considerably. Together with John A. Hoff, another longtime employee who started with the firm as a messenger and rose to become New York sales manager for municipals in 1954, and in 1961 a partner in charge of general sales, Vostal revitalized Kidder, Peabody's tax-exempt business, turning several years of decline into impressive gains.[17]

Outside of New York the Philadelphia office launched the firm's most innovative sales technique for municipals. In September 1953 the tax-exempt group at Philadelphia negotiated the sale of $300,000 of Akron Borough (Lancaster County, Pennsylvania) School Authority bonds. Instead of selling the lot in bonds of $1,000 each, the traditional denomination for issues of this type, Kidder, Peabody offered some in denominations of $100 and $500, advertising their availability in five local newspapers. The response proved so encouraging that the experiment was repeated in the Philadelphia office's next municipal offering, a $285,000 issue of Williamsburg Community (Blair County, Pennsylvania) Joint School Authority bonds. This time the entire offering was sold in bonds of $500 and $1,000 denominations. "We expect to continue this type of financing in Pennsylvania," said Willard M. Wright, Jr., the manager of the Philadelphia office's municipal department. The smaller denomination bond, Wright explained, attracted investors interested in helping finance their own community's improvements, publicized municipals among individuals generally unfamiliar with the tax-exampt features of these securities, and widened the firm's list of clients.[18]

Still more strength was added to Kidder, Peabody's state and municipal department in June 1966 when the firm absorbed B. J. Van Ingen & Co., Inc. Founded in 1916, the firm started as and remained a specialized bond house, heading the offerings of a distinguished clientele of government authorities, among them the Pennsylvania, Ohio, Oklahoma, and Kentucky turnpikes, as well as managing others for several large hydroelectric projects in the Pacific Northwest. The firm continued to be a major underwriter of tax-exempt bonds—in 1965 it ranked twenty-fifth, four places below Kidder, Peabody among the nation's leading managers of municipal and state securities—but its business, like that of other specialized houses, had been declining. Falling municipal bond prices had lowered Van Ingen's profits, forcing it to close all of its offices outside New York City. The decision to merge with Kidder, Peabody, explained a Van Ingen executive, was "a very deliberate move on our part to become part of a large diversified firm."[19] Two of Van Ingen's senior executives, each widely experienced in consulting work for and negotiating with tax-exempt issuers, joined Kidder, Peabody's municipal finance department.

The Van Ingen takeover, like Kidder, Peabody's earlier absorption of Kissel, Kinnicutt, disclosed more than Gordon's determination to augment the firm's ability in an important area of the securities business. It also confirmed his strategy of expansion—taking up the offices of faltering houses. Such a policy, he believed, not only was easier and less expensive than opening a new office, but it also allowed Kidder, Peabody to incorporate in its own organization experienced personnel and, hopefully, hold on to the clients and goodwill of the assimilated house.[20]

Kidder, Peabody had built its strength as an originator and underwriter on its ability to sell a wide variety of securities to individuals with different investment needs and tastes, from wealthy dowagers to blue-collar workers of moderate income, and to an equally broad group of institutions that included the country's largest insurance companies as well as relatively small pension funds from coast to coast. This large and diverse clientele, built up in the 1930s and 1940s and carefully maintained and served in the 1950s and 1960s, paid the brokerage commissions that accounted for Kidder, Peabody's largest source of gross revenues, ranging from a high of 46.1 percent in 1946 to a low of 28.1 percent in 1953, with an overall annual average of about 38.6 percent for the period 1945 to 1970.[21]

Brokerage, together with underwriting, constituted Kidder, Peabody's traditional business, generating as much as three-fourths of the firm's total gross yearly revenues and occupying most of the partners' attention. Another 15 percent to 20 percent of Kidder, Peabody's annual income came from corporate and tax-exempt trading, buying and selling listed stocks and bonds and maintaining markets in nonlisted securities, activities pursued by most large, diversified, full-service investment houses.[22]

But in prosperous postwar America traditional investment banking no longer guaranteed a firm's continued success. That business failed to regain the central and privileged position it had occupied in the pre-1929 era, when the nation's leading Wall Street houses were the chief conduits for channeling savings into investments. Widespread changes on both the demand and supply sides of the capital markets and the development and increasing use of alternative methods of raising long-term capital led to a marked increase in competition among the nation's financial intermediaries. Clients that once had depended almost entirely upon investment houses for their long-term funds and financial advice found other intermediaries able and anxious to provide both. The progress of investment banking, as a result, was less marked than it was for some of the other financial institutions. Membership in the Investment Bankers Association of America (IBA), the trade group that included most of the leading firms, reached 796 in 1937—the highest point since the organization's founding in 1912—fell to 578 in 1943, then started a slow recovery up to 812 in 1955, the peak year before another downturn that continued, with only a few interruptions, until it merged with the Association of Stock Exchange Firms to form the Securities Industry Association (SIA), the new national trade body that was set up in January 1972.[23] And while the more widely inclusive National Association of Securities Dealers, the self-regulatory agency established under the 1938 Maloney Act, showed no similar decline, the 4,470 broker-dealers that belonged to the organization in 1970 represented a rise of only some 13.2 percent from the 1938 peak of 3,871 members.[24]

Lack of a significant increase in the number of investment banking firms reflected not only the highly competitive conditions that prevailed in the post-World War II securities industry and throughout the financial community but also what one analyst called the declining "influence" of Wall Street houses vis-a-vis their issuer clients.[25] Corporations no longer found the services of investment banks indispensable. In 1950, for instance, internal sources, chiefly undistributed profits and capital consumption allowances, accounted for slightly less than 43 percent of the total funds used by nonfarm and nonfinancial corporations; by 1960 that share was up to 71.5 percent, and for the years 1965 through 1969 it averaged about 59.3 percent. More important still, when these corporations looked to the financial community for the funds they required, they did not rely only upon investment firms. Very often these companies turned to commercial banks for term loans. In some years, for instance in 1950 and 1965, bank loans exceeded the amounts raised by the sale of stocks and bonds, but even when more funds were raised by security issues than by bank loans, the latter rarely fell below 13.9 percent of all externally generated funds. Total bank loans to nonfarm and nonfinancial corporations during the six years from 1964 through 1969 amounted to $46.8 billion, or about 20 percent of all funds raised from outside sources, while the total dollar value of stocks and bonds sold by these companies during the same period ($67.4 billion) accounted for nearly 29 percent of all external funds used.[26]

Equally significant changes also occurred on the supply side of the capital markets. Among the most notable of these was the growing prominence of institutional investors, not only such longtime clients of investment houses as life insurance companies and trust funds but also the newer financial intermediaries that came of age after World War II, particularly private noninsured pension funds and investment companies. The assets of all financial intermediaries grew significantly during the prosperous postwar years—those of life insurance companies, for example, up from slightly less than $44.8 billion in 1945 to $199 billion in 1970. But it was the noninsured pension funds and investment companies that registered some of the most striking increases of the era. The assets of these two groups of intermediaries, which stood at about $1 billion each in 1950, soared during the next twenty years, reaching $107.2 billion for the pension funds and $47.6 billion for the investment companies.[27] Institutions of this type, together with the life and general insurance companies, were large buyers of corporate securities, not only bonds but after 1960 of stocks as well. Total stock holdings of the four leading institutional investors—private noninsured pension funds, open-end investment companies (mutal funds), and insurance companies (life, property, and liability)—more than tripled, from $44.4 billion in 1960 to $139.6 billion in 1970, with the largest increases being registered by the pension funds ($50.6 billion) and open-end investment companies ($28.5 billion).[28] Managed by experts, these institutional clients required varied and complex services. To win and hold the business of these giants, investment houses developed new and highly specialized services. Some firms responded to the growing volume of institutional trading—in the early 1960s it accounted for more than 30 percent of all stock exchange trades and would double by the 1970s—by limiting their operations almost entirely to buying and selling securities for institutions.

Kidder, Peabody met the challenge of changes in the demand for its services in several ways. To satisfy a growing, increasingly diverse and nationwide clientele of individuals and institutions, the firm added to its exchange memberships outside of New York and Boston by joining the Midwest (1949), Pacific Coast (1957), and Philadelphia–Baltimore–Washington (1958) exchanges, and it expanded and reorganized its branch system. The older branches, Boston and Philadelphia, were enlarged and turned into regional offices, each with its own new business, underwriting, sales, and trading departments, and staffed to serve individual and institutional investors as well as local corporations and governments in need of raising capital.

Similar organizational changes were implemented at the firm's newer offices. In 1948 the Chicago branch was reorganized and made into a regional office with a resident partner as its manager. This was the first time in Kidder, Peabody's history that a partner held a permanent assignment outside of New York or Boston. Subsequently four other regional offices were established: two in California—San Francisco (November 1952) and Los Angeles (January 1956)—another in Atlanta (December 1965), and still another in Dallas (September 1966). In April 1967 the firm opened a branch in Detroit and expanded into the Pacific Northwest, the only region of the country where it did not have any offices of its own. The addition of branches in that growing section of the nation followed Gordon's tested policy of expanding, whenever practicable, through the acquisition of an established house. In this case Kidder, Peabody took over the investment banking and brokerage business of the Pacific Northwest Company, a Seattle firm with thirteen branches in three states—Washington, Oregon, and Idaho. Kidder, Peabody kept open the Seattle, Spokane, and Portland offices and closed the others. By the end of the decade the firm's New York City headquarters, with four branches of its own, supervised a nationwide operation of seven regional offices with a total of twenty-three branches scattered from coast to coast and from Fort Lauderdale, Florida, in the South to Minneapolis in the North.[29] At none of these locations did the firm maintain facilities for clients to watch the continuously changing prices of securities on the nation's principal exchanges. The absence of a board room at Kidder, Peabody's offices, Gordon explained, "lies primarily in the fact that we believe that what you buy or sell is more important than when you buy or sell."[30]

Direct, more comprehensive representation in the nation's chief financial centers reflected the partners' growing awareness of the many important changes occurring in the structure and operations of the country's capital markets, among them the relative decline of New York City as an investment outlet. Recognition of these changes also accounted for the firm's decision to give top priority to achieving as quickly as possible effective nationwide underwriting and sales ability.

Another of the firm's early postwar policy decisions was to diversify operations still further. Regional offices and branches added to Kidder, Peabody's recognized strength as a national distributor of securities; diversification promised to attract a greater variety of individual and institutional clients and enable the firm to provide them and its corporate underwriting customers with a wider range of services. Neither policy—nationwide offices or diversified services—was entirely new. Nor were they unrelated. Both were in the firm's tradition, and each was designed to complement the other, to meet the competition of other intermediaries, and help keep Kidder, Peabody among the leading full-service, national investment banking houses in the industry.

One of the firm's first major postwar efforts to widen its services occurred in February 1949, when Kidder, Peabody established a specialized mutual fund department at its midtown Manhattan branch. Mutual funds, or open-end investment companies, were not an innovation of the post-World War II era; they appeared in early nineteenth-century Britain at about the same time they appeared in Boston. The modern period in the history of these institutions started with the organization of the Massachusetts Investment Trust in March 1924.[31]

Unlike closed-end and other types of investment companies which expanded so spectacularly both in numbers and assets during the later 1920s, mutual funds grew at a much slower pace. At the end of 1929 only 19 of the 770 investment companies then in existence were mutual funds, and their combined assets ($140 million) represented only a trifling share of the assets of the entire group (nearly $7.2 billion).[32] Mutual funds not only survived the stock market crash better than most other types of investment companies, they also recovered from the depression more rapidly, their assets climbing from a low of $64.3 million in 1931 to $75 million in 1932, before soaring to $506 million at the end of 1936. Their greatest growth occurred with the onset of wartime prosperity, and they continued to expand at an accelerating pace through the postwar boom years. Between 1950 and 1960 the number of investment companies registered with the Securities and Exchange Commission, some two-thirds of which were mutual funds, increased from 366 to 570, and their combined assets grew fivefold, from $4.7 billion to $23.5 billion. By 1970 both their number and assets had more than doubled from the 1960 peak, to 1,328 companies with assets of $56.3 billion.[33]

The dramatic growth of mutual funds, like the investment trust boom of the 1920s, was fed by thousands of investors, many of them as gullible and greedy as the speculators of the 1920s. The hope of quick riches swelled the number of mutual fund shareholders to some 3 million by 1965, with many of the more venturesome among them investing in the so-called performance funds, the companies that posted the quickest and largest gains in assets. Investment and brokerage houses earned commissions merchandising mutual fund shares to investors, and they collected still larger ones buying and selling securities for the funds themselves. In 1960 these companies bought and sold almost $4.8 billion of common stock, or nearly 49.2 percent of the total stock transactions of the four leading institutional investors; in 1965 their common stock purchases and sales reached nearly $11.7 billion, almost 50.5 percent of the total volume of the top four group of institutions; and the comparable figures for 1969, the peak year for the decade, were nearly $42 billion, representing some 52.4 percent of such trades.[34] Some funds, intent upon realizing large and quick profits, traded so often and in such quantities that the term "go-go" was used to refer to their stock market operations.[35]

Kidder, Peabody was not among the "go-go" promoters and

sellers of mutual fund shares. Gordon's recollections of the old firm's unhappy experience with its own investment trusts, the Kidder Participations, and his own judgment of what he considered proper and correct conduct dictated a more cautious approach to this increasingly popular investment medium. Amyas Ames, who served as Kidder, Peabody's sales manager at the time the mutual fund department was organized, explained the firm's basic policy and purpose. The mutual fund department, he said in a memorandum to the partners, "will engage in the promotion, through advertising and mail follow-up, of a group of 'open-end' investment company shares," but unlike some firms, which touted certain specific funds, Kidder, Peabody's entire program, Ames said, was to be "keyed to talking about, writing about, selling, and advertising the *Mutual Fund Industry*—rather than any particular Fund or group of Funds." The thrust of the firm's mutual fund business, he concluded, was to make prospective clients aware of the many types of fund shares available—balanced portfolio, general stock, long-term growth—and to make customers conscious of Kidder, Peabody "as an impartial purveyor of the highest grade of investment company shares."[36]

Several considerations determined the partners' decision to locate the mutual fund department at the firm's midtown Manhattan office. Business there had been lagging and it was hoped that the mutual fund department would improve the office's entire sales performance. New York City was one of the largest markets for mutual fund shares in the country, and Kidder, Peabody's office at 10 East 45 Street appeared ideally situated to attract the type of client interested in these securities.[37]

At first the partners had planned to use the mutual fund department to train salespeople for eventual assignment to the firm's general stock department, but it soon became apparent that the marketing of investment company shares required a specialized and experienced staff. The original plan was dropped and the firm recruited young people with some experience selling mutual fund shares and, in time, it added other experts in advertising and merchandising this type of securities. To acquaint investors with the risks and opportunities of buying investment company shares, the mutual fund department arranged special lectures at its office, the first of which was given by a representative of Calvin Bullock, the oldest investment management firm in the country. In May 1952 Kidder, Peabody launched a thirteen-week series of fifteen-minute radio interview programs to advertise mutual fund investments.[38] By then the firm was retailing the shares of some forty investment companies and had added mutual fund departments to its Boston, Philadelphia, and Chicago offices.[39]

Besides its retail sales to individuals, Kidder, Peabody also developed institutional markets for these securities. The firm's institutional approach to mutual funds as an investment medium appealed to the managers and trustees of corporate and union retirement, pension, and profit-sharing plans. The financial officers of these pension trusts looked to Kidder, Peabody's research reports on the past performance and future projections of various investment companies, as well as for investment advice. Both of these services often led to Kidder, Peabody becoming the intermediary through which these benefit funds bought and sold their investment company shares, adding to the firm's commission business.

Current research on the investment company industry, together with a strong nationwide sales capacity, also made kidder, Peabody an attractive house to help plan and organize new funds and underwrite their offerings. In April 1952 the firm comanaged a syndicate of 101 houses that underwrote a 900,000-share offering of Canadian Fund, Inc., a new open-end investment company. Chartered in Maryland and managed by Calvin Bullock, the fund was designed to provide Americans with a medium of "diversified investments in Canada." This successful flotation, one of the first by a member firm of the New York Stock Exchange, led to other similar underwritings as well as to additional calls upon the firm's advisory services, including some from abroad. In 1967 Kidder, Peabody helped plan and organize the first wholly managed Italian investment company, the International Securities Fund. By then the firm was a major national distributor of mutual fund shares, one of the few top investment banking houses to have made itself a specialist in selling this class of securities. Between 1950 and 1970, the years of the mutual funds' most striking expansion, Kidder, Peabody's business in sponsoring and selling the shares of these companies accounted for between 8 percent and 10 percent of the firm's annual gross revenue.[40]

During that same period Kidder, Peabody diversified its services still further, expanding some it had not developed extensively and adding others not previously provided. The firm's long experience in arranging mergers and acquisitions, which dated back to the end of the nineteenth century, was used to cultivate this rapidly expanding business. During the postwar years the trend toward consolidations and mergers and the growth of conglomerates expanded at an accelerated pace. Not since the 1920s, when some 6,800 major mergers and acquisitions were accomplished, had the rate of these consolidations grown so significantly. Between 1960 and 1969 the number of mergers and acquisitions among manufacturing and mining concerns with assets of $10 million or more alone totaled upwards of 12,500, more than 2½ times as many as had been negotiated in the previous decade.[41] Kidder, Peabody assisted in many of these transactions, bringing possible new acquisitions to the attention of corporate clients interested in diversifying, analyzing and evaluating companies, and negotiating terms. Some of these transactions involved concerns with assets of hundreds of millions of dollars, such as occurred in August 1968 when Kidder, Peabody negotiated the combination of Control Data Corporation and the Commercial Credit Company. The newly combined corporation's total assets exceeded $860 million. But most of the firm's merger-related services were for small and medium-sized companies valued between $3 million and $50 million.[42]

Another growing area of business which Kidder, Peabody

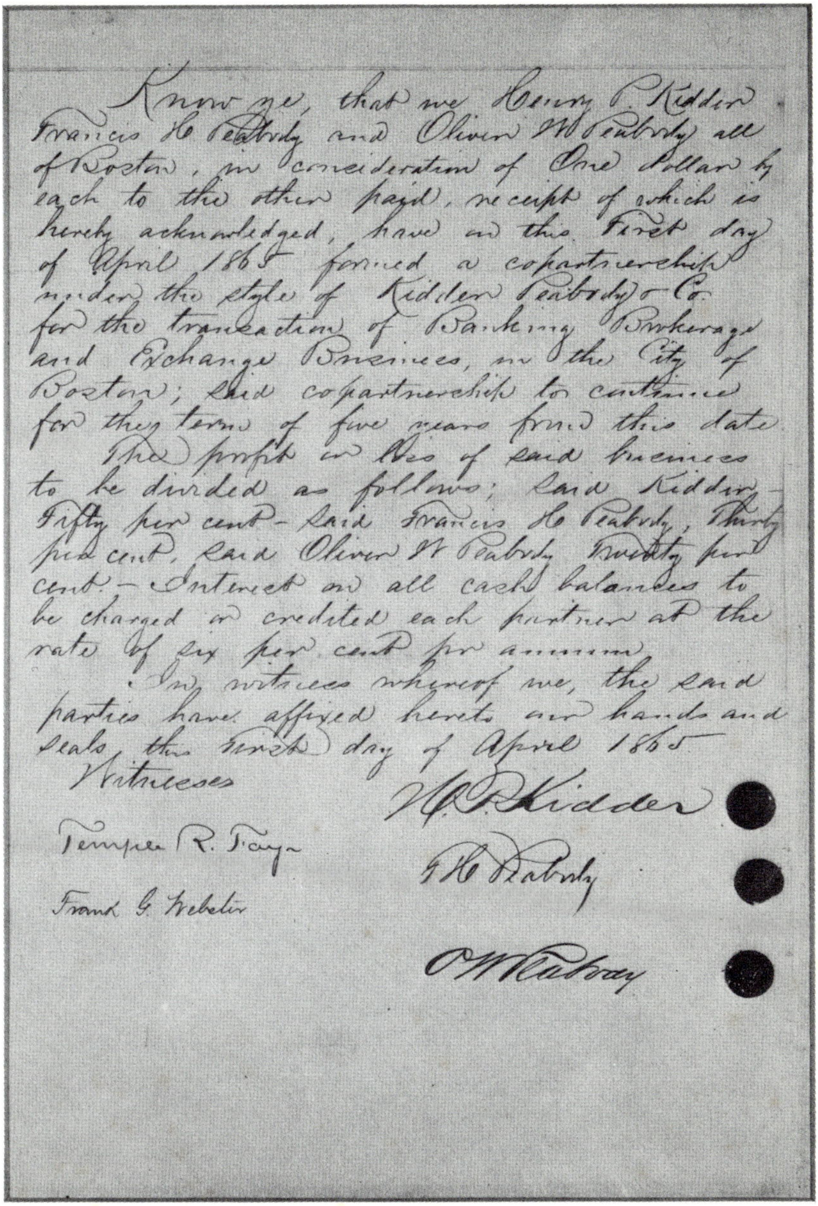

Know ye, that we Henry P. Kidder Francis H. Peabody and Oliver W. Peabody all of Boston, in consideration of One Dollar by each to the other paid, receipt of which is hereby acknowledged, have on this First day of April 1865 formed a copartnership under the style of Kidder Peabody & Co for the transaction of Banking Brokerage and Exchange Business, in the City of Boston; said copartnership to continue for the term of five years from this date

The profit or loss of said business to be divided as follows; said Kidder Fifty per cent - said Francis H Peabody, Thirty per cent, said Oliver W Peabody Twenty per cent - Interest on all cash balances to be charged or credited each partner at the rate of six per cent per annum.

In witness whereof we, the said parties have affixed hereto our hands and seals, the First day of April 1865

Witnesses

Temple R. Fay

Frank G. Webster

H. P. Kidder

F. H. Peabody

O. W. Peabody

The original partnership agreement, signed by the three founding partners on April 1, 1865, with Frank G. Webster serving as one of the witnesses.

Robert Winsor joined Kidder, Peabody & Co. in July 1880, shortly after graduating from Harvard College. He was made a partner in January 1894; after World War I, when Frank G. Webster became increasingly inactive in the business, Winsor took over as senior active head of the firm. (Courtesy of Mr. Philip W. Trumbull.)

Frank G. Webster started with Kidder, Peabody in March 1865, the month the firm opened for business, was made a partner in July 1886, and continued to serve in that capacity until his death in January 1930.

The three partners who reorganized Kidder, Peabody & Co. in 1931: Chandler Hovey (left); Edwin S. Webster, Jr. (center); and Albert H. Gordon (right).

Erwin A. Stuebner (left), Albert H. Gordon (center), and Amyas Ames (right), the three senior partners of the firm's policy group from November 1957 through December 1964. The portrait on the wall is of Frank G. Webster.

Kidder, Peabody's 1975 policy committee, Erwin A. Stuebner, President (right); Albert H. Gordon, Chairman, Board of Directors (left); and Ralph D. DeNunzio, Chairman of the Executive Committee (center).

developed was providing, on a fee basis, financial advisory services to wealthy individuals, fiduciaries, and privately owned corporations. This business, like its work in planning and negotiating mergers, combinations, and acquisitions, grew out of Kidder, Peabody's nineteenth century experience when the firm had served the investment needs of Boston's wealthy elite families. In the post-World War II era the firm continued to advise individuals of inherited wealth and manage their investments, but it also sought new clients requiring professional management of their stock and bond portfolios, such as high-salaried corporate executives, trust estates, and educational and charitable institutions. By the end of the 1960s the firm was providing continuous, specialized investment services to several hundred individual and institutional clients.

Kidder, Peabody's advisory services, particularly those for institutions, helped increase the firm's block trading business. Most of these operations were secondary distributions conducted off the floor of the exchanges. The number of secondary distributions soared after 1956, the first year these transactions involved more than 10 million shares valued in excess of $50 million shares valued at over $1.2 billion. Block distributions on the nation's exchanges arranged by member firms also the security markets, both the number and dollar value of secondaries more than tripled, from a low of 11.4 million shares worth $424.7 million in 1960 to a 1969 peak for the decade of 38.2 million shares valued at over $1.2 billion. Block distributions on the nation's exchanges arranged by member firms also increased substantially, exceeding a million shares for the first time in 1961 and reaching almost 3.5 million shares in 1967. The number and dollar value of these sales always remained considerably less than those arranged off the floor of the exchanges.[43] Kidder, Peabody participated in both types of operations. The average annual value of its secondary distributions during the 1960s amounted to about $30.6 million. The greatest dollar volume for the decade, nearly $74.9 million, was reached in 1961; six years later the firm executed the single largest block distribution on the floor of the New York Stock Exchange, trading 1 million shares of Pacific Petroleums Inc.[44]

But Kidder, Peabody did not limit itself only to expanding and updating the firm's traditional investment banking services. It also moved into new areas, among them real estate financing and investments. The huge demand for capital by the real estate industry, which in the 1960s exceeded $100 billion yearly, attracted corporations seeking to diversify, investors looking for above average rates of return, and investment houses searching for new clients and profits. Some firms, like Kidder, Peabody, considered real estate financing a natural extension of their investment banking activities and decided to add real estate to the list of industries they served. Though Kidder, Peabody was not totally inexperienced in real estate financing, it did not set up a special department for the purpose until November 1960 when Richard Hurd joined the firm. The son of a prominent real estate financier, Hurd, who was then in his mid-thirties, developed the firm's business in this area, and in September 1962 the partners, determined to limit the firm's liabilities in these operations, organized the Kidder, Peabody Realty Corporation, a wholly-owned subsidiary of the partnership.[45] The Realty Corporation assisted builder-developers and property owners seeking capital by helping them plan and place their financings with wealthy individuals, partnerships, and institutions. Through the use of sale and leasebacks, limited partnership interests, first mortgage loans, and secured and collateral trust notes, the Realty Corporation arranged the acquisition and construction of apartment complexes, shopping centers, and similar projects.

In addition to its financings which totaled $30.3 million in 1968, the peak for the decade, the Realty Corporation also cooperated closely with the firm's activities in distributing and making a market in certificates of the Government National Mortgage Association (GNMA), a corporate entity of the federal government under the Department of Housing and Urban

Development.[46] Authorized by the National Housing Act of August 1968, GNMA was designed to stimulate residential construction by making it attractive for institutions to invest in first mortgages. The means to achieve this objective was the GNMA-guaranteed mortgage-backed certificate, a debt security, usually issued by the mortgage banking firm qualified to organize the pool of approved residential mortgages. The certificates, generally issued in amounts greater than $25,000, carried the federal government's guarantee on "the timely payment of both principal and interest." These instruments fitted the portfolio needs of a wide group of individual and institutional investors. GNMA certificates added a new investment medium to Kidder, Peabody's growing assortment of securities the firm distributed.

Urban renewal provided Kidder, Peabody with still another area of business opportunities. During the 1960s, while the federal government spent billions on slum clearance and the construction of low-income dwellings, private developers also were involved in projects designed to rehabilitate the downtown sections of the nation's older cities. In November 1964 Lewis Kitchen, a prominent Kansas City, Missouri, developer with several successful projects to his credit, joined with Kidder, Peabody and the Prudential Life Insurance Company to organize the City Reconstruction Corporation. The company, a subsidiary of Kidder, Peabody Realty which owned 10 percent of its preferred and 50 percent of its common stock, was designed to recruit long-term capital for large downtown urban renewal projects. Kidder, Peabody, which previously had raised $3 million for Kitchen's Mansion House project in St. Louis, was expected to provide City Reconstruction with the long-term equity capital it required by recruiting it from individuals in high tax brackets, partnerships, and other sophisticated investors, not from public sales of the company's securities. Kendall Lutes, a vice president of Kidder, Peabody Realty and chairman of City Reconstruction's finance committee, also saw the firm's role in the new company as one of adding "the discipline of investment banking" to a new and increasingly important area of business and finance.[47]

City Reconstruction yielded few of the profits its organizers had anticipated. Soaring construction costs and high interest rates made real estate ventures increasingly less profitable. This together with differing views among the company's top officials convinced Kidder, Peabody to quit financing redevelopment projects. Early in 1967, less then three years after it had helped organize City Reconstruction, the firm took the first step that led to the company's final dissolution in 1976. By then Kidder, Peabody Realty also had become less active, its chief function being to hold the equities in properties it had financed.[48]

Kidder, Peabody's real estate operations proved to be one of the firm's least successful activities. "We broke even," said one of the firm's retired partners, "and that was no small accomplishment."[49]

Displeasure with its experience in real estate financing was more than compensated by the firm's success in planning and negotiating leasing arrangements that allowed companies to secure the use of expensive capital equipment—computers, jet airplanes, oil tankers, chemical plants—without using their own or borrowed funds to pay for it. The job of the investment banker in a lease financing—whatever the type, leveraged or nonleveraged—was similar to the responsibility of arranging a public offering or direct sale of securities. Whatever the method employed in raising the required capital, the investment banker was expected to serve the best interests of both borrowers and lenders. In a leasing transaction the banker had to weigh a host of complex variables and decide, in the words of a *Fortune* analyst, the "optimal point at which the lessee has the lowest cost and the lessors the highest yield."[50] Kidder, Peabody moved into lease financing in the early 1960s when this centuries-old method of raising capital regained favor. And though the "cost" of leasing equipment almost always was greater than its total purchase price, many companies found it to their advantage to employ their capital in ventures that yielded profits in excess of the cost of the rental. This, together with possible tax benefits, mounting inflation, tight money, and the desire of some companies to limit the amount of debt appearing on their balance sheets, sparked a leasing boom that by the end of the decade attracted to the business not only investment houses, commercial banks, and credit companies, but also some large industrial corporations that found it profitable to add this kind of financial intermediation to their usual operations. During the three-year period between 1967 and 1969, when the volume of lease financings soared to new highs reaching close to $50 billion, Kidder, Peabody managed thirty-seven plant and equipment transactions ranging in size from $204,000 to $10.7 million. The firm's total for that three-year period exceeded $120.7 million and was growing rapidly. By the early 1970s, according to a *Fortune* survey, the firm ranked eighth among the top twenty-five institutions in the country engaged in financing leases.[51]

Expansion and diversification of Kidder, Peabody's domestic financial and investment services were matched by a similar widening of the firm's international operations. The quarter-century following the end of World War II witnessed a huge outflow of American capital overseas. Between 1950 and 1970 direct private investments in Europe grew by more than 6½ times, from nearly $11.8 billion to about $78.2 billion, while during that same twenty-year period private long-term portfolio investments increased 4½ times, from $5.7 billion to $26.6 billion.[52] Servicing the needs of American companies and investors throughout the world and particularly in Europe provided investment houses with widening opportunities. It was only natural that Kidder, Peabody with its long tradition in international finance—for nearly the first fifty years of its history the firm advertised itself and was generally classified by contemporary compilers of financial institutions as a foreign and domestic banking house—should be among the first securities concerns to revive and strengthen its overseas operations.

Until June 1956 when Kidder, Peabody opened its first international office at London, the firm had conducted its foreign business through correspondents, some of which, such as Barings and Hope & Co., were houses with which ties dated back to the immediate post-Civil War decades. Kidder, Peabody continued to maintain some of these old relationships, but as American business activities abroad expanded in the 1950s, the partners decided to develop independent international strength by expanding the firm's foreign operations to include a comprehensive range of financial and investment services, duplicating overseas the structure of representative and branch offices that had been implemented in the United States. "We wanted to provide throughout the world," said a partner, "the same range of services to individuals, corporations, institutions, and governments that we supplied our American clients."[53]

Expansion and restructuring of the firm's international operations started early in 1960 with the organization of Kidder, Peabody & Co., Limited, a wholly-owned and controlled Swiss holding company with administrative offices in Zug, Switzerland. Several considerations dictated the organization of this subsidiary. It provided the New York partners with important tax benefits and allowed them to use retained earnings to build the firm's capital base in Europe. By organizing its own wholly-owned subsidiaries, the holding company also served as the vehicle through which to administer Kidder, Peabody's international operations and reaffirm forcefully the firm's commitment to international business and finance.[54]

The Swiss company started expanding almost at once. In 1960 it organized its first subsidiary, Kidder, Peabody S. A. (Paris), to operate in France, and opened a representative office in Hong Kong. That year it also took over the New York firm's London office, making it a branch of its own. The Swiss company's growth continued rapidly. By the end of the decade it had established subsidiaries at Geneva (Kidder, Peabody Geneva S.A) and Johannesburg (Kidder, Peabody [Pty] Limited), opened a branch in Cairo to concentrate on Arab investment problems, and organized its own wholly-owned Swiss company (Kidder, Peabody Securities, Limited). This subsidiary, with administrative offices at Glarus and a branch in London, was set up to trade in Eurobonds, particularly those denominated in Eurodollars. The London office's trading department, with twenty-one employees at the end of 1969, was a miniature version of the one at Kidder, Peabody's main New York office. Early in 1972 the Swiss holding company formed still another wholly-owned subsidiary, Kidder, Peabody International Limited. The purpose of this company, the only Kidder, Peabody company organized in Great Britain, was to originate and manage underwritings outside the United States.[55]

Kidder, Peabody's network of foreign subsidiaries cooperated closely with the firm's international group in New York, which was substantially strengthened in the 1960s by the addition of several experts in international finance from commercial banks and businesses with overseas operations.[56] Improved ties with European institutions together with an enlarged and experienced staff made it possible for the international group in New York to provide the firm's network of foreign subsidiaries with the investment and research services they required to respond effectively to the impact of changing economic and political conditions on the needs of the firm's foreign and American clients. Private telephone and telex lines connected the offices in London, Paris, Geneva, and Hong Kong with Kidder, Peabody's New York headquarters, which supervised and managed the firm's entire international operations.[57]

The Swiss company's subsidiaries, with their branches and representatives in key financial centers throughout the world, turned Kidder, Peabody into an international investment banking house, equipped to provide its foreign clients—both institutional and individual—with a range of services similar to those available to its American customers. Demand for the firm's worldwide brokerage, investment banking, and financial advisory services increased rapidly. By the end of the decade foreign operations accounted for some 12 percent of Kidder,

Peabody's gross annual income.[58] Most of the firm's foreign revenues came from brokerage, trading in Eurosecurities, with underwriting and direct sales becoming increasingly more important later in the decade. In April 1962 Kidder, Peabody placed with institutions in the United States $25 million of fifteen year, 6¾ percent notes of the Kokusai Denshin Denwa Co., Ltd. of Tokyo, which used the funds to finance most of the construction costs of a new submarine cable between Japan and Hawaii. The next year in June 1963 Kidder, Peabody also placed with institutional investors $13.5 million of convertible debentures for the Mitsubishi Electric Corporation, the first time this Japanese company borrowed abroad.[59] Private placements usually exceeded the number of the firm's public offerings by about two to one, with the total annual dollar value of the two types of transactions often about equal. Kidder, Peabody's offerings, both public and private, were issued in various currencies: pounds sterling, deutsche marks, Swiss francs, French francs, as well as United States dollars (both domestic and Eurodollars). The volume of these transactions grew steadily, from nearly $71.6 million in 1967 to more than $268.1 million in 1969. Some of the largest public offerings headed by Kidder, Peabody in the later 1960s were for the government of New Zealand. These issues, five in all—two each in 1967 and 1968 and one in 1969—amounted to almost $98 million of which only one loan of $20 million was issued in United States currency. The balance was offered in deutsche marks, with one issue denominated in both deutsche marks and pounds sterling.[60] Most of the firm's other large public offerings were for foreign corporations and American companies doing business abroad, among them Gulf & Western International and the Dreyfus Offshore Trust.

In addition to providing foreign corporations and governments with traditional investment banking services, Kidder, Peabody often was asked to act, on a fee basis, as financial consultant and adviser. In July 1958, for example, the government of Venezuela appointed the firm and Kuhn, Loeb & Co. as its financial advisers. The two houses were assigned the task of establishing the country's "credit in the international investment market. The appointment," *The New York Times* commented, "is believed to be the first time in many years that a foreign government has formally designated private bankers as financial counsel."[61]

Probably Kidder, Peabody's most unusual and complex foreign transaction occurred in Beirut, Lebanon. It involved saving from liquidation the country's largest bank, the Intra Bank, with assets of $500 million. Some of its largest depositors included the government and royal family of Kuwait, the government of Qatar, an independent sheikdom on the Persian Gulf, and the United States Commodity Credit Corporation. The latter had extended the bank a credit of some $22 million to finance purchases of surplus American wheat.[12]

Several considerations contributed to Intra Bank's difficulties. Some of its depositors, attracted by high European interest rates, moved their funds out of the bank, and large withdrawals by oil-rich Arabs from neighboring countries helped weaken Intra still further. Perhaps even more important was the fact that the bank's officers had used deposits to invest in the equities of companies in and out of Lebanon. Intra soon found itself unable to meet the demands of its depositors. Knowledge of its troubles led to a run, and in October 1966 the bank was forced to close its doors. After several proposals to salvage the bank had failed to win the approval of all parties, Kidder, Peabody on its own initiative and with no previous connections with Intra advanced a plan in October 1967.[63]

Kidder, Peabody's interest in salvaging the embattled bank originated with the firm's international group in New York. Convinced that Intra could be refloated, the firm sent representatives to Beirut to study and report on the situation. They, together with outside experts hired by Kidder, Peabody, analyzed the bank's assets and sought and won the cooperation of its major depositors. It took Kidder, Peabody almost fourteen months of delicate negotiations, with several of its executives shuttling back and forth between New York and Beirut, to prepare a plan that was satisfactory to all parties. The rescue package was designed largely by Richard F. Coons, an experienced investment banker who, at the time, comanaged Kidder, Peabody's corporate finance department.[64] Coons' plan called for dividing the bankrupt Intra Bank into two institutions, an investment company to be called Intra Investment Company, and a commercial bank owned by the investment company and to be named the Bank al Mashrek. The depositors in the collapsed bank were to be paid in cash and in the stock of the new company. The completed plan was approved, according to *The New York Times,* "almost literally at the 11th hour." An official of the Commodity Credit Corporation in Beirut described the situation as the old bank's creditors waited anxiously for all sides to approve Kidder, Peabody's rescue plan. "We're sitting here with bated breath waiting for somebody to come in and save us," he said.[65]

Kidder, Peabody collected a substantial fee for its work in Beirut. But more important than its compensation which, according to some accounts was at least a million dollars less than the firm originally had asked, was the fact that salvaging Intra opened new opportunities for Kidder, Peabody in an increasingly important part of the world.[66] "We saw the growing importance of the Middle East," said a Kidder, Peabody officer, "and we wanted to become established there." The transaction also yielded the firm enough new business to justify its Swiss affiliate to set up a subsidiary in Beirut, Kidder, Peabody & Co. (S.A.L.), opened in 1973 and closed less than three years later. Arab investors with their bulging coffers of petrodollars preferred to invest their funds with bankers in New York, London, and Zurich. With its own foreign subsidiaries operating in these and other world financial centers, Kidder, Peabody no longer found it necessary or profitable to maintain an office in Beirut.[67]

Expansion and diversification at home and abroad necessitated a reorganization of Kidder, Peabody's internal management and controls. Until the end of World War II Kidder,

Peabody, like most investment banking houses, was a small informal organization. The total staff in its Wall Street office in 1945 numbered 261, with another 147 men and women in the firm's Boston, Philadelphia, and Chicago branches. There were no formal departments and individual responsibilities were not strictly defined. The partners and the senior staff moved from one area of operations to another depending upon an individual's talents and what needed to be done at the moment. "Every one participated in everything," said one of the firm's senior employees.[68] Each of the partners had several primary responsibilities. Gordon, for example, headed the new business group, as well as the committee dealing with underwriting and direct placements; others directed the sales, trading, and commission business; and Webster and Ames were designated managing partners and were charged with supervising the firm's internal operations.[69] Overall responsibility rested with Gordon and Webster, Kidder, Peabody's top policy team from 1931 through 1945. But it was Gordon more than any one else who kept close watch over the entire firm. Weekly reports from the chief accountant, first Brick then Loverd, kept Gordon and Webster fully informed about the firm's income, expenses, and which areas of the business were making or losing money. "In those days," Gordon said of the pre-1945 era, "we enjoyed the luxury of a small organization."[70]

It was not only Kidder, Peabody's growing volume of business that made this small, informal organization no longer practicable. The SEC and the New York Stock Exchange also contributed to the firm's internal restructuring and to the adoption of tighter supervisory measures over office practices and procedures. In May 1945 Webster informed the partners that "the rules of the Stock Exchange, S.E.C., and other government bodies" required a "definite allocation . . . of the partners responsibilities," not only in the New York office but in the firm's branches as well. The plan he proposed and adopted at all Kidder, Peabody offices established seven major departments.[71] One or more partner was assigned to supervise the various functions of each department. Russell, the partner assigned to the stock exchange department, for example, supervised enforcement of the various SEC and New York Stock Exchange regulations dealing with manipulation, long and short sales, and bookkeeping practices. He defined the jobs of every member of his staff and conducted "periodic reviews" of the entire department's performance, not only to ensure compliance with all federal, state, and stock exchange regulations but also to determine income and expenses. Each department's performance was reviewed at the partners' weekly meetings where overall policies were established.

Frequent, comprehensive review of the firm's internal procedures and practices led to other changes designed to equip Kidder, Peabody to deal with its mounting stock exchange business more efficiently and at less cost, without reducing services to clients. In June 1947 Ames, one of the partners charged with supervising the firm's internal operations, initiated a broad review of back office practices that eliminated much duplication, simplified several procedures, and concentrated many of the support services in New York, among them the Boston branch's billing, bookkeeping, and payroll work.[72] None of these changes or similar ones adopted subsequently, important as they were in cutting costs and increasing efficiency, affected the way Kidder, Peabody conducted its business as much as the decision taken early in 1945 to convert much of the firm's back office operations to punched card tabulating equipment, the first step toward its complete automation. Kidder, Peabody not only employed the new technology to improve its support services, but also—after testing it for two years and finding it satisfactory—made early and full use of it in other areas of the firm's operations. In 1961, when R.C.A. set up its Data Processing Center in New York, the firm subscribed to its service. Not all of Kidder, Peabody's business systems were coordinated with the R.C.A. Center's computers; the firm continued to use several of its own tabulating machines, but its stock exchange transactions after 1961 were assigned entirely to R.C.A.'s computers. The machines took care of all the firm's trades and at the end of each day the Center sent Kidder, Peabody the customers' bills and buy or sell confirmations. Conversion to computers not only brought greater order and efficiency to the firm's back office, reduced the size of its clerical staff, and cut the cost of handling each trade but, unknown at the time the system was adopted, made it possible for Kidder, Peabody to avoid serious difficulties later in the decade when a huge increase in the volume of stock market transactions created an avalanche of paperwork that nearly toppled some firms unable to cope with it.[73]

Mechanization and the ongoing restructuring of the firm's internal operations, combined with a huge increase in personnel—total employees in the New York office alone increased from 261 in 1945 to 840 in 1969—turned Kidder, Peabody into a much more tightly structured organization.[74] The restructuring did not, however, alter the roles of Gordon and Webster. They remained as in the past the two chief policy makers, the firm's seniors in every sense of the word. In 1952 they invited the forty-seven-year-old Erwin Stuebner to join the small high-level group. He had been the manager of Kidder, Peabody's Philadelphia office, leaving it in 1938 to accept a vice presidency with the Fidelity-Philadelphia Trust Company. In October 1947 he returned to Kidder, Peabody as managing partner of the firm's Chicago regional office, and in 1952 he was elevated to senior partner and made a member of the policy committee. No further changes occurred in the group's membership until Webster's death in November 1957. The next year Ames, who had taken up much of Webster's capital in the firm, was made a senior partner and joined Gordon and Stuebner as a member of the policy group.[75]

Ames' elevation came at a time of transition when the firm, like so many others, was moving toward incorporation. During the 1950s many investment banking houses abandoned the securities industry's traditional forms of organization (sole proprietorships and partnerships) and started to incorporate. In 1950 securities corporations accounted for slightly less than 28.5 percent of the 3,908 broker-dealers registered with the SEC; by 1970 incorporated houses represented nearly 73.8 percent of the 3,982 registrants.[76] Tax benefits for the shareholders (the former partners), continuity of the firm, the ability to use retained earnings to build capital, the fact that the shareholders' financial liabilities were limited whereas those of general partners were unlimited, and, most importantly, the opportunity to widen ownership—to retain and attract able young employees by giving them an interest in the business—made incorporation increasingly attractive, particularly after May 1953 when the New York Stock Exchange amended its old rule denying seats to corporate officers and directors.[77]

Kidder, Peabody's decision to incorporate was not reached easily or quickly. Some of the partners, proud of the prestige associated with the positions they had attained, were reluctant to abandon the traditional form of organization; others feared incorporation would destroy the close flexible relationship that distinguished investment banking partnerships and lead to rigid institutionalization and increased costs. Opposition within the firm and uncertainty about the tax advantage offered by incorporation led to a compromise decision, the organization of a corporate affiliate (Kidder, Peabody & Co. Incorporated) to take over the firm's corporate underwriting business. Set up in January 1956, the affiliate offered some of the more important advantages of full incorporation—limited liability in a high risk area, executive positions to key employees, and organizational continuity—without sacrificing the tangible and intangible benefits of the partnership which continued, as in the past, to conduct the firm's other activities: brokerage, corporate and municipal over-the-counter trading, and municipal underwriting.[78]

Organization of the underwriting affiliate marked the beginning of Kidder, Peabody's slow transition to full incorporation, which was finally accomplished late in 1964. Two considerations probably more than any others made full incorporation desirable: the "unanticipated great success" of the underwriting affiliate and the cut in federal income tax rates approved by Congress earlier in the year. Some thought was given to continuing the partnership and having it conduct only the firm's brokerage business. That arrangement presented such "extraordinarily difficult operating problems," in the words of the firm's counsel, that the proposal won little support. Forced to decide between changing back to a full partnership or moving toward complete incorporation, the partners opted for the latter.[79]

Kidder, Peabody & Co. Incorporated, a Delaware corporation, took over the entire business of the old partnership in January 1965. The shift to the corporate form of organization involved no fundamental changes except, of course, in the firm's legal entity. The thirty-two general and nine limited partners became the corporation's stockholders. Their holdings in the corporation were determined by the share of the business they formerly held in the partnership. Gordon, the head of the house at the time of incorporation, became chairman of the board of directors, and the other two senior partners—Stuebner and Ames—were made president and vice president and chairman of the executive committee, respectively. Most of the other general partners became vice presidents, and another twenty-seven members of the firm also were elevated to that rank, not all of whom were stockholders. The number of common stockholders, the equivalent status of former partners, grew from thirty-two, at the time of incorporation, to thirty-six by the end of the decade.[80]

Nor did incorporation bring about any significant changes in Kidder, Peabody's functions. The firm remained what it had been, a diversified investment banking house, serving the needs of a varied clientele—individuals, corporations, and governments—both at home and abroad.

More traumatic, perhaps, than the decision to incorporate fully was the one compelling the firm to give up its Wall Street address. Since 1891, when Baring, Magoun & Co., Kidder, Peabody's New York partnership until 1908, occupied offices at 15 Wall Street, the firm had held space on that famous, narrow thoroughfare. The decision to move, dictated in part by the need for more space, was forced upon the partners by the New York Stock Exchange which also needed larger facilities and owned the building at 17 Wall Street where Kidder, Peabody had occupied offices for more than a half century. The first member to move into the Exchange's new building, Kidder, Peabody also was the last one to vacate it, moving to 20 Exchange Place in November 1961. Its new location allowed the firm to bring together in one building all of its departments.[81]

Loss of its Wall Street address, while disturbing to some of the firm's more sentimental partners, did not impair Kidder, Peabody's ability to conduct its business or recruit new clients. By the end of the 1960s it ranked among the top corporate banking houses in the country. Unlike some investment firms whose corporate clients were concentrated mostly in a single industry or composed chiefly of mature companies in or about to enter the so-called billion dollar club, Kidder, Peabody's listing reflected the firm's long-time commitment to serving the needs of ably managed, growing businesses. Some of the companies it financed repeatedly—Burroughs Corporation, Cessna Aircraft, General Tire & Rubber, Carnation, among others—chose Kidder, Peabody as their banker because of the diversified services it could provide and its ability to distribute all types of securities throughout the Unites States and the world. During the 1960s the firm ranked tenth in dollar volume ($6.7 billion) and eighth in the number (375) of security offerings managed or comanaged by the top forty investment houses in the country that headed issues in that decade amounting to $500 million or more. The firm's underwriting participations in that ten-year period—2,017 with a value of nearly $2.3 billion—put it in third place in number of participations and ninth in dollar value.[82] The firm's private placements between 1960 and 1969, valued at nearly $3.7 billion, also placed it among the top houses in the business. In 1969 Kidder, Peabody ranked first in the number of direct sales (eighty) and third in dollar volume ($440.7 million).[83]

For Kidder, Peabody, the quarter-century following the close of World War II was a time of remarkable accomplishment. In 1945 the firm was a recognized national distributor of securities; by 1969 it had become top originator and underwriter of corporate and government offerings as well as a leader in private sales. The marked increase in Kidder, Peabody's capital from $4.5 million in 1945 to $30 million in 1969 provided compelling evidence of the firm's progress, as did *Finance*'s widely read yearly survey of the capital positions of the country's 100 leading underwriters. In 1969 that monthly's listing ranked Kidder, Peabody in twenty-eighth place.[84] No one contributed more to the firm's rise to prominence than Gordon, who steered Kidder, Peabody back to a position of leadership at least equal to if not surpassing the one it had occupied in its greatest pre-World War I days. But neither he nor the other senior executives were content to rest on past accomplishments or the firm's long history. "We are proud of our whiskers," said one of them, "but we are too concerned with the present and future of the business to sit back and admire them."[85]

There was good reason for their concern, despite the great underwriting and brokerage booms that made 1968 one of the most profitable years in Wall Street history. The optimism generated by soaring profits—the total capital of 424 underwriters surveyed by *Finance* increased 31 percent in 1968, reaching almost $3.5 billion—failed to dispel the widespread uneasiness and uncertainty that blanketed much of the country as the "go-go" decade of the 1960s drew to a close. The divisive war in Vietnam and racial violence, civil disorder, and assassination at home disheartened millions of Americans and undermined their confidence in the nation's institutions, including Wall Street, which faced serious problems of its own. Kidder, Peabody, along with the rest of the securities industry, was about to enter another period of difficult testing, in some respects the most serious since the far-away depression years of the 1930s.

CHAPTER
SEVEN

The Last Half-Dozen Years

The United States approached its bicentennial decade a seriously divided and troubled country, a nation "coming apart," in the words of a knowledgeable observer. A long, widely unpopular war in Vietnam and a host of difficult social and economic problems at home led many Americans, particularly the generation born after World War II, to turn against traditional values and standards. To the disaffected the country's leaders in and out of government were selfish, materialistic, and hypocritical, responsible for the killing in Southeast Asia and all the ills and anachronisms in American society—racism, poverty, urban decay, and ecological damage. "Trust no one over thirty" summed up the views of the youth revolt of the late 1960s. Some young rebels rejected everything their parents' generation considered important—money, material possessions, position, status, way of life—and dropped out of conventional society.

And it was not only the young who were dissatisfied with

American life and society. Their disaffection was shared by enough older people so that virtually no socioeconomic group was without its critics of the contemporary American scene and of the government's policies at home and abroad. And since all the angry voices, not only in the United States but throughout the world, held the business system primarily responsible for everything that was wrong, Wall Street—the citadel of capitalism—was a chief target of their attacks. In the 1930s the villains had been called the "merchants of death"; in the 1960s the culprit was the "military-industrial complex." At both times Wall Street was a chief target.

Though long accustomed to such attacks, the recent wave of anti-Wall Street criticism came at a time when the financial district was on the verge of deep trouble. Not since the long depression of the 1930s had it faced such serious difficulties as it did at the end of the 1960s, when the great bull market of 1968 expired in mid-1969.

Some of Wall Street's worst difficulties stemmed from the prolonged stock market boom of the 1960s. By the end of the decade total annual trades on the New York Stock Exchange alone soared from 1.8 billion shares in 1965 to almost 2.9 billion shares in 1967 before peaking at nearly 3.3 billion shares in 1968. Neither the Exchange nor the brokerage community anticipated such a massive increase in trading volume. Daily transactions on the Big Board in 1967 averaged slightly less than 10.1 million shares, a figure the Exchange had predicted would not be reached until 1975. In 1968 the daily average shot up to 12.4 million shares. That year the old record of 16.4 million shares traded on a single day—on October 24, 1929—was not only repeatedly exceeded but on April 10, for the first time in the Exchange's long history, more than 20 million shares changed hands. Still bigger days were to follow.[1]

Many brokerage houses were unprepared to deal with so high a volume of trades. For some of them booming business and profits proved to be their undoing. The upsurge in stock market transactions generated so much paper work that it exceeded the capacity of many brokerage houses to transfer or deliver stock certificates within the established five-day settlement period. The root cause of the problem stemmed from the outmoded manual bookkeeping procedures still employed in the "cages," the back offices of many brokerage houses. Such firms found themselves unable to tag and move thousands upon thousands of stock certificates. Unlike the spacious, airy, elegantly decorated front offices, the cages of most firms were crowded and disorganized, with securities stacked on tables, counters, or wherever there was a place for them. The back offices of most brokerage firms, according to a study by an independent management and accounting firm, belonged to the "green eyeshade era," places where Charles Dickens' "Scrooge and Bob Cratchitt would still feel at home."[2]

Antiquated back office procedures resulted in millions upon millions of "lost" (misplaced) securities. By the end of 1967 the volume of "fails," the term used to refer to incompleted transactions, assumed crisis proportions, and the worst was still to come. In January 1968 the Securities and Exchange Commission (SEC) warned brokerage houses to improve their back office practices to achieve "prompt transfer and delivery of securities" and to adjust their net capital figures to reflect their fails. "The long length of time in which amounts due are carried in the failed-to-deliver accounts of the various broker-dealers," the SEC warned, "exposes them to undue risk of market fluctuations in the securities, as well as to the possibility of financial difficulties of the broker on the other side of the transaction."[3]

That same month the New York Stock Exchange also took steps to ease the paper crunch. It shortened trading hours by ninety minutes a day. The restriction accomplished little and was lifted in March. Then in June, when the volume of fails reached almost $3.8 billion, nearly 2¾ times greater than the generally accepted level, the Exchange decided to stay closed for a full day, which it did through December. But neither a shortened trading week nor the Exchange's efforts to persuade the most troubled firms to curtail "voluntarily" their brokerage business proved useful. By December 1968 the volume of fails reached its peak, $4.1 billion.[4]

Kidder, Peabody survived the fails crisis better than most houses. Unlike some firms which shifted their brokerage and accounting operations to computers only after the onset of the paper work mess, Kidder, Peabody's back office was fully automated and, just as important, staffed with experienced personnel qualified to use the new technology effectively. "We either planned well or guessed right," said William Loverd, the firm's treasurer.[5] Whichever it was, Kidder, Peabody's back office never ran into any severe operational problems. Throughout the worst of the paper crunch it succeeded in sending out daily statements to customers, and it did so without adding scores of untrained clerks as did some houses with less efficient back offices. Most of the firm's staff had been with Kidder, Peabody since the mid-1940s when it first started to experiment with new back office machines and procedures. With great loyalty, the firm's employees worked throughout most of the night to stay abreast of the expanding volume of transactions; during the day other employees and officers stayed after hours, telephoning customers, brokers, banks, and institutions to get them to deliver the certificates they owed the firm.

Efficient back office operations saved Kidder, Peabody from SEC warnings and kept it off the New York Stock Exchange's "watch list," which included at one time or another almost fifty firms. Effective management, however, did not allow Kidder, Peabody—or any other well-managed house—to escape the fails crisis altogether. Firms whose own operations were in reasonably good shape had to deal with brokerage houses with back office snarls. The deficiencies of the latter affected the performance of all firms. Kidder, Peabody's chief concern during the massive paper work mess of 1968 stemmed largely from the failure of other houses to make deliveries on time; their delinquencies, in turn, prevented the firm from settling with its own clients. Late in April 1968, before the worst of the crisis, the value of the firm's fails to receive and deliver, as reported to the New York Stock Exchange, amounted to $33.8 million and $35.6 million, respectively. A year later both figures were down substantially: fails to receive fell to $23.3 million and fails to deliver shrank to $17.5 million.[6]

Kidder, Peabody's drop in fails was not atypical. Almost all houses showed a decline, and not only because of a marked increase in back office efficiency. Nor was the decrease attributable chiefly to the New York Stock Exchange's Central Certificate Service (CCS) set up early in 1969 to reduce the actual movement of certificates by establishing a central depository that, in the words of Big Board president Robert W. Haack, would provide for "securities a fluidity of movement comparable to the way checks move money through the banking system."[7] The principal reason for the decrease in fails, from $4.1 billion in December 1968 to $2.3 billion in April 1969, was the decline in the volume of trades. "The same elements that made the problem have continued to exist," said a prominent Wall Street operations expert, Junius W. Peake of Shields & Co. "I just don't think anything has changed," he continued. "Any time you increase your sales capacity you should increase your operations capacity. The industry has not done that."[8] And the improvements that had been achieved, such as the Exchange's automated central depository system, affected only listed securities, not those traded over-the-counter where the most acute problems had occurred. That market's automated quote system, NASDAQ (National Association of Securities Dealers Automated Quotations), did not go into effect until January 1971.

Resolved or not, the fails problem in 1969 was eclipsed by another more serious crisis, the great Wall Street money squeeze that accompanied the downturn in stock prices. In January 1969, at the time of Richard Nixon's inauguration as President, Standard & Poor's index of 500 common stocks (1941–43=10) stood at 102.04, down 4.44 points from its December 1968 peak. By May 1969 it was up again to 104.62; then it started on a steep decline, sinking to 99.14 in June, down to 91.11 in December, and dropping to a low of 75.59 in June 1970.

In the eighteen months between December 1968 and June 1970 the index lost 30.89 points, a decline of some 29 percent, while the market value of all listed stock (common and preferred) fell from $759.5 billion in 1968 to $680.7 billion in 1970, a loss of almost 10.4 percent.[9]

The eighteen-month-long bear market that started with the June 1969 break owed much to the Nixon administration's decision to fight a mounting inflation by continuing the tight money policy initiated during Lyndon Johnson's last months in office. The monetary curbs, combined with the war in Vietnam, threats of new conflicts in the Middle East and elsewhere, and uneasiness about the general state of the economy drove investors out of the stock market and into bonds, where interest rates on high-grade corporate debt (Moody's AAA-rated bonds) rose from a yearly 6.18 percent in 1968 to 7.03 percent in 1969, and up to 8.04 percent in 1970. Stock sales on the nation's exchanges which had peaked at 5.40 billion shares in 1969 were down to 4.83 billion shares by the end of 1970.[10] The steep drop in share volume shrank the profits of investment houses at a time of increased operational costs, when many firms had added expensive computer equipment to meet an expanding brokerage business that suddenly declined sharply. Computers, unlike clerks, could not be dismissed so easily when trading volume plunged as it did after June 1969. And while most firms did succeed in reducing expenses, the cuts usually did not match the drop in income, with the result that the industry suffered a severe profit and capital squeeze that forced upwards of 100 houses to liquidate or to seek life-saving mergers.[11]

It was not only small houses that closed or had to merge to prevent collapse. The capital squeeze threatened some of Wall Street's largest and most respected firms, among them Hayden, Stone, Inc., Goodbody & Co., and Francis I. duPont & Co. The failure "of any one of them," wrote *The New York Times'* financial reporter Terry Robards, "could have triggered a run on all brokerage firms," a view widely shared by most of the industry's leaders.[12]

Timely action by the New York Stock Exchange prevented the crisis from turning into a financial panic, the kind that had occurred earlier in American history when a prominent Wall Street brokerage house suspended operations and its customers suffered heavy losses. During the 1969 to 1970 crisis the New York Stock Exchange's Special Trust Fund, established in 1964 after the widely publicized Ira Haupt & Co. failure, stood ready to protect an insolvent firm's clients. The money in the Fund, originally $25 million—$10 million in cash and the balance in standby bank credit—was raised by assessing the Exchange's members 0.375 percent of their annual net commissions.[13] Late in October 1970, when the Fund's pool was near exhaustion and the need for emergency cash was still large and growing, the Exchange imposed a special surcharge of 0.50 percent. Congress, meanwhile, also concerned itself with Wall Street's crisis, and in December boosted the sagging confidence of brokers' clients by passing the Securities Investor Protection Act. The law provided investors with government-backed insurance against broker insolvency, much as the Federal Deposit Insurance Corporation protected depositors against bank failures.

Money from the Exchange's Special Fund also went to provide emergency capital to tottering member houses that might be saved by a hurriedly arranged merger. Salvage operations of this kind were entrusted to a special Surveillance Committee, better known as the Crisis Committee. Set up in May 1970, the six-person top-level group was headed by Felix Rohatyn, a partner in Lazard Freres & Co., and included Bernard J. Lasker, the chairman of the New York Stock Exchange, and Ralph D. DeNunzio, vice chairman of the Exchange and then executive vice president of Kidder, Peabody. The three of them conducted the long, difficult negotiations that resulted in saving Hayden, Stone, one of the Street's largest houses, from liquidation by merging it with Cogan, Berlind, Weill & Levitt, Inc. to create the new house CBWL-Hayden, Stone. That rescue, accomplished in September, was followed immediately by two others, each involving major firms. Goodbody & Co. was saved from collapse in October when Merrill Lynch, Pierce, Fenner & Smith was persuaded to take it over; and in November Rohatyn, DeNunzio, and Lasker succeeded in preventing the failure of Francis I. duPont & Co., a house closely connected with and bearing the name of one of America's oldest and wealthiest industrial families. The duPont rescue, the last of the Crisis Committee's major operations, was accomplished by a merger with Glore, Forgan & Staats and Hirsch & Co., and a huge infusion of Texas money from H. Ross Perot.[14]

Catastrophe had been averted, but the Crisis Committee's work did not strike at the fundamental cause of Wall Street's troubles: the dangerously thin and impermanent nature of so many firms' capital. Much of it was in securities whose value eroded quickly in a falling market, or in subordinated loans which the lenders could demand on relatively short notice, in some cases no more than ninety days. "Many Wall Street firms," said Merrill Lynch chairman Donald T. Regan, "have what they call a capital structure, but which more closely resembles a scaffold."[15] The very fact that the New York Stock Exchange had to establish a special committee to monitor its members' capital position, a job regularly performed by the Big Board's staff, not only appeared to confirm the truth of Regan's comment but it also disclosed the extent to which so many of the country's investment firms—the acknowledged experts in raising capital for giant businesses and governments—seemed unable to finance themselves.

Kidder, Peabody was not among the inadequately capitalized houses. Nor did it suffer a cash squeeze. The fact that the firm escaped embarrassment owed much to Gordon, De Nunzio, and other senior officers, some of whom had not forgotten the difficult years of the 1930s. Gordon, still an active policymaker particularly in matters of money, had decided at the time of the 1931 reorganization that no effort would be spared to avoid the kinds of situations that had brought the old Kidder, Peabody to the brink of bankruptcy. That experience, followed by the Pure Oil and Bethlehem Steel underwriting debacles of September

1937, made lasting impressions. Never again, Gordon resolved, would the firm get caught with inadequate capital. If there was one topic on which he and the policy group were in complete agreement, it was to make certain that Kidder, Peabody had adequate permanent capital and sufficient cash. To achieve this Gordon urged the partners to add to their investment in the firm by not withdrawing all their annual profits and after incorporation, he and the policy committee relied heavily on retained earnings to strengthen the firm's capital position. Gordon's financial conservatism—"he's as tight with the firm's money as he is with our clients' funds," said one of the old partners—not only allowed Kidder, Peabody to survive the great money squeeze of 1969 and 1970 but made it possible for the house to add a million dollars to its capital, from $30 million in December 1969 to $31 million in December 1970.[16] And Kidder, Peabody continued to add to its capital every year after then, reaching $53.7 million in 1975. The firm's capital position in the 1970s placed it among the top 25 of the country's 100 leading underwriters, usually among the first 20 houses in the industry. In November 1975 the firm's ratio of net capital to the New York Stock Exchange's net capital rule reached 5.61 to 1, or almost six times more than the Big Board's requirement.

Building capital depended upon profits, and it was the lack of these that bankrupted some houses and drove others to the brink of collapse. "Inadequate profits is the central problem," said Clifford W. Michel, a Loeb, Rhoades & Co. partner and head of the Association of Stock Exchange Firms, the group that included the industry's leading houses. The same view was expressed by a senior member of another major house, Reynolds & Co. "The one thing we need in this business," he said, "is profitability and it's obvious there is a tie-in between profits and capital. The very firms that need it most are the ones that are hardest pressed to get it."[17]

Profitability, of course, accounted for Kidder, Peabody's ability to add to its capital at a time when other firms were being squeezed. Efficient internal management and care in conserving capital and maintaining its liquidity, refusing to allow capital to be tied up in unsold securities even if it meant taking a loss, prevented the firm from incurring deficits. But these policies, important as they were, did not increase profits. Only new business could accomplish that, and then only if the firm had diversified strength so that losses in one area could be offset by gains in another. Diversification made it possible for Kidder, Peabody to register gains even during the long two-year stock market downturn that precipitated the severe Wall Street capital crunch of 1970. Between 1969 and 1970 the securities commission income of the country's broker-dealers fell by almost 26 percent, from $2.93 billion to $2.18 billion. Kidder, Peabody's stock market business stood up much better than the industry's average. Gross income from brokerage commissions in 1969 and 1970 remained almost the same, about 44 percent each year.[18]

But it was the firm's investment banking activities—syndicate managements, underwriting participations, and direct sales—that swelled its total 1970 profits. That year, one of Wall Street's worst since the depths of the great depression, Kidder, Peabody registered a large increase in the dollar value of the corporate public offerings it managed (from $1.74 billion to $3.08 billion), a more modest rise in the municipal financings it headed (from $1.46 billion to $1.78 billion), and a considerable

TABLE 7.1 *Corporate Public Offerings Managed or Comanaged by Kidder, Peabody, 1970–1975* (in billions of dollars)

Year	Total number	Total dollar value
1970	72	3,083
1971	111	4,495
1972	107	4,155
1973	70	4,822
1974	76	4,664
1975	122	6.202
Totals	558	27,421

SOURCE: Kidder, Peabody & Co., Records—New York City.

TABLE 7.2 *Private Placements by Kidder, Peabody, 1970–1975* (in millions of dollars)

Year	Total number	Total dollar value
1970	72	317.9
1971	68	359.2
1972	72	625.5
1973	72	724.1
1974	48	591.9
1975	85	768.1
Totals	417	3,386.7

SOURCE: Kidder, Peabody & Co., Records—New York City.

gain in the volume of its underwriting participations (from \$3.64 billion to \$5.18 billion).[19] The firm's leadership in these areas, as well as the mounting volume of its tax-exempt offerings, were exceeded only by its preeminence in private placements. In three of the six years between 1970 and 1975 Kidder, Peabody ranked first in the number of private placements, and only once in that period did it drop below second place; in 1974 it occupied third place.[20] By the end of 1975 the firm ranked ninth among the nation's twenty-five leading underwriters, measured in terms of the dollar volume of total negotiated corporate managements, and sixth if ranked on the basis of

TABLE 7.3 *Municipal Financings Managed or Comanaged by Kidder, Peabody, 1970–1975* (in billions of dollars)

Year	Total number	Total dollar value
1970	77	1,782
1971	75	2,104
1972	74	2,336
1973	85	1,774
1974	78	2,090
1975	124	3,991
Totals	513	14,077

SOURCE: Kidder, Peabody & Co., Records—New York City.

TABLE 7.4 *Underwriting Participations of Kidder, Peabody, 1970–1975* (in billions of dollars)

Year	Total number	Total dollar value
1970	221	5,183
1971	254	6,958
1972	253	7,116
1973	227	7,319
1974	202	7,347
1975	331	10,961
Totals	1,488	44,884

SOURCE: Kidder, Peabody & Co., Records—New York City.

leadership in competitive sales. That year the editors of *Institutional Investor,* a widely cited trade journal, credited Kidder, Peabody with being the investment banker of fifty-two of the country's largest companies, a number which placed the firm in seventh place among the thirty-seven top houses in the United States.[21]

During the 1970s Kidder, Peabody's international financings also grew substantially. The increased liquidity of the banking system—particularly in Eurodollars—provided international investment houses with new business opportunities which they were quick to cultivate. Kidder, Peabody's close, continuous ties with the world's principal capital markets, maintained through a network of foreign subsidiaries that also kept it informed of the needs of both users and suppliers of long-term funds, gave it strength as an international investment house, as did its "marketing muscle" in the United States and abroad. The fact that it was a diversified firm able to design and place different types of securities and provide a variety of financial and investment advisory services also added to Kidder, Peabody's ability to recruit foreign clients. Kidder, Peabody's long experience in mergers and acquisitions, for example, allowed it to compete effectively for the business of United States corporations interested in acquiring foreign companies and, when the dollar weakened, for overseas concerns seeking to buy American businesses. Transactions of this type helped swell the volume of Kidder, Peabody's foreign security issues. In the six-year period 1970 through 1975 the firm and its foreign subsidiaries managed public offerings and negotiated direct sales of corporate and government securities totaling nearly $1.45 billion, making Kidder, Peabody one of the top twenty-five international investment banking houses in the United States.[22]

Foreign and domestic investment banking activities helped moderate the trauma of radical, far-reaching changes in the brokerage business, not only for Kidder, Peabody but for other large houses as well. In December 1968 the SEC ordered the New York Stock Exchange to rescind its 179-year rule on fixed commissions and permit negotiated rates on trades of $500,000 or more. The new era of competitive pricing, which started in April 1971 after the Exchange's members bowed to the inevitable and voted it into effect, brought an immediate and considerable reduction in commission charges—in some instances 50 percent or more. Such large cuts in fees, obviously, forced down the profits brokerage houses earned from this business. Least affected were diversified firms like Kidder, Peabody whose brokerage clients included both individuals and institutions—insurance and investment companies, pension funds, and bank trust departments.[23]

But even some of these firms, though not badly hurt by negotiated commissions on large trades, were concerned that the SEC, intent upon making the brokerage business more competitive and reducing the New York Stock Exchange's long dominance over the country's securities markets, would press for an early lowering of the $500,000 level, perhaps bringing it down as far as $100,000, the amount originally considered.[24] Continuing pressure from a reform-minded SEC and some Capitol Hill leaders, consumer advocates, as well as a few Wall Street spokespeople anxious to stem the flow of business away from the Big Board by making it more competitive, soon led to a further breakdown in fixed commissions. In April 1973 the

Exchange, adhering to SEC orders, extended negotiated rates to trades of $300,000 or more, and on May 1, 1975, the Big Board accepted the inevitable and abolished fixed commissions on all transactions of whatever size.

Competitive rates brought small investors few immediate benefits; in some cases they actually had to pay a higher fee to buy and sell stock than they did under the old fixed-rate structure. Many firms, including Kidder, Peabody, established a minimum per-trade fee, usually $25. These and other efforts to hold the line, to avoid a "rate-cutting war" on small individual trades like the one that yielded institutional clients huge discounts, proved unsuccessful. Once a few small houses hoping to add to their volume started cutting fees, other firms followed and by the end of the year the commissions charged individuals also started to fall, sometimes reaching as much as 40 percent below the previously fixed rate.[25]

Negotiated rates combined with sagging stock prices and diminished share volume cut deeply into brokerage earnings and prompted much concern about the future profitability of investment firms. Evidence of that apprehension was not hard to find. Investors showed little interest in the stock of publicly owned securities firms, all of which were selling at steep discounts from their original offering prices earlier in the decade when it was widely held that public ownership was the solution to Wall Street's capital shortage. Donaldson, Lufkin & Jenrette, Inc., the first brokerage house to go public, saw the price of its stock, originally offered in the spring of 1970 at $15 a share, drop to 4⅞—its 1975 high—then down to 2 in October 1975.[26] The stock of most other publicly owned houses, including some well-managed and profitable firms such as Merrill Lynch, Pierce, Fenner & Smith, Inc., also registered declines. Hardest hit were the small and medium-sized houses, particularly those heavily committed to research in a narrow range of stocks. Some of these houses were forced to close, quit the brokerage business, or merge with large full-service firms. The future seemed to rest with the financially strong, diversified houses. "They can offset the rate cutting with underwriting business, they can obtain the underwritings because they have distribution," said a brokerage house official, "and they can eat up the small firms with economics of scale."[27]

Because Kidder, Peabody was just such a house it survived the wrenching experience of the shift from fixed minimum commissions to negotiated rates without too much immediate hardship. Its gross revenue from commissions declined from 47.8 percent in 1974, the peak for the decade, to 46.6 percent in 1975.[28] The decline, modest compared to some firms, stemmed chiefly from the loss of some small accounts that either left the market entirely or chose to do business with one of the small discount houses with which Kidder, Peabody did not try to compete. The firm, like most other major houses, did more for individual clients than only execute their buy or sell orders. It provided advice, research, and other assistance. Some brokerage customers, not wanting these services, found it cheaper to place small orders (up to 500 shares) with a discount house than with Kidder, Peabody. The firm, like the other top houses with which it competed, offered discounts only on orders above 500 shares.[29] Whether Kidder, Peabody or any other major house would continue to adhere to a "standard" rate remained to be seen, particularly since some commercial banks seemed prepared to cultivate the small investors' business by providing them with a discount securities service. In September 1976 New York City's Chemical Bank, the nation's sixth largest commercial bank, announced it was testing just such a plan for some of its checking account clients.[30]

Negotiated rates were but one of the many profound changes that helped transform Wall Street in the late 1960s and early 1970s. There were other equally far reaching ones. Included among these were: the increasing institutionalization of stock ownership and trading; a substantial decrease in the number of individual shareholders (down 18.3 percent between 1970 and 1975); the emergence of a nationwide central trading market for stocks that weakened the New York Stock Exchange's previously undisputed primacy as the nation's chief trading market; the growing number and rising importance of foreign investment firms in America's security markets, making both the brokerage and underwriting business more international and competitive; and the mounting challenge posed to investment houses by other financial intermediaries, particularly the large commercial banks which competed with security firms in several important areas: the underwriting of state and local general obligation bonds, Eurobonds, and others, most notably private placements. These developments, coming at a time of an erratic stock market and a reform-minded SEC, forced investment houses to adapt their policies and practices to a new financial and investment environment.[31]

Adjustment to these changes served to reconfirm the correctness of several of Kidder, Peabody's earliest and most fundamental policies. Strong distribution, diversification, and adequate capital, the three basic principles that had guided the partners' actions for two generations, made it possible for Kidder, Peabody to weather the most recent crises that beset the securities business. And since these policies appeared to be equally valid for the future, they continued to determine the firm's direction.

Kidder, Peabody strengthened its distribution still further in June 1974 when it acquired Clark, Dodge & Co., an old, respected house founded in 1845. Faced with rising costs and declining income, Clark, Dodge's officers sought to unite their twenty-two-branch firm with a full-service house.[32] The merger gave Kidder, Peabody three additional offices in California (Palo Alto, Sacramento, and Carmel), two in Ohio (Cleveland and Toledo), and for the first time direct representation in the upper South, at Norfolk, Virginia. Most of Clark, Dodge's senior officers and employees joined Kidder, Peabody.[33]

Effective nationwide distribution, particularly access to large numbers of individual buyers, proved itself in July 1975 when Kidder, Peabody, together with Salomon Brothers, Merrill Lynch, and three of New York City's largest commercial banks

(Morgan Guaranty Trust, Chase Manhattan, and First National City), served as senior comanagers of the huge bond issue brought out by the Municipal Assistance Corporation for the City of New York, better known as "Big Mac." The $1 billion offering, the first of three designed to provide New York City with enough cash to pay its bills and avoid default, proved difficult to sell. Investors both large and small had little confidence in the city's ability to manage its affairs, and Kidder, Peabody's salespeople not only had to stress price and yield but, more importantly, had to persuade clients that the bonds appeared to be a safe investment because of their strong prior claim to city revenues. Most of the firm's initial sales, upwards of $26.1 million, went to clients in the Northeast with the next largest number going to buyers in Atlanta and Dallas. Kidder, Peabody's leadership in selling "Big Mac" bonds for a hard-pressed city continued through most of that year. In August it distributed an additional $3.5 million; the next month, together with the First National City Bank, the firm jointly placed some $80 million with various institutions; and in November Kidder, Peabody sold another $5 million. By the end of 1975 Kidder, Peabody alone was responsible for distributing some $34.7 million of Big Mac bonds.[34]

"We have a large machine," Gordon once said, "and we find a great many securities have to be fed through it if we want to break even."[35] That statement, made some twenty years earlier during the antitrust trial, applied with even more force in the 1970s when competition from commercial banks and other financial intermediaries moved into areas once considered exclusively the domain of investment houses. To hold on to its old clients and win new ones while serving them both efficiently, as well as to guard against possible steeper declines in brokerage income, the most vulnerable source of an investment firm's earnings, Kidder, Peabody strengthened its traditional services and added new ones, two of the most important being project financing and trading in options.[36] Between 1970 and 1975 the firm's lease financings of plant and equipment totaled

$502.3 million and the volume of its options transactions also grew substantially, particularly after April 1973 when the Chicago Board of Options opened for business.[36]

Option trading—a contract to buy or sell a specified number of shares of a certain stock at a determined price within a defined period—was an old business, the instruments themselves dating back to antiquity. Options regained popularity in the early 1970s because, in the words of the Chicago Board of Options, they offered investors opportunities for a "potentially large profit from a relatively small investment with a known and predetermined risk," provided the buyer made the right decision (some preferred the word bet) on a stock's future movement and acted on it in time. Options, like other investments, also carried the risk of losses. But whether the option buyer made or lost money the brokers dealing in these instruments earned handsome commissions, sometimes as many as three or four in a single operation.

Options trading was a profitable business. Dealers in these securities, said SEC chairman Roderick M. Hills, "make more money from options than they foresee making from new stock issues." Hills was concerned the option business would siphon off seed money from new enterprises. "I'd like to get some of the horse-betting money on stocks," he said in July 1976 when he announced plans to have the SEC study the economic effects of option trading.[38] Kidder, Peabody not only traded in options—these operations helped offset some 50 percent of the firm's decline in commission earnings—but also included the instruments in its portfolio management service. Gary L. Gastineau, the manager of Kidder, Peabody's options portfolio service, was an experienced security analyst and portfolio manager whose book *The Stock Options Manual* (McGraw-Hill, 1975) analyzed the various techniques for evaluating option contracts, with special reference to the computerized model he developed with Professor Albert Madansky of the University of Chicago's Graduate School of Business Administration.

Investment management and advisory functions provided

still other opportunities to expand Kidder, Peabody's income-producing services. Although investment management was a highly competitive business with several types of financial intermediaries seeking to serve a relatively small clientele of individuals and institutions, it allowed Kidder, Peabody to employ more fully and effectively its resources and expertise. The decision to expand this area of its operations was strengthened by the acquisition of Clark, Dodge & Co., which had a substantial and well-staffed management service. Five of its top managers joined Kidder, Peabody and together with its own advisory group provided the firm with a large experienced staff. In January 1976 Kidder, Peabody reorganized and consolidated all its investment management and advisory services, assigning them to a new and separate subsidiary called the Webster Management Corporation. The new corporate entity, named after Edwin S. Webster, Jr., Kidder, Peabody's senior partner from 1931 until his death in November 1957, was designed to provide the benefits of outside investment research and in the words of the corporation's officers, assure its fourteen senior and five associate portfolio managers the required "autonomy and independence in decision making." At the time of its organization Webster Management took over accounts valued in excess of $460 million, some 50 percent of which belonged to individuals with the rest almost equally divided between tax-exempt funds and those of corporations and other institutions.[39]

Providing diversified services effectively in the rapidly changing and highly competitive environment of the early 1970s required expertise in many areas, far more than any single individual or department could provide. Kidder, Peabody sought to keep abreast of the vast changes in the nation's security markets and the impact of these changes on its clients' financial needs by reorganizing and expanding its research department. The first major departure from past practice came in March 1972 when the research department, originally separated from the new business group by Amyas Ames in the mid-1930s, was relieved of its remaining responsibilities to the corporate finance section. Until then members of the research staff occasionally had been called upon to investigate and analyze the firm's new offerings. Under the new setup this work was assigned to analysts in corporate finance, and the research department devoted itself entirely to preparing industry and company analyses, with regular follow-ups to update the original studies. The research staff also prepared portfolio strategy materials, "think pieces," for money managers, research directors, and analysts of institutional buyers. Using computer facilities of their own, the department's three economists and sixteen fully chartered analysts built various types of industry and company models to forecast future performance. The information contained in the department's various publications was based entirely on its own investigations and when necessary on the findings of outside specialists, particularly consulting accountants. But the final product was its own. "We make it a point not to use other people's research," said Douglas West, the vice president responsible for quality control of the department's publications.[40]

The other major change in the firm's research program, also accomplished in March 1972, was to shift the primary emphasis of its product and services away from the individual client and toward institutional buyers, the largest owners and traders of equities. By improving the quality of its research to meet the sophisticated needs of institutional buyers, Kidder, Peabody maintained that the firm's individual clients also would benefit from superior reports and recommendations that had been specially prepared for the institutional buyers. The firm's research, in other words, was made to serve two markets—individuals and institutions.

By the end of 1975 Kidder, Peabody's research department, headed by Johann Gouws, a thirty-six-year-old analyst formerly with H. C. Wainwright & Co., was one of the largest on Wall Street, not only among investment houses but also among commercial banks and trust companies. Nearly half of it's total staff of some 110 men and women were professionals—economists and analysts. The department's annual budget which had reached almost a million dollars in 1968 continued to grow steadily; by 1975 it exceeded $4 million a year. And the group's publications, among the largest and most diverse of those of any investment firm on the Street, were distributed selectively to some 2,000 individuals and institutions.[41]

But it was not only Kidder, Peabody's clients that benefited from the research department's findings. By providing the firm with in-depth knowledge on a wide range of economic and financial subjects, the research group's analyses also strengthened the firm's ability to recruit new clients and better serve old ones. The research department's work often proved highly useful also to the corporate finance group in its investigation of new public offerings and in arranging direct sales.

Research, with its specialists studying the present and future needs of various industries, put a premium on expert, detailed information on a wide range of complex financial topics. Kidder, Peabody and other diversified houses like it soon came to be composed of teams of specialists in every type of financial transaction and investment medium. Experts in one department cooperated closely with specialists in others, and all of them operated under the general supervision of the firm's three-man policy committee headed by Gordon. The other two members in 1975 were Erwin Stuebner, Kidder, Peabody's president who was stationed in Chicago, and Ralph D. DeNunzio, the chairman of the firm's executive committee. DeNunzio joined the policy group in 1969 at the age of thirty-eight replacing Ames, who gave up most of his responsibilities at Kidder, Peabody to become Chairman of the Board of the Lincoln Center for the Performing Arts, Inc.

A Princeton graduate with a major in classics, DeNunzio once considered a career as a sports broadcaster but chose instead to become an investment banker. In July 1953, a month after earning his bachelor's degree, he joined Kidder, Peabody's training program and has been with the firm since then, rising rapidly from institutional sales in Chicago to syndicate manager in New York. In 1962 at age thirty he was made a partner, and in 1969 when he joined Gordon and Stuebner on the policy committee, he also became the firm's chief operating officer, a post he continued to hold even after he was made president in January 1977.

Intelligent—"a razor-sharp intellect," said one Wall Street observer—knowledgeable and level-headed—"one of the coolest cats I've ever watched in action," said a New York Stock Exchange official—and possessed of a seemingly infinite capacity for hard work, DeNunzio has earned the respect and confidence of both the senior members of his own firm and the leaders of the securities industry.[42] In 1968 he was elected a governor of the New York Stock Exchange; the next year he was elevated to vice chairman of the board of governors; and in May 1971 he was made chairman, the youngest person to hold that post in the Big Board's entire history. DeNunzio's service on the New York Stock Exchange's board occurred at a terrible time in Wall Street's history, when the back office and capital crises shook the financial district to its roots and the Big Board itself was under attack for having failed to foresee and avert the worst problems. DeNunzio presided over the sweeping reorganization that resulted in the election of the first public members to the Exchange's board of directors, and he played a major role on its Crisis Committee, the group that helped arrange the lifesaving mergers that kept afloat some of Wall Street's largest houses. DeNunzio also headed the industry task force that helped draft the Securities Investor Protection Act, as well as serving on several committees of the Investment Bankers Association and its successor organization, the Securities Industry Association.[43]

DeNunzio's long and difficult work on behalf of the Exchange and the securities industry was accomplished without neglecting his mounting responsibilities at Kidder, Peabody. Since 1969 when he joined the firm's policy group, DeNunzio has carried the major responsibility for supervising the worldwide operations. As its chief operating officer in the New York City headquarters, he has occupied himself with every aspect of

Kidder, Peabody's business. He serves on the commitment committee which decides what the firm will underwrite and at what price; and he reviews the many weekly reports submitted to him from department heads, regional office managers, and the heads of overseas subsidiaries. The firm's present-day internal management and control system, which DeNunzio himself helped plan and establish, allows him to keep as close and effective a watch on Kidder, Peabody's underwriting commitments, trading position, and operating costs as Gordon had done in the days before incorporation.[44]

That DeNunzio is qualified to run Kidder, Peabody is generally accepted both within and outside the firm. He has participated in all the large policy decisions of the last decade, often assuming the chief responsibility for implementing them. He took a lead in negotiating the Van Ingen, Pacific Northwest, and Clark, Dodge mergers, and he was largely responsible for restructuring the firm's back office procedures. In 1968, a year before he joined the policy group, it took some 550 operational employees to process fewer than 2,000 trades a day; by the end of December 1975, with slightly fewer than 400 workers, the firm's back office was processing an average of about 5,000 trades a day. DeNunzio's commitment to improved productivity and service and his readiness to invest heavily in expensive new computers and other sophisticated office machinery made it possible for Kidder, Peabody in 1975 to conduct more business more effectively with fewer clerical workers than ever before.[45] Kidder, Peabody's high reputation among Wall Street leaders—that it is a well-managed, carefully balanced, profitable house—owes much to DeNunzio's constant striving for operational efficiency and conservative, steady growth.

If there is one aspect of the investment banking business in which DeNunzio has yet to distinguish himself, say some Wall Street observers, it is in recruiting large corporate clients, a talent that Gordon possessed in such abundance that *The New York Times'* Michael C. Jensen labeled it "legendary."[46] Whatever the merits of that observation, DeNunzio is fully aware of

Kidder, Peabody's need to win and hold large corporate clients; now that he has succeeded in making the firm more responsive to the many changes that have occurred on Wall Street in the last decade, he is spending more and more of his time with the corporate finance group. And though he still may not be on close terms with as many top company executives as is Gordon, the fact remains that DeNunzio, like his mentor, is an informed, perceptive, and persuasive banker able to call upon a skilled staff for whatever information and support he requires.

DeNunzio's rise to power at Kidder, Peabody is due, of course, to his own intelligence, competence, and drive. But it is also true that his substantial accomplishments in preparing Kidder, Peabody for the challenges of the next decade would not have been possible without the full cooperation and support of the firm's senior officers, particularly Gordon, who worked closely with him for some fifteen years, helping to train him for a position of leadership. Unlike some Wall Street leaders, Gordon showed himself willing not only to yield responsibility but authority as well. And while he continued to head the firm, serving as its chief executive officer longer than any of his predecessors, it has been DeNunzio who, in Gordon's words, "has been running the place for the last half-dozen years."[47]

A veteran of more than a half century on Wall Street, Gordon, seventy-four years of age in April 1975, was one of the few active investment bankers whose career spanned two eras. When he first arrived on Wall Street investment banking was not too far removed from what it had been at the turn of the century when the elder Morgan presided over much of American finance. Firms then, and for almost another two generations, reflected the personalities and talents of a few key partners. Investment houses still were relatively small organizations, their business conducted mostly by a few partners aided by several clerks, assistants, and stenographers. In 1931 when Gordon took over as active head of Kidder, Peabody, the firm occupied the same Wall Street offices it had in 1922, and the composition of the staff, both in New York and in its Boston headquarters, was just about the size it had been a decade or so earlier.

By 1975 investment banking, like the country and the world, had changed drastically. For one thing, few of Wall Street's recent leaders occupied the positions of authority and influence formerly held by some of the financial district's earlier giants. There appeared to be, observed a *Fortune* writer in 1973, few "strong personalities" left, people who so dominated their houses that it could be said they constituted the firm. Gordon was such a figure, this author said, one of the very few of them left, with little likelihood there would be others like him. In 1975 investment banking had ceased to be a one-person operation; it had become a "team effort," with scores of specialists using expensive and sophisticated technology, including computers. These were the people who presided over departments previously headed by a partner or two.[48] And the firms themselves, once nearly all partnerships, now are mostly corporations, many of them publicly owned. In 1975 corporations accounted for more than half of all broker-dealers registered with the SEC. Expansion and diversification altered not only the organization and operations of investment firms but their appearance as well. Kidder, Peabody's present location at Hanover Square, the firm's headquarters since March 1972, occupies eleven floors, many of them crowded with advanced technological equipment accomplishing jobs few had considered possible at the time Gordon started on his career in finance.

Not only did Gordon himself accommodate to Wall Street's transformation, but he as much as any one helped prepare Kidder, Peabody's transition from one era to the other. Aware that no business could survive much less grow and prosper if its fortune remained tied to a single individual, Gordon from the start sought to develop leaders for the future by recruiting and holding on to good people, "individuals," to use his words, "able to lead the firm into the next generation."[49] The informal policy group set up shortly after the 1931 reorganization was used to recognize and reward talent, a process that became more structured after incorporation and the size of the staff had grown strikingly. The addition of numerous experts able to meet the varied and complex needs of the firm's corporate and other institutional clients made Kidder, Peabody an employer of highly trained specialists, not all of whom appeared likely to achieve the status of former partners. In 1975 when the firm's total employees at home and abroad stood at 2,600, only 150 of them were common shareholders in the corporation, the equivalent position of a former partner.[50] An improved retirement plan, expanded benefits, together with Gordon's policy of developing top-level leaders assured Kidder, Peabody the highly trained personnel necessary to operate a large, full-service international investment banking house.

The firm's present-day management team headed by DeNunzio is one of the youngest on Wall Street. The age of most of its members ranges between forty and fifty years. All of them have an investment in the firm. "There are no fat cats with high salaries at Kidder, Peabody," DeNunzio stressed. "Compensation comes to us at the end of the year when the books are balanced," a policy that has prevailed since the founding of the house over a century ago.[51]

Kidder, Peabody's record of more than a century of investment banking experience is one of the longest in the history of American finance. Not only has the firm participated in most of the major developments that helped shape the growth and character of the securities business, but very often it stood at the forefront of these changes. From the time of the Thayers in the mid-nineteenth century when railroad finance gave birth to many modern investment banking practices, through the era of great mergers and consolidations at the beginning of the twentieth century, on down through World War I, the boom and bust of the 1920s, the new era of federal regulation in the 1930s, and the spectacular changes of the last quarter-century, the firm has occupied a central and influential position in the nation's capital markets.

The corporations Kidder, Peabody has helped finance over

the past 110 years read like a *Who's Who* in American business. Included among these are the leading companies in every major industry, from some of the earliest railroad, industrial, utility, and communications corporations to the most recent pioneers in electronics and computers.

Kidder, Peabody's record in raising capital for both domestic and foreign governments has been equally impressive. The firm has helped finance many state and city governments, providing them with the funds to build all kinds of public facilities, most recently pollution control and hospital and medical care institutions. In 1976, according to *The Daily Bond Buyer,* Kidder, Peabody led all other houses both in the number (twenty-five) and dollar value ($609.6 million) of its management or comanagement of hospital and medical care offerings.[52] And the firm also has continued to be among the leading sponsors of foreign government and corporate securities.

Many profound changes have occurred in the world since Kidder, Peabody was founded at the end of the Civil War. At that time investment bankers, like most business people, operated almost totally free of any legal restraints. Today investment firms "work in a goldfish bowl," said Amyas Ames, the former chairman of Kidder, Peabody's executive committee. In 1865 the firm's corporate clients were almost entirely railroads and the buyers of its securities chiefly wealthy Bostonians and foreign capitalists. Kidder, Peabody's present-day clientele is not only highly varied but scattered across the United States and throughout the world. The firm has been forced to adapt to many changes in its long history. The fact that it has done so not only accounts for its longevity—from shortly after the onset of the age of steam and rails to the era of the atom and space travel—but also suggests that it will continue to adjust to changing financial conditions and requirements.

Notes on the Sources and Secondary Literature

Because of the substantial notes accompanying the text it appears unnecessary to repeat all the works cited in a formal bibliography. The purpose of this note is to explain the nature and extent of Kidder, Peabody's records, single out the principal published documents upon which the text rests, and acknowledge some of the books and articles that were of particular value, either for information on specific topics or for providing insights into the ways investment firms conducted their affairs.

Kidder, Peabody's pre-1931 records, now held by Baker Library, Harvard Graduate School of Business Administration, include an incomplete set of John E. and Nathaniel Thayer's account books, the most important of which are John E. Thayer's "Ledger, 1836–1857" and "Cash Book, 1840–1844," and Nathaniel Thayer's "Ledger A, 1858–1868," and Estate of Nathaniel Thayer, "Ledger, 1883–1913." George E. Ellis, *Mem-*

oir of Nathaniel Thayer, A.M. (J. Wilson, Cambridge, 1885) provides some of the basic facts on an influential, relatively obscure Boston capitalist.

The partnership records of the pre-1931 Kidder, Peabody (1865–1931), also housed at Baker Library, are more numerous than those of the Thayers, but these too are far from complete. They include some of the partners' correspondence, "Confidential Letters" (6 vols., 1883–1929), a set "Record of Clerks" (6 vols., 1880–1927), and two collections, "Circulars" (10 vols., 1895–1927) and "Histories" (16 vols., 1911–1943), each containing mostly announcements and prospectuses of some of the firm's underwritings. This collection, together with a few other isolated items such as the papers dealing with Kidder, Peabody's "Bank Consolidation of 1898," represent most of the early firm's records. A useful supplement to the founders' correspondence at Baker Library is the volume of typescript letters held by the present firm at its New York City office and prepared by Charles H. Wyman, Compiler, "A Souvenir of Henry P. Kidder, Francis H. Peabody, and Oliver W. Peabody from Verbatim Shorthand Notes taken . . . at the Office of Kidder, Peabody & Co., Boston, Mass. (1881–1896)."

Most of the firm's post-1931 records are stored in New York City. These include several partners' files, interoffice memoranda, syndicate agreements, account books, ledgers as well as miscellaneous correspondence with some of the firm's clients. These papers, together with copies of prospectuses of new offerings, trading and brokerage records, and other documents, constitute the single most important collection of the firm's written records. Since so much of Kidder, Peabody's business, like that of most other investment houses, was conducted informally, often by telephone or at meetings with no one taking minutes, the written record needs to be enriched with personal interviews and the oral reminiscences of the participants. Thus far only Frederick L. Moore, among the firm's former partners and present officers, has put his recollections on paper. His "42 Happy Years at Kidder, Peabody" provides information not available elsewhere.

Other essential primary materials are to be found in the hearings and reports of various federal probes into the affairs and practices of the country's major investment houses. Kidder, Peabody partners testified at several of these investigations, all of which are cited in the chapter notes. Probably the most important public source on Kidder, Peabody's history and operations, particularly during the years 1933 through 1947, is the massive trial transcript and extensive documentary exhibits incorporated in the investment banking antitrust case, U.S. District Court, Southern District of New York (Civil No. 43-757), *United States of America v. Henry S. Morgan, et al.*, especially the "Corrected Opinion of Harold R. Medina" (February 4, 1954). The latter has been published by the Arno Press in its series *Wall Street and the Security Markets* (58 vols., New York, 1975). Important material on the new partnership, as told by Albert H. Gordon and others connected with Kidder, Peabody's 1931 reorganization, as well as information on the firm's long association with American Telephone & Telegraph Company bond and stock offerings and other corporate financings, can be found in U.S. Temporary National Economic Committee, *Investigation of Concentration of Economic Power: Hearings . . .* (31 pts., Washington, 1939–1941). Four other federal probes also contain valuable information on Kidder, Peabody. These include the well-publicized investigation headed by Arsène Pujo, U.S. Congress, House, 62d Cong., 3d Sess., *Investigation of Financial and Monetary Conditions in the United States: Hearings . . .* (3 vols., Washington, 1913) and the conclusions drawn from that inquiry, *Report of the Committee Appointed . . . to Investigate the Concentration of Control of Money and Credit* (Washington, 1913); the equally well-known Wall Street probe conducted by Ferdinand Pecora, which made headlines during the darkest years of the depression, U.S. Senate, Committee on Banking and Currency, 73d Cong., 2d Sess., *Stock Exchange Practices: Hearings . . .* (7 pts., Washington, 1931–1933) and its accompanying *Report* (Washington, 1934); and two other widely cited inquiries, one dealing with the activities of American bankers doing business with the Allies prior to the United States' entry into World War I, U.S. Senate, Special Committee Investigating the Munitions Industry, 73d and 74th Congs., *Munitions Industry: Hearings . . .* (40 pts., Washington, 1934–1943) and the second, which delved into Wall Street's postwar international financings, U.S. Senate, Committee on Finance, 72d Cong., 1st Sess., *Sale of Foreign Bonds or Securities in the United States: Hearings . . .* (4 pts., Washington, 1931–1932).

Wall Street bankers long have been the object of much interest, and there is a substantial secondary literature of mixed quality touching upon their activities and affairs. For both information and insights on the pre-1913 period, none is more valuable than Fritz Redlich's, *The Molding of American Banking: Men and Ideas* (2 vols., Hafner Publishing, New York, 1947, 1951). Another particularly helpful work is Margaret G. Myers' volume, "Origins and Development," in Benjamin H. Beckhart, ed., *The New York Money Market* (4 vols., Columbia University Press, New York, 1931–1932). Some of the same topics are touched upon, though less comprehensively, in Robert Sobel's general survey, *The Big Board: A History of the New York Stock Market* (Free Press, New York, 1965). The author's earlier work *Investment Banking in America: A History* (Harvard University Press, Cambridge, Mass., 1970), focuses on change and continuity in the securities business, from the mid-nineteenth century to the 1960s. George W. Edwards, *The Evolution of Finance Capitalism* (London, 1938), continues to be useful for a comparative view of investment banking developments in the United States and Europe. The Federal Reserve Bank of Boston's brief survey, *A History of Investment Banking in New England* (Boston, 1965), contains some interesting details on Kidder, Peabody and its competitors.

Three specialized works on the nineteenth century proved particularly useful. Ralph W. Hidy, *The House of Baring in American Trade & Finance. English Merchant Bankers at Work, 1763–1861* (Harvard University Press, Cambridge, Mass., 1949), and Edwin J. Perkins, *Financing Anglo-American Trade: The House of Brown, 1800–1880* (Harvard University Press, Cambridge, Mass., 1975), provide much valuable information on the way international banking houses conducted their affairs, while Arthur M. Johnson and Barry E. Supple, *Boston Capitalists and Western Railroads: A Study in the Nineteenth Century Railroad Investment Process* (Harvard University Press, Cambridge, Mass., 1967), added many specific details to the Thayer stories and the nature of Kidder, Peabody's role in the affairs of the railroads it financed, notably the Atchison, Topeka & Santa Fe.

For background information on post-World War I developments in the securities business, see John Brooks, *Once in Golconda: A True Drama of Wall Street, 1920–1938* (Harper & Row, New York, 1969), and Robert Sobel, *The Great Bull Market: Wall Street in the 1920's* (Norton, New York, 1968). A specialized work of special relevance to the Kidder, Peabody story is John B. McFerrin, *Caldwell and Company: A Southern Financial Empire* (Vanderbilt University Press, Nashville, Tenn., 1939).

Several works provided much useful material on the many changes that have occurred in the nation's security markets since the end of World War II. Irwin Friend, James R. Longstreet, et al., *Investment Banking and the New Issues Market* (World, Cleveland, 1967), is indispensable. More general analyses of the tumultuous events that shook Wall Street in the 1960s and 1970s include John Brooks, *The Go-Go Years* (Weybright, New York, 1973), Michael C. Jensen, *The Financiers: The World of the Great Wall Street Investment Houses* (Weybright & Talley, New York, 1976), and Robert Sobel's two books, *N.Y.S.E.: A History of the New York Stock Exchange, 1935–1975* (Weybright & Talley, New York, 1975), most of which covers the years after 1942, and, *Inside Wall Street: Continuity and Change in the Financial District* (Norton, New York, 1977), which also focuses on recent developments.

Periodical articles, as the chapter notes make clear, provided much material of both general and specific value. Some of the most useful of these were Richard Sylla, "Forgotten Men of Money: Private Bankers in Early United States History," *The Journal of Economic History*, vol. 36, (March 1976), pp. 173–188;

Frederic C. Jaher, "The Boston Brahmins in the Age of Industrial Capitalism," in Frederic C. Jaher, ed., *The Age of Industrialism in America: Essays in Social Structure and Cultural Values* (Free Press, New York, 1968), pp. 188–262; two pieces by Marian V. Sears, "A Michigan Bureaucrat Promotes the State's Economic Growth: George F. Porter Sells Michigan's Central Railroad to Eastern Capitalists, 1846," *Explorations in Entrepreneurial History*, 2d ser., vol. 3 (Spring–Summer 1966), pp. 200–219; and her equally interesting article, "The National Shawmut Bank Consolidation of 1898," *Business History Review*, vol. 39 (Autumn 1965), pp. 368–390; Dolores Greenberg, "Yankee Financiers and the Establishment of Trans-Atlantic Partnerships: A Reexamination," *Business History*, vol. 16 (January 1974), pp. 17–35; Donald L. Kemmerer, "The Marketing of Securities, 1930–1952," *The Journal of Economic History*, vol. 12 (Fall 1952), pp. 455–469; and Samuel L. Hayes III, "Investment Banking: Power Structure in Flux," *Harvard Business Review* (March–April 1971), pp. 136–152.

Two specialized journals—*The Commercial & Financial Chronicle* and *Finance*—and three newspapers—*The New York Times*, *Herald Tribune* (New York City), and *The Wall Street Journal*—not only added much detail on many topics but also helped shape the entire story.

Notes for Chapter One

1. The principal primary source for the Thayer story is an incomplete set of miscellaneous manuscripts—letterbooks, ledgers, and other account books—deposited in Baker Library, Harvard Graduate School of Business Administration, and hereafter cited as Thayer Mss.
2. *Boston Evening Transcript*, September 29, 1857. See also George E. Ellis, *Memoir of Nathaniel Thayer, A. M.* (Cambridge, 1885), p. 11, and [Abner Forbes], *The Rich Men of Massachusetts* (2d. ed., Boston, 1852), p. 66.
3. John E. Thayer, "Ledger, 1836–1857," Thayer Mss.
4. For an important reappraisal of the role of private banking in the antebellum era, see: Richard Sylla, "Forgotten Men of Money: Private Bankers in Early United States History," *The Journal of Economic History*, vol. 36 (March 1976), pp. 173–188, and the comments by Lance E. Davis and Thomas C. Cochran which follow the article.
5. *Boston Evening Transcript*, September 29, 1857.
6. Frederic C. Jaher, "The Boston Brahmins in the Age of Industrial Capitalism," in

Frederic C. Jaher, ed., *The Age of Industrialism in America: Essays in Social Structure and Cultural Values* (New York, 1968), pp. 188–262, treats the role and activities of Boston's elite in finance and business.

7. John E. Thayer, "Ledger, 1836–1857," Thayer Mss. See also Arthur M. Johnson and Barry E. Supple, *Boston Capitalists and Western Railroads: A Study in the Nineteenth Century Investment Process* (Cambridge, 1967), 41n, 45n.
8. John E. Thayer, "Ledger, 1836–1857," Thayer Mss.
9. Ibid. See also Forbes, *Rich Men of Massachusetts,* p. 66, and *Boston Evening Transcript,* September 29, 1857.
10. [Clarence W. Barron and Joseph G. Martin], *The Boston Stock Exchange* (Boston, 1893), pages unnumbered. See also Ellis, *Memoir of Nathaniel Thayer,* passim.
11. Ellis, *Memoir of Nathaniel Thayer,* passim; State Street Trust Company, *Other Merchants and Sea Captains of Old Boston* (Boston, 1919), p. 15.
12. John E. Thayer, "Cash Book, 1840–1844," Thayer Mss.
13. John E. Thayer, *The Will of John Eliot Thayer* (Boston, 1857).
14. [Barron and Martin], *The Boston Stock Exchange,* passim.
15. Nathaniel Thayer, "Ledger A, 1858–1868," Thayer Mss.
16. Ralph W. Hidy, *The House of Baring in American Trade and Finance. English Merchant Bankers at work, 1763–1861* (Cambridge, 1949), p. 366; Gerald T. White, *A History of the Massachusetts Hospital Life Insurance Company* (Cambridge, 1955). p. 88.
17. Marian V. Sears, "A Michigan Bureaucrat Promotes the State's Economic Growth: George F. Porter Sells Michigan's Central Railroad to Eastern Capitalists, 1846," *Explorations in Entrepreneurial History,* 2d. ser., vol. 3 (Spring–Summer 1966), pp. 203, 213. See also Dorothy R. Adler *British Investments in American Railways, 1834–1898,* ed. Muriel E. Hidy (Charlottesville, 1970), 54n.
18. Nathaniel Thayer, "Ledger A, 1859–1868," Thayer Mss. See also Johnson and Supple, *Boston Capitalists and Western Railroads,* 45n, pp. 49–50, 57, 90, 100, 103, 116.
19. Hidy, *House of Baring,* pp. 447–448, 462–463, and Adler, *British Investments in American Railways,* 52n.
20. Nathaniel Thayer, "Ledger A, 1858–1868," Thayer Mss.
21. Ibid. See also Johnson and Supple, *Boston Capitalists and Western Railroads,* pp. 179, 228, 238, passim; Adler, *British Investments in American Railways,* 52n.
22. Nathaniel Thayer, "Ledger A, 1858–1868," and Estate of Nathaniel Thayer, "Ledger, 1883–1913," Thayer Mss.
23. Francis H. Peabody to Oliver W. Peabody, April [?], 1883, in Charles H. Wyman, comp., "A Souvenir of Henry P. Kidder, Francis H. Peabody, and Oliver W. Peabody from Verbatim Shorthand Notes taken by Charles A. Wyman at the Office of Kidder, Peabody & Co., Boston, Mass. (1881–1896)," typescript in Kidder, Peabody & Co., Inc., Records, New York City.
24. Brown, Shipley & Co. (London) to Brown Brothers & Co. (New York), November 9, 1864, in Brown Brothers-Harriman Historical File, New-York Historical Society.

Notes for Chapter Two

1. Kidder, Peabody & Co. Records, New York. See also the *Boston Evening Transcript,* April 3, 1865.
2. Edwin A. Stone, *A Century of Boston Banking* (Boston, 1894), p. 56. The figures

cited for the different types of institutions were derived from listings in the *Bankers' Almanac and Boston Almanac* for 1865.

3. Henry Hall, ed., *America's Successful Men of Affairs* (2 vols., New York, 1895–1896), vol. 2, pp. 458–59. See also *The New York Times*, January 29, 1886.
4. The Boston Herald, *Commercial and Financial New England* (Boston, 1906), p. 29. See also "Kidder, Peabody & Company," *The Bankers' Magazine*, vol. 76 (February 1904), p. 266.
5. "In Memory of Companion Oliver White Peabody, Lieutenant Colonel, Forty-fifth Regiment Mass. Volunteers," in Kidder Peabody & Co. Records, New York City. This reference is to a collection of miscellaneous letters, typescripts, memoranda, and other papers in the firm's New York City offices. Hereafter cited as KP & Co., Records—NYC. See also *Appleton's Annual Cyclopaedia*, vol. 2, n.s., 1896 (New York, 1897), p. 578.
6. Kidder, Peabody & Co., "Partnership Agreement," in Kidder, Peabody & Co., Records, Baker Library, Harvard Graduate School of Business Administration. Hereafter cited as KP & Co., Records—Baker.
7. "Frank George Webster," *Stone & Webster Journal*, vol. 46 (February 1930), pp. 193–195, and *The Commercial & Financial Chronicle*, vol. 130 (January 25, 1930), p. 572.
8. Kidder, Peabody & Co., "Regulations" (December 7, 1868), in KP & Co., Records—NYC.
9. KP & Co., Records—Baker.
10. Quoted in Edwin J. Perkins, *Financing Anglo-American Trade: The House of Brown, 1800–1880* (Cambridge, 1975), p. 145.
11. KP & Co., Records—NYC. See also "Kidder, Peabody & Company," *The Banker and Tradesman*, vol. 33 (June 10, 1905), pp. 1139–1141; *Finance and Industry: The New York Stock Exchange: Banks, Bankers, Business Houses, and Moneyed Institutions of the Great Metropolis of the United States* (New York, 1886), p. 74; *The Banker's Magazine*, n.s., vol. 14 (July 1879), p. 46; ibid., vol. 40 (February 1886), p. 626, and *The New York Times*, January 29, 1886.
12. Fritz Redlich, *The Molding of American Banking: Men and Ideas* (2 vols., New York, 1947, 1951), vol. 2, p. 365.
13. Francis W. Peabody to Henry P. Kidder, August 9, 1883, Kidder, Peabody & Co., "Confidential Letters," vol. 1, p. 79, KP & Co., Records—Baker.
14. KP & Co., Records—Baker.
15. Frank G. Webster to Francis H. Peabody, September 20, 1886, Kidder, Peabody & CO., "Confidential Letters," vol. 1, pp. 43–51, KP & Co., Records—Baker.
16. Ibid.
17. Arthur M. Johnson and Barry E. Supple, *Boston Capitalists and Western Railroads: A Study in the Nineteenth-Century Investment Process* (Cambridge, 1967), pp. 291–293, 298–317; and *Boston Evening Transcript*, May 13 and 17, 1882. See also Clarence W. Barron, *More They Told Barron: Conversations and Revelations of an American Pepys in Wall Street* (New York, 1931), p. 118.
18. Kidder, Peabody & Co. to Baring Brothers & Co., October 19, 1887, in Kidder, Peabody & Co., "Letterbooks," vol. 1, pp. 100–107, KP & Co., Records—Baker.
19. Frank G. Webster to Francis H. Peabody, September 30, 1886, "Confidential Letters," pp. 46–47, KP & Co., Records—Baker.
20. Kidder, Peabody & Co. to Atchison, Topeka & Santa Fe Finance Committee, July 30, 1888; Kidder, Peabody & Co., to Wm. B. Strong, October 2 and 16, 1888; Kidder, Peabody & Co. to Baring Brothers & Co., October 9, 1882; Francis H.

Peabody to J. J. McCook, October 20, 1898, "Confidential Letters," vol. 2, pp. 59, 68–73, KP & Co., Records—Baker. See also Johnson and Supple, *Boston Capitalists and Western Railroads,* pp. 323–326.

21. Born in Cambridge, Massachusetts, on August 23, 1841, Magoun prepared to enter Harvard University but chose to go into business, beginning his career as a clerk in a Boston varnish factory. From there he went to Kidder, Peabody in 1867, starting as a clerk. The next year he represented the firm in New York, and in 1872 he was made a partner. See KP & Co., Records—Baker, and *The Commercial & Financial Chronicle,* vol. 57 (December 23, 1893), p. 1060.
22. Johnson and Supple, *Boston Capitalists and Western Railroads,* pp. 326–327; Barron, *More They Told Barron,* p. 131, and Dorothy R. Adler *British Investments in American Railways, 1834–1898,* ed. Muriel E. Hidy (Charlottesville, 1970), pp. 171–172.
23. Johnson and Supple, *Boston Capitalists and Western Railroads,* p. 326, and Barron, *More They Told Barron,* p. 131.
24. *The Commercial & Financial Chronicle,* vol. 57 (December 23, 1893), p. 1060.
25. Francis H. Peabody to Edwin H. Abbott, October 23, 1889, and Francis H. Peabody to George C. Magoun, December 12, 1889, "Confidential Letters," vol. 2, pp. 100–103, 106; KP & Co., Records—Baker.
26. On the European connections of American private bankers, see: Dolores Greenberg, "Yankee Financiers and the Establishment of Trans-Atlantic Partnerships: A Re-examination," *Business History,* vol. 16 (January 1974), pp. 17–35.
27. Oliver W. Peabody to [Thomas?] Baring, December 3, 1886, "Confidential Letters," vol. 1, p. 62; Kidder, Peabody & Co. to Baring Brothers & Co., October 19, 1887, ibid., vol. 2, p. 107; Francis H. Peabody to Thomas Baring, January 5, 1898, ibid., vol. 3, p. 228.
28. Vincent P. Carosso, *Investment Banking in America: A History* (Cambridge, 1970). See Chapter 2 for the major techniques bankers employed to finance corporations.
29. Francis H. Peabody to John Murray Forbes, August 31, 1882, in Charles H. Wyman, comp., "A Souvenir of Henry P. Kidder, Francis H. Peabody, and Oliver W. Peabody from Verbatim Shorthand Notes taken by Charles A. Wyman at the Office of Kidder, Peabody & Co., Boston, Mass. (1881–1896)," typescript in Kidder, Peabody & Co., Records, New York City.
30. *Boston Evening Transcript,* May 26, 1882, and *The New York Times,* January 29, 1886. See also *The Bankers' Magazine,* vol. 14, n.s. (July 1879), p. 45; and Clarence W. Barron and Joseph G. Martin, *The Boston Stock Exchange* (Boston, 1893), p. 78.
31. Herbert L. Satterlee, *J. Pierpont Morgan, An Intimate Portrait* (New York, 1939), pp. 249–250; Edward C. Kirkland, *Charles Francis Adams, Jr., 1835–1915: The Patrician at Bay* (Cambridge, 1965), pp. 119–120, and *The Commercial & Financial Chronicle,* vol. 43 (January 12, 1889), pp. 67–68.
32. Francis H. Peabody to President Benjamin Harrison, December 29, 1882, in Wyman, comp., "Souvenir of Henry P. Kidder, Francis H. Peabody, and Oliver W. Peabody," pp. 149–150.
33. Francis H. Peabody to Oliver W. Peabody, July 7, 1893, in ibid., p. 173. See also Stone, *A Century of Boston Banking,* 28n.
34. Oliver W. Peabody to William Everett, March 31, 1894, in Wyman, comp., "Souvenir of Henry P. Kidder, Francis H. Peabody, and Oliver W. Peabody," pp. 184–186.
35. Frank G. Webster to Elijah A. Morse, December 28, 1894, in ibid., pp. 195–197.
36. Francis H. Peabody to Oliver W. Peabody, July 21, 1896, in ibid., pp. 201–203.

37. KP & Co., Records—Baker. See particularly the firm's "Circulars."
38. U.S. Temporary National Economic Committee, *Investigation of Concentration of Economic Power, Hearings. . . .* (31 pts., Washington, 1939–41), vol. 23, p. 12125; U.S. Federal Communications Commission, *Telephone Investigation: Proposed Report. . . .* (Washington, 1938), pp. 96–97; *The Commercial & Financial Chronicle,* vol. 73 (December 12, 1901), p. 1316, and ibid., vol. 74 (January 4, 1902), pp. vi–vii. See also Jonas W. Stehman, *The Financial History of the American Telephone and Telegraph Company* (Boston, 1925), pp. 100–103, and N. R. Danielian, *AT&T: The Story of Industrial Conquest* (New York, 1939), pp. 49–50.
39. Robert Winsor to Lord Revelstoke, March 25, 1904, KP & Co., Records—Boston, Henry Spencer Files; *The Commercial & Financial Chronicle,* vol. 80 (March 4, 1905), p. 999, and ibid. (March 18, 1905), pp. xiv, 1113.
40. U.S. Temporary National Economic Committee, *Investigation of Concentration of Economic Power,* 23, pp. 11849–11852; U.S. Federal Communications Commission, *Telephone Investigation, Proposed Report,* pp. 504–505; *The Commercial & Financial Chronicle,* vol. 82 (February 17, 1906), p. 394, and ibid. (March 10, 1906), pp. 571.
41. New York State, *Final Report of the Joint Committee . . . on Telephone and Telegraph Companies* (Albany, 1915), pp. 176–177.
42. Kidder, Peabody & Co. to Russell, Brewster & Co., July 27, 1909, KP & Co., Records—NYC.
43. KP & Co., Records—Baker and NYC. See also Federal Reserve Bank of Boston, *A History of Investment Banking in New England* (Boston, 1965), pp. 19–21.
44. KP & Co., Records and "Circulars"—Baker. See also Benjamin H. Beckhart, ed., *The New York Money Market* (4 vols., New York, 1931–32), vol. 1, p. 292, and *The Commercial & Financial Chronicle,* vol. 72 (April 27, 1901), p. 799.
45. Chandler Hovey to author October 26, 1961.
46. KP & Co., Records—Baker.
47. Thomas Baring to Oliver W. Peabody, August 20, 1886, and Oliver W. Peabody to Thomas Baring, September 12, 1886, "Confidential Letters," vol. 1, pp. 36–42; KP & Co., "Record of Clerks," In KP & Co., Records—Baker. See also *The Banker's Magazine,* vol. 40 (February 1886), p. 626. The newly admitted Boston partners included Frank G. Webster and two sons of the founders: Charles A. Kidder, twenty-eight years old and the first college graduate (Harvard) to join the firm, and Francis Peabody's thirty-year-old son, Frank E., who had been with Kidder, Peabody since 1875. The two newly appointed New York partners, George F. Crane and Herbert L. Griggs, had started with Kidder, Peabody in the late 1860s upon graduating from high school, moving to New York after the firm's office had been made a branch.
48. KP & Co., Records—Baker. See also *The Banker's Magazine,* vol. 45 (April 1891), p. 811, and *The Commercial & Financial Chronicle,* vol. 52 (May 2, 1891), p. 669.
49. KP & Co., Records—Baker, and *The Commercial & Financial Chronicle,* vol. 82 (March 24, 1906, p. 666. Baring, Magoun & Co. was dissolved in March 1906, thirteen years after Magoun's death and after all four of the other original partners had retired. The new firm that took its place, Baring & Co., organized by Hugo Baring, served as Kidder, Peabody's New York agent until January 1908, when Hugo Baring returned to England and the partnership he headed was discontinued. Kidder, Peabody took over Baring & Co.'s business and operated it as a branch of the Boston partnership with four resident managers, two of whom (William L. Benedict and Charles S. Sargent) were made partners in January 1911.
50. Charles A. Kidder, who had become a partner in July 1886 shortly after his father's

death, resigned in April 1889, returning to the firm in June 1901, but not as a partner. See KP & Co., "Record of Clerks"—Baker.

51. KP & Co., "Record of Clerks"—Baker. See also *Who Was Who in America . . . 1897–1942* (Chicago, 1939), p. 1367. Oliver Peabody died in October 1896, but no new partners were added for nine years. In October 1905, a month after Francis Peabody's death, William Endicott III and Frank W. Remick were made partners. Both had been clerks for a long time: Endicott joined the firm upon graduating from Harvard in 1887, and Remick, Kidder, Peabody's member of the Boston Stock Exchange since 1900, started with the firm in 1879.
52. "Kidder, Peabody & Company," *The Bankers Magazine*, vol. 76 (February 1908), p. 267. See also "Boston Financiers Honored," *American Banker*, vol. 69 (February 6, 1904), p. 254, and *The Commercial & Financial Chronicle*, vol. 71 (September 23, 1905), p. 949. Clarence W. Barron, the founder of the *Boston News Bureau* (1887) and other financial journals, provided another explanation for "the secret of why Winsor runs the firm." Barron attributed it to the fact that he had invested $500,000 in the firm, borrowing $150,000 from his two brothers and the balance from William Gaston, board chairman of the National Shawmut Bank. See Barron, *More They Told Barron*, p. 198.
53. Frank G. Webster to Frank W. Remick, n.d. [July 1920?], KP & Co., Records—NYC.
54. Ibid.
55. KP & Co., "Record of Clerks"—Baker, and Chandler Hovey to author, October 26, 1961.
56. *Boston Evening Transcript*, April 1, 1882.
57. "Kidder, Peabody & Company," p. 269. See also the Boston Herald, *Commercial and Financial New England* (Boston, 1906), pp. 28–32.
58. KP & Co., Records—Baker. See especially "Confidential Letters," vol. 4, pp. 66–67. Consult also Frank W. Remick to Charles S. Sargent, Jr., July 20, 1920, KP & Co., Records—NYC. In March 1905, at the time he executed his last will, Francis Peabody established a $700,000 trust fund for his wife, an amount his son said represented "about a third of his [father's] active partnership capital." Peabody's will authorized the trustees (his son and Endicott) to keep the $700,000 "in the partnership business of Kidder, Peabody & Co. for not over a year," after which the money was to be invested. See Francis H. Peabody to Lawrence A. Ford, March 28, 1905, and Frank E. Peabody to Lord Revelstoke, October 18, 1905, "Confidential Letters," vol. 3, pp. 624–625, 635–636, KP & Co., Records—Baker.
59. Kidder, Peabody & Co. to Minister of the Treasury (Rome), December 18, 1907, "Confidential Letters," vol. 4, p. 54.
60. U.S. House of Representatives, Committee on Banking and Currency, *Report of the Committee Appointed . . . to Investigate the Concentration of Control of Money and Credit* (Washington, 1913), pp. 76–77.
61. For a brief review of the impact of the Pujo investigation on subsequent Wall Street probes, see: Vincent P. Carosso, "The Wall Street Money Trust from Pujo through Medina," *Business History Review*, vol. 47 (Winter 1973), pp. 421–437.
62. U.S. House, *Report of the Committee . . . to Investigate the Concentration of Control of Money and Credit*, p. 56.
63. Kidder, Peabody & Co. to Samuel Untermeyer (sic), December 5, 1912, "Confidential Letters," vol. 6, p. 17. KP & Co., Records—Baker.
64. U.S. House, *Report of the Committee . . . to Investigate the Concentration of Control of Money and Credit*, pp. 76–77. See also U.S. House of Representatives, Commit-

tee on Banking and Currency, *Investigation of Financial and Monetary Conditions in the United States: Hearings. . . .* (3 vols., Washington, 1913), vol. 2, pp. 2051–2087.

65. U.S. House, *Report of the Committee . . . to Investigate the Concentration of Control of Money and Credit,* p. 77; and U.S. House, *Investigation of Financial and Monetary Conditions,* vol. 2, p. 2053.
66. U.S. House, *Report of the Committee . . . to Investigate the Concentration of Control of Money and Credit,* p. 159.
67. Ibid., p. 161.
68. Carosso, *Investment Banking in America,* chap. 8, deals with the organization of the Investment Bankers Association.

Notes for Chapter Three

1. Herbert D. Seibert & Co., *The Business and Financial Record of World War Years* (New York, 1939), pp. 2, 5–6. See also Board of Governors of the Federal Reserve System, *Banking and Monetary Statistics* (Washington, 1943), p. 485.
2. Kidder, Peabody & Co. to Baring Brothers, February 19, 1914, "Letterbooks," vol. 6, p. 62, KP & Co., Records—Baker.
3. Gordon B. Anderson, "The Effect of the War on New Security Issues in the United States," *The Annals,* vol. 68 (November 1916), p. 119.
4. U.S. Treasury, *Annual Report . . . 1914* (Washington, 1915), pp. 24–25; *The Commercial & Financial Chronicle,* vol. 99 (August 8, 1914), p. 385.
5. Arthur S. Link, *Wilson: The Struggle for Neutrality, 1914–1915* (Princeton, 1960), p. 100. A descendant of a Mayflower family, Benedict joined Kidder, Peabody in October 1878 at the age of eighteen. In December 1907, after the dissolution of Baring, Magoun & Co., he was made manager of the firm's New York City office. Four years later he became a partner. See Kidder, Peabody & Co., "Record of Clerks," KP & Co., Records—Baker, and *Who Was Who in America . . . 1897–1942* (Chicago, 1936).
6. Kidder, Peabody & Co. to Baring Brothers, October 9, 1914, "Confidential Letters," vol. 6, pp. 86–88, KP & Co., Records—Baker.
7. William J. Shultz and M. R. Caine, *Financial Development of the United States* (New York, 1937), pp. 505–506.
8. Kidder, Peabody & Co., "Circulars," vol. 2, pp. 170, 178, KP & Co., Records—Baker.
9. Harold F. Williamson, *Winchester: The Gun that Won the West* (Washington, 1952), pp. 218–24, 260; *The Commercial & Financial Chronicle,* vol. 102 (January 29, 1916), p. 443; ibid. (February 26, 1916), p. 810; and ibid. (March 4, 1916), p. 891.
10. Kidder, Peabody & Co. to Baring Brothers, January 27, 1916, "Confidential Letters," vol. 6, p. 101, KP & Co., Records—Baker.
11. Kidder, Peabody & Co., "Circulars," vol. 2, pp. 193–194, and vol. 3, pp. 15–23, 46–47, 54, KP & Co., Records—Baker.
12. Ibid., vol. 3, p. 56.
13. John S. Snyder, "Security Issues in the United States: 1909–1920," *The Review of Economic Statistics,* vol. 3 (May 28, 1921), p. 102; and *The Daily Bond Buyer,* November 27, 1950. See also Seibert & Co., *Business and Financial Record of World War Years,* pp. 254–255.
14. Kidder, Peabody & Co., "Record of Clerks," KP & Co., Records—Baker.
15. Kidder, Peabody & Co., "Circulars," vol. 3, p. 99, KP & Co., Records—Baker.
16. U.S. Department of Commerce, *Historical Statistics of the United States Colonial Times to 1957* (Washington, 1961), pp. 126, 139.

17. Ibid., pp. 658–659, and George W. Dowrie and Douglas R. Fuller, *Investments* (2d. ed., New York, 1950), p. 32.
18. Henry Spencer to author, June 18,1975, and Walter H. Trumbull to author, June 18, 1975.
19. Arthur Pound and Samuel Taylor Moore, eds., *They Told Barron: Conversations and Revelations of an American Pepys in Wall Street* (New York, 1930), p. 305.
20. Kidder, Peabody & Co., "Histories," KP & Co., Records—Baker.
21. KP & Co., Records—NYC.
22. Walter H. Trumbull to author, June 18, 1975.
23. Charles Francis Adams to H. B. Thayer, July 15, 1921, and H. B. Thayer to Robert Winsor, July 28, 1921, KP & Co., Records—NYC.
24. H. B. Thayer to Robert Winsor, November 10, 1922, KP & Co., Records—NYC. See also John Brooks, *Telephone: The First Hundred Years* (New York, 1976), pp. 165–166.
25. Kidder, Peabody & Co., "Circulars," vol. 11, p. 94, KP & Co., Records—Baker.
26. Donald Ward to author, June 25, 1975, and U.S. Senate, Committee on Finance, 72d Cong., 1st Sess., *Sale of Foreign Bonds in the United States: Hearings. . . .* (4 pts., Washington, 1931–1932), vol. 1, pp. 56–57.
27. Donald Ward to Author, June 25, 1975.
28. [Walter S. Gifford?] to H. Blair-Smith, July 21, 1921, KP & Co., Records—NYC.
29. Walter H. Trumbull to author, June 18, 1975; Henry Spencer to author, June 18, 1975; Donald Ward to author, June 25, 1975; and *The Commercial & Financial Chronicle*, vol. 114 (May 6, 1922), pp. 1955–1956.
30. Albert H. Gordon, "Memorandum to Partners," December 23, 1937, KP & Co., Records—NYC.
31. U.S. Temporary National Economic Committee, *Investigation of Concentration of Economic Power: Hearings. . . .* (31 Pts., Washington, 1939–1941), vol. 23, pp. 12210–12211, 12218.
32. Albert H. Gordon, "Memorandum to Partners," December 23, 1937, KP & Co., Records—NYC.
33. KP & Co., Records—NYC.
34. "Kidder, Peabody & Co.," booklet, dated January 1923, KP & Co., Records—NYC.
35. Henry Spencer to author, June 18, 1975; Donald Ward to author, June 25, 1975, and KP & Co., Records—NYC.
36. Henry Spencer to author, June 18, 1975, and Donald Ward to author, June 25, 1975.
37. KP & Co., Records—Baker; U.S. Securities and Exchange Commission, *Investment Trusts and Investment Companies: Report. . . .* (5 pts., Washington, 1939–1942), vol. 1, pp. 81–83.
38. American Acceptance Council, *Facts and Figures Relating to the American Money Market* (New York, 1934), p. 94.
39. Clyde W. Phelps, *The Foreign Expansion of American Banks* (New York, 1927). p. 174, and KP & Co., Records—Baker.
40. KP & Co., Records—Baker.
41. U.S. Securities and Exchange Commission, *Investment Trusts and Investment Companies: Report*, vol. 1, p. 36.
42. KP & Co., Records—Baker.
43. Walter H. Trumbull to author, June 18, 1975, and Donald Ward to author, June 25, 1975.
44. Quoted in *The New York Times*, August 18, 1937.
45. KP & Co., Records—Baker. See also *The New York Times*, June 10, 1926.
46. KP & Co., Records—Baker.

47. Ibid. See also William H. Steiner, *Investment Trusts: American Experience* (New York, 1929), pp. 132–134.
48. KP & Co., Records—Baker.
49. Kidder, Peabody & Co., "Circulars," vol. 10, p. 129; and ibid., vol. 11, p. 79, KP & Co., Records—Baker.
50. *The Commercial & Financial Chronicle*, vol. 125 (July 9, 1927), p. 201.
51. KP & Co., Records—Baker. In 1939 The Kidder Peabody Trust Company became part of Boston's State Street Trust Company.
52. Ibid.
53. Quoted in *The New York Times*, August 18, 1937.
54. Walter H. Trumbull to author, June 18, 1975, and Henry Spencer to author, June 18, 1975.
55. *The New York Times*, March 8, 1921, Julv 18, 1922, and March 10, 1927.
56. Donald Ward to author, June 25, 1975, and Alfred E. Borneman to author, June 25, 1975.
57. Walter H. Trumbull to author, June 18, 1975; Frederick L. Moore, "42 Happy Years at Kidder, Peabody," Typescript reminiscences in KP & Co., Records—NYC; U.S. Temporary National Economic Committee, *Investigation of Concentration of Economic Power*, vol. 23, p. 11943.
58. KP & Co., Records—NYC. Walter H. Trumbull to author, June 18, 1975.
59. "Notes taken by Henry Spencer at a Meeting with Gaston B. Snow," May 14, 1968, in Henry Spencer Files, KP & Co., Records—Boston. The story of the Nashville firm is told in John B. McFerrin, *Caldwell and Company: A Southern Financial Empire* (Chapel Hill, 1939).
60. Walter H. Trumbull to author, June 18, 1975, and Herbert Spencer to author, June 18, 1975. The eleven partners admitted to the firm with their dates of admission were: William Holway Hill and Alexander Winsor (November 1926), John R. Chapin, Walter H. Trumbull, Richard R. Williams, Daniel W. Weeks, John Elliott (January 1928), and Robert Winsor, Jr., John A. Remick, William B. Snow, and Howard N. Flanders (August 1929). Only Alexander Winsor, the youngest son of the head of the house, and his son-in-law, Trumbull, had been with Kidder, Peabody less than 10 years. Five of the others—Hill, Williams, Weeks, Robert Winsor, Jr., and Flanders—had been with the firm for more than twenty years. See Kidder, Peabody & Co., "Record of Clerks," KP & Co., Records—Baker.
61. Albert H. Gordon to John M. Olin, November 10, 1939, in *U.S. v. Henry S. Morgan, et al.*, "Plaintiff's Exhibit, No. 1072" (April 6, 1949), pp. 4215–4216.

Notes for Chapter Four

1. The other members of the revolving credit, with the amount each contributed, were: First National Bank of Boston ($1.25 million), Bankers Trust Company ($1 million), Guaranty Trust Company ($1 million), National Shawmut Bank of Boston ($750,000), First National Bank of the City of New York ($500,000), Merchants National Bank of Boston ($250,000), and Second National Bank of Boston ($250,-000). See Albert H. Gordon to John M. Olin, November 10, 1939, in *U.S. v. Henry S. Morgan, et al.*, "Plaintiff's Exhibit No. 1072" (April 6, 1949), pp. 4215–4216; and Stuart W. Cragin to Henry W. Spencer, January 22, 1970, in Henry W. Spencer Files, Kidder, Peabody & Co., Boston.
2. Albert H. Gordon to John M. Olin, November 10, 1939, in *U.S. v. Henry S. Morgan, et al.*, "Plaintiff's Exhibit No. 1072" (April 6, 1949), p. 4216; and ibid., "Transcript of Trial, Defendants' Opening—Mr. Webster" (March 6, 1951), p.

4016. The other contributors included Lee, Higginson & Co. ($500,000), J. L. Richards ($250,000), Frederic E. Snow ($250,000), Mortimer L. Schiff ($250,000), National Shawmut Bank ($125,000), First National-Old Colony Corporation ($125,000), Mrs. Susan R. Chapin ($200,000), Homer Loring ($100,000), Hornblower & Weeks ($100,000), Harris, Forbes & Co. ($100,000), and Koppers Co. ($100,000). See *The New York Times,* July 27, 1937.

3. Arthur Young & Co., Audit, December 5, 1930, KP & Co., Records—NYC. See also Albert H. Gordon to John M. Olin, November 10, 1939, in *U.S. v. Henry S. Morgan, et al.,* "Plaintiff's Exhibit No. 1072" (April 6, 1949), p. 4216.
4. Albert H. Gordon to John M. Olin, November 10, 1939, in *U.S. v. Henry S. Morgan, et al.,* "Plaintiff's Exhibit No. 1072" (April 6, 1949), pp. 4216–4217; U.S. Temporary National Economic Committee, *Investigation of Concentration of Economic Power: Hearings. . . .* (31 pts., Washington, 1931–41), vol. 23, 11945–11949, and "Edwin S. Webster, Jr.," *Stone & Webster Journal,* vol. 48 (April 1931), p. 235.
5. *U.S. v. Henry S. Morgan, et al.,* "Transcript of Trial, Defendants' Opening—Mr. Webster" (March 6, 1951), p. 4051; Chandler Hovey to author, October 26, 1961, and *The New York Times,* March 17, 1931.
6. *U.S. v. Henry S. Morgan, et al.,* "Transcript of Trial, Defendants' Opening—Mr. Webster" (March 6, 1951), p. 4099; Albert H. Gordon to John M. Olin, November 10, 1939, in ibid., "Plaintiff's Exhibit No. 1072" (April 6, 1949), p. 4217, and *Harvard Class of 1923: Fiftieth Anniversary Report* (Cambridge, 1973), p. 213.
7. Chandler Hovey to Edwin S. Webster, Jr., February [?], 1931, and February 16, 1931, KP & Co., Records—NYC.
8. *U.S. v. Henry S. Morgan, et al.,* "Transcript of Trial, Plaintiff's Case—Deposition of Gordon" (May 3, 1951), p. 6083.
9. Albert H. Gordon to John M. Olin, November 10, 1939, *U.S. v. Henry S. Morgan, et al.,* "Plaintiff's Exhibit No. 1072" (April 6, 1949), p. 4217, and U.S. Temporary National Economic Committee, *Investigation of Concentration of Economic Power,* vol. 23, p. 11945.
10. Albert H. Gordon to John M. Olin, November 10, 1939, in *U.S. v. Henry S. Morgan, et al.,* "Plaintiff's Exhibit No. 1072" (April 6, 1949), p. 4218, and ibid., "Transcript of Trial, Defendants Opening—Mr. Webster" (March 6, 1951), p. 4017. The executors of Frederic E. Snow, one of the contributors to the $5 million pool that organized itself as the Commonwealth Corporation, subsequently sued J. P. Morgan & Co. on the grounds that at the time the loan was made the Wall Street house had guaranteed repayment, which was not the case at all. Snow's executors lost the suit, and during the course of the proceedings the auditor who reviewed the Commonwealth Corporation's books testified that "none of the five million had been repaid;" nor did he "think it would be." Quoted in *The New York Times,* July 27, 1937.
11. "Agreement of Partnership," dated March 6, 1931, in Henry Spencer Files, KP & Co., Records—Boston.
12. Chandler Hovey to author, October 25, 1961, and Donald Ward to author, July 25, 1975.
13. Robert Sobel, *The Big Board: A History of the New York Stock Market* (New York, 1965), pp. 280–281.
14. Albert H. Gordon to author, July 25, 1975. See also Albert H. Gordon to John M. Olin, November 10, 1939, in *U.S. v. Henry S. Morgan, et al.,* "Plaintiff's Exhibit No. 1072" (April 6, 1949), p. 4220.
15. Albert H. Gordon to Chandler Hovey, October 26, 1931, in KP & Co., Records—NYC; *U.S. v. Henry S. Morgan, et al.,* "Transcript of Trial, Defendants' Opening—

Mr. Webster" (March 6, 1951), pp. 4046, 4051–4052, and Frederick L. Moore, "42 Happy Years at Kidder, Peabody," typescript reminiscences in KP & Co., Records—NYC. See also *The New York Times,* December 24, 1931.

16. Moore, "42 Happy Years at Kidder, Peabody," p. 6; and E. Merrill Darling to Alfred E. Borneman, March 23, 1966, KP & Co., Records—NYC.

Notes for Chapter Five

1. Vincent P. Carosso, *Investment Banking in America: A History* (Cambridge, 1970), Chaps. 15 and 16. See also Susan E. Kennedy, *The Banking Crisis of 1933* (Lexington, 1973), Chap. 5.
2. Quoted in *The New York Times,* August 18, 1937. See also ibid., May 30 and November 7, 1931, and September 29, 1933.
3. Carosso, *Investment Banking in America,* pp. 352–368. See also Michael E. Parrish, *Securities Regulation and the New Deal* (New Haven, 1970), Chaps. 1–4, and George Stigler, "Public Regulation of the Securities Markets," *The Journal of Business,* vol. 37 (April 1964), pp. 117–142, and "Comment," ibid., vol. 37 (October 1964), pp. 414–422.
4. Carosso, *Investment Banking in America,* pp. 368–376. See also Kennedy, *The Banking Crisis of 1933,* Chap. 9, and Helen M. Burns, *The American Banking Community and the New Deal Banking Reforms, 1933–1945* (Westport, 1975), Chaps. 3 and 4.
5. *U.S. v. Henry S. Morgan, et al.,* "Transcript of Trial, Defendants' Opening—Mr. Webster" (March 6, 1951), pp. 4052–4057, and ibid., "Corrected Opinion of Harold R. Medina" (February 4, 1954), p. 78. See also *The New York Times,* April 27, 1933, and June 2 and 15, 1934.
6. Carosso, *Investment Banking in America,* pp. 376–379. See also Parrish, *Securities Regulation and the New Deal,* Chaps. 5, 6 and Ralph DeBedts, *The New Deal's SEC* (New York, 1964), Chap. 3.
7. U.S. Senate, Committee on Banking and Currency, 72d and 73d Congs., *Stock Exchange Practices: Hearings. . . .* (20 pts. in 9 vols., Washington, 1932–1934), vol. 15, p. 6868.
8. Carosso, *Investment Banking in America,* pp. 382–407.
9. U.S. Department of Commerce, *Historical Statistics of the United States Colonial Times to 1957* (Washington, 1961), pp. 658–659. See also Stuart Chase, "Shadow Over Wall Street," *Harper's Magazine,* vol. 180 (March 1940), p. 364.
10. Donald Ward to author, June 25, 1975, and Frederick L. Moore, "42 Happy Years at Kidder, Peabody," typescript in KP & Co., Records—NYC.
11. Donald Ward to author, June 25, 1975.
12. Albert H. Gordon to author, July 17, 1975.
13. Alfred E. Borneman to author, June 21, 1976.
14. *U.S. v. Henry S. Morgan, et al.,* "Transcript of Trial, Defendants' Opening—Mr. Webster" (March 6, 1951), pp. 4015–4016. See also U.S. Temporary National Economic Committee, *Investigation of Concentration of Economic Power: Hearings. . . .* (Washington, 1939–1941), vol. 23, pp. 11942–11950, and *The New York Times,* December 19, 1939.
15. *U.S. v. Henry S. Morgan, et al.,* "Transcript of Trial, Defendants' Opening—Mr. Webster" (March 6, 1951), pp. 4019–4023, 4027–4037.
16. U.S. Department of Commerce, *Historical Statistics of the United States Colonial Times to 1957,* p. 658, and KP & Co., Records—NYC.

17. U.S. Department of Commerce, *Historical Statistics of the United States Colonial Times to 1957*, p. 658.
18. Donald Ward to author, June 25, 1975.
19. Ibid., and Alfred E. Borneman to author, June 21, 1976.
20. Albert H. Gordon to John M. Olin, November 10, 1939, *U.S. v. Henry S. Morgan, et al.*, "Plaintiff's Exhibit No. 1072" (April 6, 1949), p. 4223.
21. U.S. Temporary National Economic Committee, *Investigation of Concentration of Economic Power*, vol. 23, p. 11944. See also *The New York Times*, December 19, 1939.
22. U.S. Temporary National Economic Committee, *Investigation of Concentration of Economic Power*, vol. 23, pp. 11953–11954.
23. "Memorandum to Messrs. Webster, Hovey, Kinnicutt, Gordon, Moore, Flint," *U.S. v. Henry S. Morgan, et al.*, "Plaintiff's Exhibit No. 1091" (April 7, 1949), pp. 4287–4288, and *Herald Tribune*, October 4, 1935.
24. U.S. House, Committee on Interstate and Foreign Commerce, 82d Cong., 2d Sess., *Study of the Securities and Exchange Commission: Report. . . .* (Washington, 1952), p. 127, and Donald L. Kemmerer, "The Marketing of Securities, 1930–1952," *The Journal of Economic History*, vol. 12 (Fall 1952), pp. 457–459.
25. U.S. Department of Commerce, *Historical Statistics of the United States Colonial Times to 1957*, pp. 640, 673.
26. E. Raymond Corey, *Direct Placement of Corporate Securities* (Boston, 1951), Chaps. 2–6.
27. Albert H. Gordon to author, July 17, 1975; Donald Ward to author, June 25, 1975, and "Freeport Texas Company, Creation and Issue of 6% Cumulative Convertible Preferred Stock . . . 1933," in KP & Co., Records—NYC.
28. KP & Co., Records—NYC.
29. Albert H. Gordon to John M. Olin, November 10, 1939, in *U.S. v. Henry S. Morgan, et al.*, "Plaintiff's Exhibit No. 1072" (April 6, 1949), p. 4221, and KP & Co., Records—NYC. See also *Herald Tribune*, October 10, 1944, and September 20, 1945.
30. Vincent P. Carosso, "The Wall Street Money Trust from Pujo through Medina," *Business History Review*, vol. 47 (Winter 1973), pp. 429–431.
31. Orus J. Matthews to Fred L. Moore, February 24, 1936, *U.S. v. Henry S. Morgan et al.*, "Plaintiff's Exhibit No. 1094" (April 7, 1949), p. 4221.
32. Ibid., "Transcript of Trial, Defendants' Opening—Mr. Webster" (March 7, 1951), pp. 1074–1075; and *Herald Tribune*, November 2, 1943, February 15, 24, and 25, 1944, and March 21, 1945.
33. Moore, "42 Happy Years at Kidder, Peabody," p. 13.
34. KP & Co., Records—NYC, and Alfred E. Borneman to author, June 16, 1976.
35. KP & Co., Records—NYC. and Albert H. Gordon, "Memorandum to Partners," December 23, 1937, KP & Co., Records—NYC.
36. *U.S. v. Henry S. Morgan, et al.*, "Corrected Opinion of Harold R. Medina" (February 4, 1954), p. 78. See also Albert H. Gordon, "Memorandum to Partners," December 23, 1937, KP & Co., Records—NYC.
37. Moore, "42 Happy Years at Kidder, Peabody," p. 13; and Albert H. Gordon to author, July 17, 1975. See also *U.S. v. Henry S. Morgan, et al.*, "Corrected Opinion of Harold R. Medina" (February 4, 1954), pp. 44–45, 68; and ibid., "Issuer Summaries: Security Issues in the United States—July 26, 1933 to December 31, 1939" (2 vols.), vol. 1, p. 42 and vol. 2, p. 324.
38. Albert H. Gordon to Hon. A. G. C. Villiers, D. S. O., April 25, 1931, KP & Co., Records—NYC.

39. Albert H. Gordon to author, July 17, 1975.
40. Moore, "42 Happy Years at Kidder, Peabody," p. 10, and Donald Ward to author, June 25, 1975.
41. Albert H. Gordon to author, June 25, 1975.
42. U.S. Department of Commerce, *Historical Statistics of the United States Colonial Times to 1957,* pp. 658–659.
43. KP & Co., Records—NYC.
44. Kidder, Peabody & Co., "Annual Report, December 31, 1945," and KP & Co., Records—NYC.
45. *The New York Times,* September 4, 1942, and Gerald T. White, "Financing Industrial Expansion for War: The Origin of the Defense Plant Corporation Leases," *The Journal of Economic History,* vol. 9 (November 1949), pp. 156–183.
46. In addition to Ames, the other two partners admitted in January 1941 were: William C. Wilkes, the head of the underwriting department, and John R. Chapin, a former partner in the old firm's Boston office with strong ties to several of that city's investment trusts. The next year's addition was H. Albert Russell, the office manager in New York who in April 1942 took Chandler Hovey's seat on the New York Stock Exchange. On January 1, 1944, the firm announced three new partners: Walter V. Moffitt, a former Guaranty Company official who had joined Kidder, Peabody in 1935; Harry C. Clifford, who had started with Kissell, Kinnicutt & Co., then served as a partner in Schmeltzer, Clifford & Co., a corporate and government bond house, before joining Kidder, Peabody; and Alfred Rauch, a former Philadelphia National Company employee who stayed on after Kidder, Peabody took over that affiliate's business and was made assistant manager of the firm's office there. The last of the eight new regular partners, Erwin A. Stuebner, was a former vice president of the Philadelphia National Company, then manager of Kidder, Peabody's Philadelphia office from 1934 through 1938, after which he headed the firm's Chicago office. KP & Co., Records—NYC, and Alfred E. Borneman to author, August 12, 1976. See also *Herald Tribune,* April 17, 1942, and October 6, 1949.
47. Alfred E. Borneman to author, August 12, 1976, and *The New York Times,* July 16, 1945.
48. "United States of America before the Securities and Exchange Commission, In the Matter of Kidder, Peabody & Co . . . Respondents' Brief," KP & Co., Records—NYC. See also *The Wall Street Journal,* April 3, 1945; *The New York Times,* April 3 and 7, 1945; and *Herald Tribune,* April 3 and 7, 1945.

Notes for Chapter Six

1. The statistics cited are from the U.S. Council of Economic Advisers, *Economic Report of the President Transmitted to Congress January 1973* (Washington, 1973), pp. 196, 213, 217, 239.
2. U.S. Department of Commerce, *Historical Statistics of the United States, Colonial Times to 1957* (Washington, 1961), p. 658; and U.S. Department of Commerce, *Statistical Abstract of the United States, 1972* (Washington, 1972), p. 458.
3. Vincent P. Carosso, "The Wall Street Money Trust from Pujo through Medina," *Business History Review,* vol. 47 (Winter 1973), pp. 421–437.
4. *U.S. v. Henry S. Morgan, et al.,* "Brief in Support of Plaintiff's Motion to Connect the Evidence, Part One," pp. 143–163, details the various specific charges against Kidder, Peabody.

5. Ibid., "Corrected Opinion of Harold R. Medina" (February 4, 1954), p. 328. See also ibid., "Transcript of Trial, Plaintiff's Case" (October 1, 1952), pp. 17150–17156; and *Herald Tribune,* October 26, 1951.
6. U.S. v. Henry S. Morgan, et al., "Investment Bankers as Underwriters, Defendants' Tables," P-1, P-2, and ibid., "Investment Bankers as Managers or Agents, Defendants' Tables," M-1, M-2, M-13.
7. Ibid., "Transcript of Trial, Statistical Analysis by Mr. [Arthur H.] Dean" (April 6, 1953), pp. 21556–21557; and ibid., "Corrected Opinion of Harold R. Medina" (February 4, 1954), p. 79.
8. Ibid., "Corrected Opinion of Harold R. Medina" (February 4, 1954), p. 417, and also ibid., "Brief on the Facts for Kidder, Peabody & Co. on the Motion to Dismiss," pp. 25, 64, 86. See also *Herald Tribune,* March 7 and 8, 1951.
9. Albert H. Gordon to author, June 17, 1976.
10. Alfred E. Borneman, "Memorandum to Operating Committee on Public Utility New Business Department," December 11, 1953, KP & Co., Records—NYC. See also *Herald Tribune,* January 13, 1953.
11. Donald Ward and Alfred E. Borneman to author, June 21, 1976. See also *The New York Times,* September 21 and 25, 1955; and *Herald Tribune,* April 3, 1958.
12. Albert H. Gordon, "Money Costs and Rate of Return," typescript copy of speech delivered before the Thirty-Sixth Annual Convention of the Edison Electric Institute, Philadelphia, June 5, 1968. Parts of this address, prepared with the assistance of Alfred E. Borneman, subsequently were published under the title, "Utilities Must Change Financing Ideas to Attract Investor Interest," *The Commercial & Financial Chronicle,* vol. 207 (June 27, 1968), pp. 1, 24–26. See also *The New York Times,* June 6, 1968.
13. Roger Hillstrom and Robert King, eds., *1960–1969: A Decade of Corporate and International Finance* (New York, 1970), p. 308.
14. KP & Co., Records—NYC.
15. Ibid.
16. "Memo to Partners" (March 3, 1964), in ibid.
17. KP & Co., Records—NYC, and *Herald Tribune,* October 1, 1952.
18. Quoted in the *Herald Tribune,* September 28, 1953. After incorporation, Hoff became a director and member of the firm's executive committee.
19. Quoted in *The New York Times,* June 1, 1966. See also *Herald Tribune,* December 8, 1966.
20. William N. Loverd and Alfred E. Borneman to author, August 16, 1976.
21. KP & Co., Records—NYC.
22. Ibid.
23. Gordon L. Calvert (vice president and general counsel, New York Stock Exchange) to author, July 15, 1975, and *IBA-Washington Bulletin,* vol. 5, (September 1971), p. 1.
24. Isabelle L. Hatton (NASD Supervisor Member Firm Section) to author, September 8, 1976.
25. Irwin Friend, et al., *Investment Banking and the New Issues Market* (Cleveland, 1967), p. 14.
26. U.S. Department of Commerce, *Statistical Abstract of the United States, 1970* (Washington, 1970), p. 478.
27. U.S. Department of Commerce, *Historical Statistics of the United States, Colonial Times to 1957,* p. 675, *Statistical Abstract of the United States, 1970,* p. 437, *Statistical Abstract of the United States, 1972,* p. 439. See also Herman E. Krooss and Martin R. Blyn, *A History of Financial Intermediaries* (New York, 1971), p. 216.

28. U.S. Securities and Exchange Commission, *Thirty-Eighth Annual Report. . . .* (Washington, 1972), p. 151.
29. George Carson to author, August 29, 1976, Kidder, Peabody & Co., "Annual Reports," 1945–1969, and *Herald Tribune*, March 2, 1967, and April 3 and 14, 1967.
30. Quoted in *The Christian Science Monitor*, October 27, 1959.
31. On the development and growth of mutual funds see, Hugh Bullock, *The Story of Investment Companies* (New York, 1959), pp. 1–23, and U.S. Committee on Interstate and Foreign Commerce, 87th Cong., 2d Sess., *A Study of Mutual Funds* (Washington, 1962), pp. 4–6.
32. Vincent P. Carosso, *Investment Banking in America: A History* (Cambridge, 1970), p. 287; and Bullock, *Investment Companies*, p. 41.
33. U.S. Committee on Interstate and Foreign Commerce, *A Study of Mutual Funds*, pp. 37–38, and U.S. Securities and Exchange Commission, *Thirty-Eighth Annual Report*, pp. 152–153.
34. U.S. Securities and Exchange Commission, *Thirty-Eighth Annual Report*, p. 150.
35. John Brooks, *The Go-Go Years* (New York, 1973), provides a lively account of the market strategy and maneuverings of some of the more active funds.
36. Amyas Ames, "Program for an Investment Trust Department," KP & Co., Records—NYC.
37. Alfred E. Borneman to author, August 13, 1976, and *Herald Tribune*, February 5, 1949.
38. *Herald Tribune*, June 24, 1949, January 15, 1952, May 26, 1952, and December 24, 1957.
39. Ibid., May 3, 1950.
40. KP & Co., Records—NYC.
41. U.S. Department of Commerce, *Statistical Abstract of the United States, 1970*, p. 483.
42. KP & Co., Records—NYC, and Alfred E. Borneman to author, September 21, 1976.
43. U.S. Securities and Exchange Commission, *Thirty-Eighth Annual Report*, p. 159.
44. KP & Co., Records—NYC.
45. Ibid., and Robert A. Krantz, Jr. and Alfred E. Borneman to author, September 20, 1976.
46. KP & Co., "Realty Financings Managed," KP & Co., Records—NYC.
47. KP & Co., Records—NYC, and Robert A. Krantz, Jr. to author, September 20, 1976. See also *Herald Tribune*, May 18, 1965.
48. Robert A. Krantz, Jr. to author, September 20, 1976, and Alfred E. Borneman to author, September 20, 1976.
49. Alfred E. Borneman to author, September 20, 1976.
50. Peter Vanderwicken, "The Powerful Logic of the Leasing Boom," *Fortune* (November 1973), p. 132.
51. Ibid., p. 134; KP & Co., Records—NYC, and Raymond J. Raff to author, September 20, 1976.
52. Mira Wilkins, *The Maturing of Multinational Enterprise: American Business Abroad from 1914 to 1970* (Cambridge, 1974), p. 331, and U.S. Department of Commerce, *Statistical Abstract of the United States, 1972*, p. 765.
53. Alfred E. Borneman to author, September 20, 1976.
54. Richard F. Coons to author, December 18, 1976, and KP & Co., Records—NYC.
55. KP & Co., Records—NYC, and William N. Loverd to author, August 16, 1976.
56. *Herald Tribune*, December 20, 1963.

57. Richard F. Coons to author, December 18, 1976.
58. William N. Loverd, "Memo to Partners," February 17, 1964, KP & Co., Records—NYC, and William N. Loverd to author, August 16, 1976.
59. KP & Co., Records—NYC, and *Herald Tribune*, June 20, 1963.
60. KP & Co., Records—NYC. See also *The Times* (London), August 5, 1968.
61. *The New York Times*, July 1, 1958.
62. KP & Co., Records8NYC, and *The New York Times*, October 3, 1967. See also Michael C. Jensen, *The Financiers, The World of the Great Wall Street Investment Banking Houses* (New York, 1976), pp. 857108, for an informed and detailed account of the lengthy negotiations, including the political and diplomatic overtones of the transaction.
63. Jensen, *The Financiers*, pp. 23, 90–95.
64. KP & Co., Records—NYC; Jensen, *The Financiers*, p. 99; and *The New York Times*, October 3, 1967.
65. Quoted in *The New York Times*, October 3, 1967.
66. Jensen, *The Financier*, pp. 99–100.
67. KP & Co., Records—NYC.
68. Donald Ward to author, August 23, 1976.
69. "New York Office Organizational Chart," KP & Co., Records—NYC, and William N. Loverd to author, August 18, 1976.
70. Albert H. Gordon to author, July 17, 1975.
71. The departments established under Webster's plan were: (1) Office Management; (2) Stock Exchange Business; (3) Statistical and New Business; (4) Trading; (5) Sales; (6) Syndicate; and (7) Partnership Matters. See ESW, Jr., "Memorandum to Partners," KP & Co., Records—NYC.
72. James E. Collins, "Memorandum to Mr. Ames," September 27, 1948, KP & Co., Records—NYC.
73. William N. Loverd to author, September 22, 1976.
74. Total employees at all the firm's offices in the United States more than tripled, from 408 in 1945 to 1,454 in 1969. George A. Carson to author, August 30, 1976.
75. KP & Co., Records—NYC, and William N. Loverd to author, August 16, 1976.
76. U.S. Securities and Exchange Commission, *Seventeenth Annual Report. . . .* (Washington, 1952), p. 200, and U.S. Securities and Exchange Commission, *40th Annual Report. . . .* (Washington, 1974), p. 148.
77. H. Lee Silberman, "To Incorporate or Not to Incorporate—That Is the Question," *Finance*, vol. 89 (March 1971), pp. 22–24, and Irwin Friend, et al., *Investment Banking and the New Issues Market*, p. 112.
78. "Supplemental Memorandum, Re: Kidder, Peabody & Co. Incorporated" (April 16, 1963), KP & Co., Records—NYC.
79. Jarvis P. Kellogg, "Memorandum Re: Full Incorporation" (March 4, 1964), KP & Co., Records—NYC.
80. William N. Loverd to author, August 18, 1976.
81. Alfred E. Borneman to author, August 16, 1976, and *Herald Tribune*, November 21, 1961.
82. Roger Hillstrom and Robert King, eds., *1960–1969: A Decade of Corporate and International Finance*, pp. 308, 338–381.
83. KP & Co., Records—NYC.
84. "The 26th Annual Survey of Net Worth and Fails," *Finance*, vol. 89 (March 1971), p. 10.
85. Alfred E. Borneman to author, May 25, 1976.

Notes for Chapter Seven

1. U.S. Department of Commerce, *Statistical Abstract of the United States, 1971* (Washington, 1971), p. 447, and *The New York Times,* December 23, 1970.
2. Quoted in *The New York Times,* December 23, 1970. See also S. M. Robards, "Fails—Dynamite in the Back Office," *Finance,* vol. 87 (March 1969), pp. 8–9, 53–61.
3. Quoted in Robards, "Fails—Dynamite in the Back Office," p. 9.
4. Robert Sobel, *N.Y.S.E.: A History of the New York Stock Exchange, 1935–1975* (New York, 1975), p. 290.
5. William N. Loverd to author, October 11, 1976.
6. Kidder, Peabody & Co., "Answers to [NYSE] Financial Questionnaire (Part I) as of April 26, 1968," KP&Co., Records—NYC.
7. Quoted in Robards, "Fails—Dynamite in the Back Office," p. 59.
8. Quoted in *The New York Times,* December 23, 1970.
9. U.S. Council of Economic Advisers, *Economic Report of the President Transmitted to Congress in February 1970* (Washington, 1970), p. 267; *Economic Report of the President Transmitted to Congress in January 1972* (Washington, 1972), p. 287; and U.S. Securities and Exchange Commission, *Thirty-Eighth Annual Report. . . .* (Washington, 1972), p. 161. See also Sobel, *N.Y.S.E.,* p. 321; and John Brooks, *The Go-Go Years* (New York, 1973).
10. U.S. Council of Economic Advisers, *Economic Report of the President Transmitted to Congress in January 1970,* p. 262; and U.S. Securities and Exchange Commission, *Thirty-Eighth Annual Report,* p. 157.
11. U.S. Securities and Exchange Commission, *Thirty-Eighth Annual Report,* p. 143.
12. *The New York Times,* December 30, 1970.
13. William N. Loverd to author, August 10, 1976.
14. On the capital crisis see Hurd Baruch, *Wall Street: Security Risk* (Washington, 1971); the series of articles by Carol Loomis, "A Squeeze on the Directors," *Fortune,* vol. 79 (May 15, 1969), pp. 146–149, 254, 261, 266; "They're Tearing Up Wall Street," ibid., vol. 80 (August 1, 1969), pp. 88–90, 137–138, 157–159; "The Capital Mess on Wass Street," ibid., vol. 82 (July 1970), pp. 141–144; "Wall Street on the Ropes," ibid. (December 1970), pp. 62–67, 136–139; "The Unbelievable Last Months of Hayden, Stone," ibid., vol. 83 (January 1971), pp. 114–116, 154–155, 158–159, as well as Chris Welles, *The Last Days of the Club* (New York, 1975), pp. 125–283; and Sobel, *N.Y.S.E.,* pp. 308–329.
15. Quoted in *The New York Times,* December 31, 1970.
16. KP & Co., Records—NYC, Willam N. Loverd and Alfred E. Borneman to author, August 18, 1976, and the annual surveys, "Top 100 Underwriting Firms in Order of Capital Position," *Finance,* vol. 90 (March 1972), p. 30, ibid., vol. 91 (March 1973), p. 18, and ibid., vol. 93 (March 1975), p. 12. See also Samuel L. Hayes III, "Investment Banking: Power Structure in Flux," *Harvard Business Review* (March–April 1971), pp. 136–152.
17. Quoted in *The New York Times,* December 31, 1970.
18. U.S. Securities and Exchange Commission, *40th Annual Report. . . .* (Washington, 1974), p. 144; and KP & Co., Records—NYC.
19. KP & Co., Records—NYC.
20. Aileen McKenna, "Memorandum, Private Placements," August 5, 1976, in ibid.
21. Institutional Investor, *1976 Annual Financing Directory* (New York, 1976), pp. 7, 16–19.

24. Ibid.; and Ezra Solomon, "Wall Street in Transition: The Emerging System and Its Impact on the Economy," in Henry G. Manne, Ezra Solomon, et al., *Wall Street in Transition: The Emerging System and Its Impact on the Economy* (New York, 1974), pp. 119–121.
25. *Time*, vol. 105 (June 30, 1975), p. 63, and *New York Magazine*, vol. 9 (March 15, 1976), p. 10.
26. *The New York Times*, October 19, 1975.
27. Quoted in ibid. See also *The New York Times*, January 11, 1976.
28. William N. Loverd to author, October 27, 1976, and KP & Co., Records—NYC.
29. Alfred E. Borneman to author, October 28, 1976.
30. *The New York Times*, September 30, 1976.
31. Solomon, "Wall Street in Transition," pp. 116–130. See also *The New York Times*, December 10, 1975.
32. *The New York Times*, May 24 and June 25, 1974.
33. KP & Co., Records—NYC, and *The New York Times*, June 25, 1974.
34. "Memorandum on 'Big Mac' Sales," KP & Co., Records—NYC.
35. *U.S. v. Henry S. Morgan, et al.*, "Brief on the Facts for Kidder, Peabody & Co., on Motion to Dismiss," p. 37.
36. KP & Co., Records—NYC.
37. Ibid.
38. Quoted in *The New York Times*, July 30, 1976.
39. KP & Co., Records—NYC.
40. Douglas West to author, August 22, 1976.
41. William N. Loverd to author, November 1, 1976.
42. H. Lee Silberman, "When the Chips Are Down . . . Call on Ralph DeNunzio," *Finance*, vol. 88 (December 1970), p. 16. See also *The New York Times*, October 16, 1977, and *New York Post*, February 21, 1978.
43. Silberman, "When the Chips Are Down," p. 16, and *The New York Times*, June 7, 1972.
44. Ibid.
45. KP & Co., Records—NYC.
46. *The New York Times*, October 16, 1977.
47. Albert H. Gordon to author, December 8, 1976.
48. Wyndham Robertson, "The Underwriters Have to Offer More," *Fortune*, vol. 87 (January 1973), p. 117.
49. Albert H. Gordon to author, July 17, 1975.
50. George Carson to author, August 30, 1976, and William N. Loverd to author, August 16, 1976.
51. Ralph D. DeNunzio to author, December 8, 1976.
52. *The Daily Bond Buyer*, October 12, 1976.

Index